THE BIOGRAPHY OF GENERAL GEORGE S.
PATTON

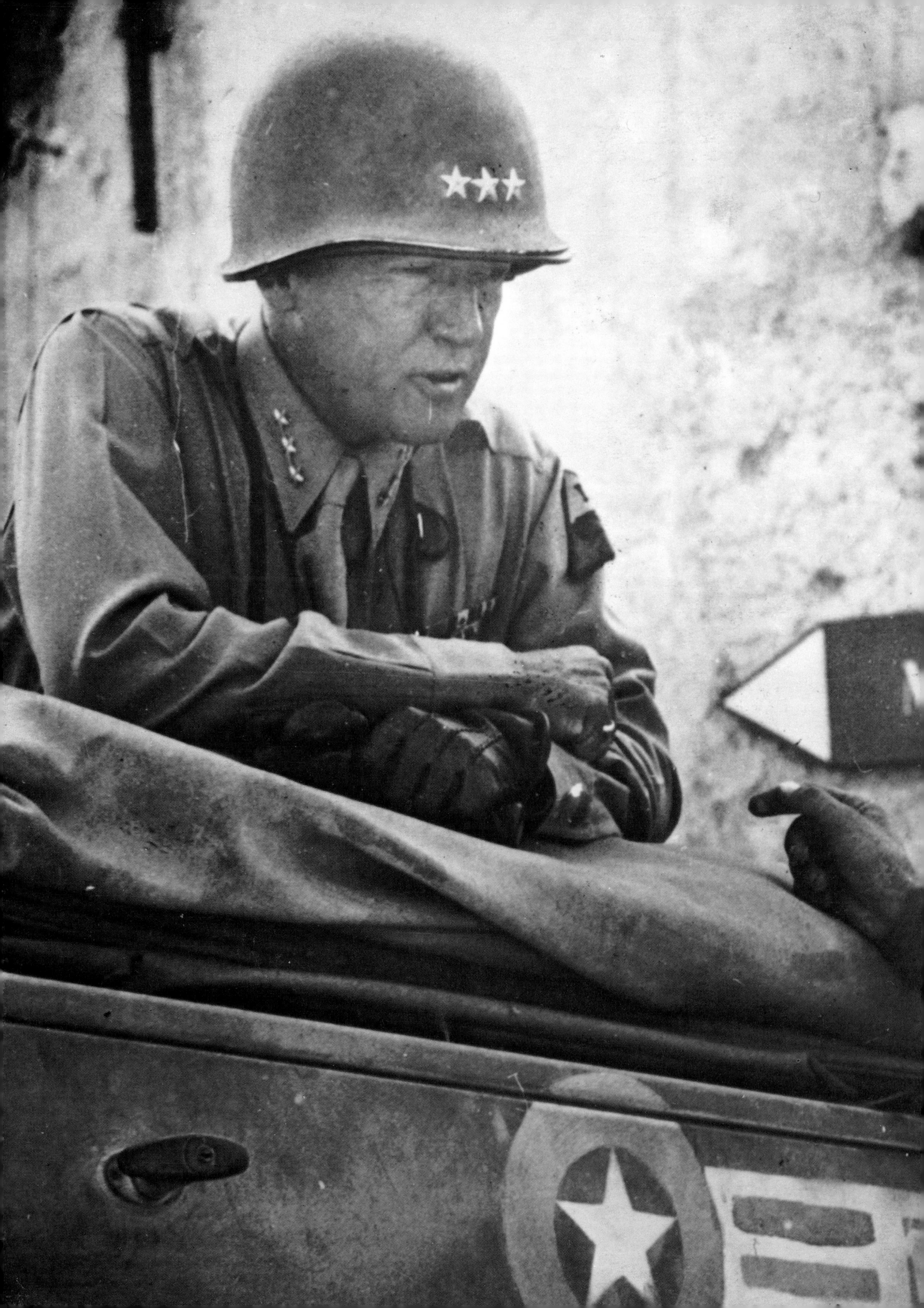

THE BIOGRAPHY OF GENERAL GEORGE S.
PATTON

IAN V. HOGG

Bison Books

Published in 1984 by
Bison Books Corp.
17 Sherwood Place
Greenwich, CT 06830

Copyright © 1982 Bison Books Corp.

ISBN 0-86124-082-0

Printed in Hong Kong

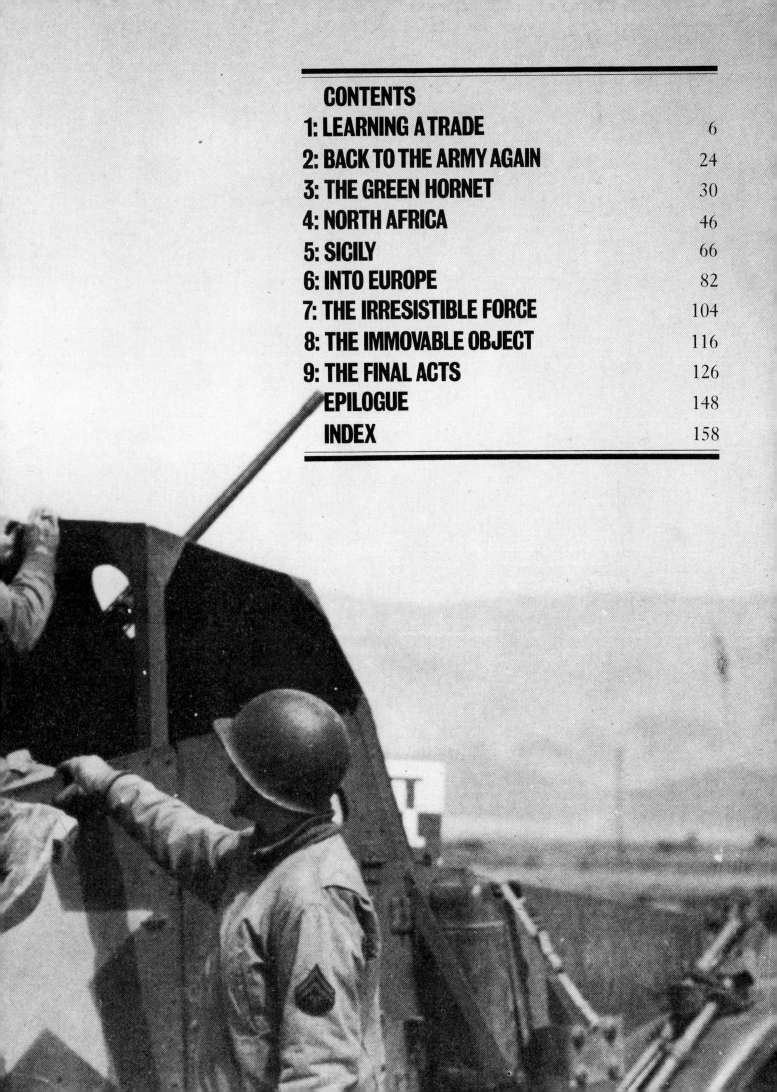

CONTENTS

1: LEARNING A TRADE

George Smith Patton Jr was born on 11 November 1885 on the Wilson-Patton ranch near Pasadena, in the San Gabriel Valley of California. He spent the early years of his life on this ranch, not even leaving it to attend school. His father did not agree with formal education for children; his idea of imparting knowledge was to read great slabs of classical literature to his children at the family fireside. Remarkably, this system did not lead to revulsion on the part of young George; on the contrary, it gave him a love of classical literature which lasted throughout his life and fired him with the ambition to be a soldier in emulation of the heroes of whom his father so often read.

Soldiering, like any other profession, demands formal education and at the age of 12 George finally had to attend school in Pasadena, where his first task was to learn to read and write. He achieved both in record time, and in later years was to achieve minor distinction as a writer, submitting finely-argued texts to military journals and heroic poetry to various magazines and newspapers. While this crash course of education managed to impart the basics, it failed to add certain vital refinements, and for the rest of his life Patton cheerfully admitted that his spelling was somewhat deficient. Mathematics, too, was scarcely a strong point with him, and both subjects were to prove obstacles in his subsequent career. He doubtless took consolation from the many examples of successful soldiers who survived a poor academic start.

Once he had mastered basic scholastic requirements Patton went to the Virginia Military Academy, that breeding ground of countless fine American officers. After a year there, he sat a competitive examination, passed, and was admitted to the United States Military Academy at West Point, entering in 1904.

His career at West Point was conventional enough, and it could scarcely have been otherwise, for unconventional behavior got short shrift in those days. However, it appears that he was not popular among his fellow-cadets. His early life had turned him into a strong and well-built youth and he was an expert horseman; athletic accomplishment was a recognized road to distinction, so he took it. He is said to have announced, shortly after arriving at West Point, that he would become a prominent member of the Academy football squad, that he would win the highest academic honor available, and that he would be the

Right: Colonel George S Patton Jr stands in front of a Renault 'Char Canon FT18' as provided for the US Tank Corps in France.

Left: George Patton as a child seems to exude the same confidence as that which was to sustain him through his military career.

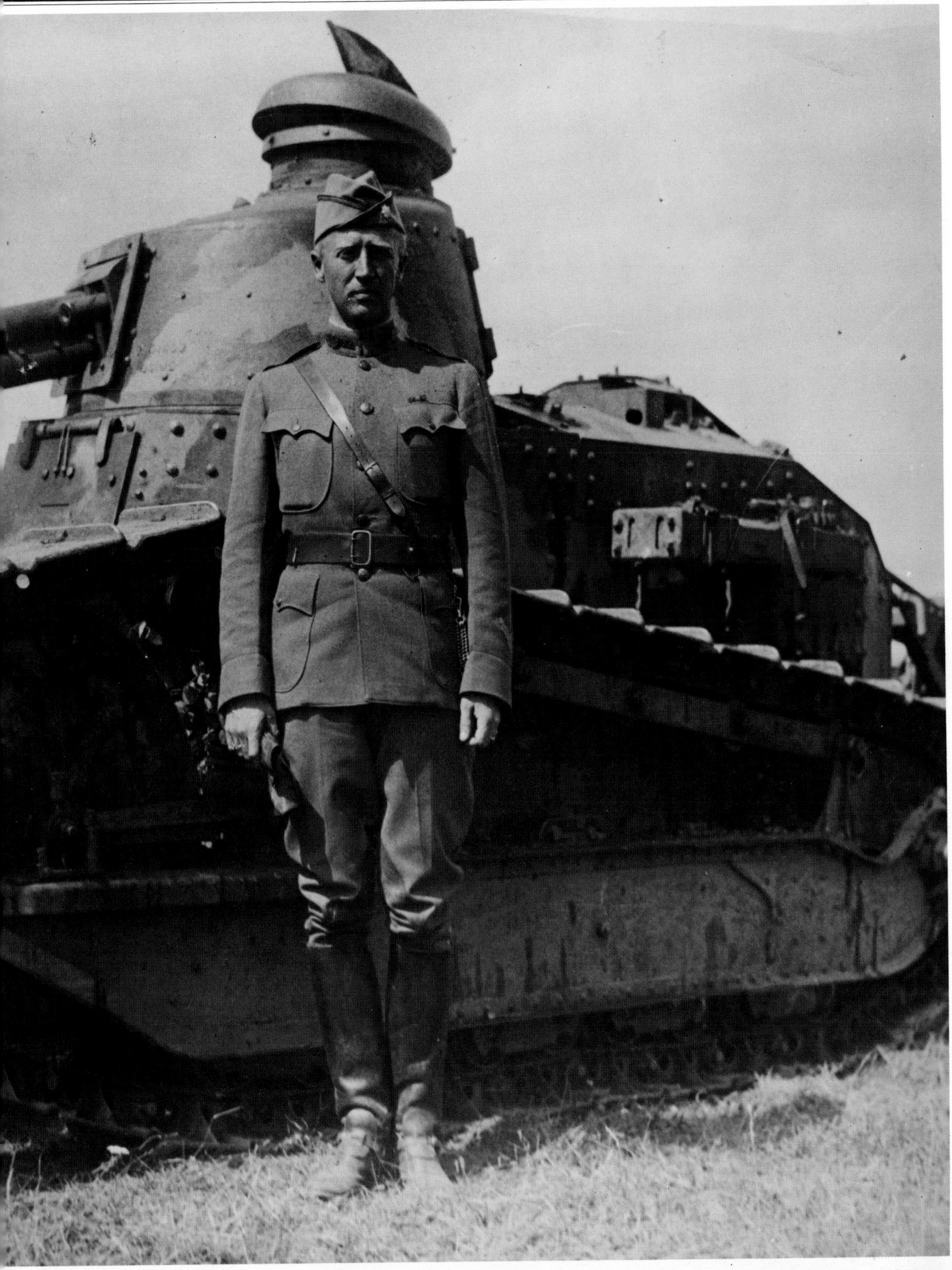

Above: The Patton family; George Jr, aged 15; his mother Ruth Wilson Patton, George Senior and sister Anne.

first of his class to reach the rank of general. It must have been a long-rankling disappointment that he failed to achieve any of these. True, he made the football squad, but his appearances on the field all too often finished with his being removed on a stretcher with something fractured. His nose was broken on three separate occasions. It has been suggested that, despite his build, he was a relative lightweight when compared with some of the football heavies in the squads of those days. It has also been suggested that the football field was a useful place for summary justice and that the rather bumptious young George asked for all he got. Whatever the truth of the matter, the fact remains that the coveted 'Major A' distinction of the football squad eluded him. So too did high academic distinction, though he did achieve the lesser accolade of Class Adjutant. Two of his classmates were appointed general before him.

Apart from his athletic achievements – he was a member of the riding, fencing, rifle and track teams – Patton's record at West Point was undistinguished. Scholastically he still labored under the handicap of his early education and he found formal learning a miserable business; he took five years to graduate instead of the usual four.

As might be expected with his background, he elected for the cavalry, and in 1909 he was commissioned second lieutenant in the 15th Cavalry Regiment. Here he seems to have had the sense to moderate his exuberance and he settled down to learn his trade and get along with his brother officers. It is likely that his mind was on other things apart from advancement; in the following year he got married.

His bride was Beatrice Ayer, daughter of a New England industrialist and financier, and on the face of it a more unlikely combination would be hard to imagine. On the one hand the flamboyant, hearty, athletic soldier, on the other a small, refined, intellectual. Nevertheless, the chemistry was there and the two were united in love and devotion which was unwavering for the rest of their lives. Pitchforked into a new world, that of the 'old army,' Beatrice Patton applied herself and mastered it, becoming an accomplished horsewoman, and her manifold social gifts frequently shielded George from the consequences of some hasty word or action.

Marriage to a rich socialite had advantages which spread beyond the confines of the home and Patton (who, it is said, was known in some circles as 'Fred Ayers' son-in-law' rather than by his rank or name) soon reaped some of the benefits. He became Aide-de-Camp to the Chief of Staff in Washington and riding companion of Henry Stimson, Secretary of War, a friendship which was to stand him in good stead in later years.

In 1912 the Olympic Games, held in Stockholm, included a new event known as the modern pentathlon. The original pentathlon was a series of five events in the athletic festivals of ancient Greece covering foot racing, long jump, wrestl-ing, throwing the discus and the javelin. These had now become individual events in the modern games, and the new Pentathlon was devised to test the classical military skills – riding, running, swimming, marksmanship and fencing. The theme behind it all was that of the faithful messenger who overcomes all obstacles to deliver his dispatches, and it was just the sort of contest to appeal to George Patton. At his own expense he travelled to Stockholm, accompanied by his wife and parents, determined to win the event. For once, nerves got the better of him. In spite of a perfect score at pistol practice, he came twenty-first out of 43 entrants in the competitive shoot-off. According to some reports he had to be rescued from the swimming pool due to exhaustion after his 300-meter swim, and he collapsed at the end of the 4000-meters cross-country run. In fencing he came first, but in riding third. Overall he rated fifth of the 43 contestants, the winner being a Swede. Today, of course, anyone not gaining a medal is a nonentity in the fiercely competitive atmosphere of the Games, but in 1912 to come fifth was a respectable achievement and Patton, if not entirely satisfied, was content to have made his mark.

Below: Cadet Sergeant Patton, during his period at the US Military Academy at West Point.

Above: The United States 1912 Olympic Team poses for its official photograph.

Right: Lieutenant Patton in his role as aide to General Pershing during the Mexican war in 1916.

At the close of the Games he indulged in a Grand Tour of Europe, which his wife looked upon as a second honeymoon, but, like most of his actions, it had an ulterior motive. The trip led them to Saumur and the French Cavalry School, where Patton stayed to take fencing lessons from the Adjutant, a renowned Master of the Sword. He returned there in 1913, this time to take lessons in the saber which formed the background for a manual he later wrote for the US Cavalry entitled 'Saber Methods.' On this second trip he went further afield and, by automobile and accompanied by his wife, spent many days touring Normandy and Brittany, a reconnaisance which, he was later to claim, greatly helped him in 1944.

Returning to the USA, Patton now took up a post as weapons instructor at the Cavalry School. He taught the use of the saber and also designed a new pattern which was promptly adopted for service. This post lasted until 1916 when he was posted to the 8th Cavalry at Fort Bliss, Texas. Almost immediately the Mexican War broke out, to give Patton his first taste of battle.

The Mexican War is a somewhat high-flown name for what was little more than a punitive foray against a bandit. Pancho Villa may have been a nationalist, but this escaped the notice of most Americans, to whom he was simply a nuisance, and after he carried out an attack on Columbus, New Mexico, and engaged the local military garrison in a running gun battle through the streets, President

Below: Cadet George Patton Jr, USMA Class of 1909, in dress gray uniform.

Above: The opposition; Pancho Villa (center, in General's uniform) and Zapata (with sombrero) in Mexico City in 1914.

Wilson instructed Brigadier General John J Pershing to go after Villa and teach him manners. What was to be a minor affair eventually escalated into a 15,000-man strong expeditionary force and severely strained relations between the USA and Mexico, though it later proved to have been a useful limbering-up exercise prior to American entry into World War I.

No sooner did Patton hear of the mounting of this expedition than he presented himself at Pershing's headquarters seeking employment. Pershing, a severe disciplinarian, promptly turned him away, but Patton persisted and eventually Pershing accepted him in the post of Headquarters Commandant and acting aide-de-camp. Considering that Patton was still only a second lieutenant at the time, this was quite a responsibility; even so, he appears to have spent as little time as possible in his administrative role, preferring to be out and about on a horse, either acting as aide to Pershing or simply galloping about the countryside. It seems to have been at this time that he adopted the habit of wearing two pistols on his belt, probably a reflection of the type of warfare in which he was indulging and the type of opponent he was seeking.

They sought Villa here and there like the Scarlet Pimpernel but never caught up with him, and such a frustrating war tended to drive Patton out in search of excitement. On 14 May 1916 he found it. Accounts disagree as to what Patton was doing when action finally found him. Some say he was on a patrol, others that he was on a routine search for fodder,

others that he was on an unofficial hunt and had tracked a band of guerillas to their lair. What is certain is that he arrived at an isolated ranch with six soldiers and two automobiles, only to be fired on as he approached. Patton and his men dismounted and took cover in the surrounding rocks, and at this juncture three mounted bandits rode up and opened fire on them. Patton drew his pistols and fired back; he shot one out of the saddle, shot the horse of the second bandit and, as the man attempted to fire, shot him dead. By this time the first rider had picked himself up and was attempting to open fire, so Patton shot him dead also. The third rider appears to have escaped while all this was taking place. With the bodies draped across the hood of his car, Patton returned to Pershing's headquarters to find that one of the dead was no less than 'General' Cardenas, chief of Villa's bodyguard.

This rapid and forceful action commended Patton to Pershing, for above all else Pershing loved 'fighters,' and an officer who could indulge in a Western-style shoot-out with bandits and bring two-thirds of them back dead certainly qualified for that title. On 26 May Patton was promoted to First Lieutenant. What was more useful was that he was marked down by Pershing, and in May 1917 he sailed to France in command of Pershing's Headquarters detachment. When Pershing arrived in the following month, Patton became his ADC and Headquarters Commandant, just as he had been in Mexico.

Unfortunately, being ADC in the enormous military machine being built up in France was a much less congenial post than it had been in Mexico; no casual touring of the countryside, no bandits to shoot, just relentless paperwork, and by September this had begun to bore Patton. He finally presented himself to Pershing and asked for a transfer to a combat post.

One of the greatest crosses which commanders have to bear is the young fire-eater who wants to get into the action, and at that time Pershing had quite enough on his mind without being called upon to alleviate Patton's boredom. It had just been agreed that the American sector of the Western Front was to be in Lorraine, and Pershing and his staff were hard at work on the planning and logistic arrangements for a forecast army of

Below: Pancho Villa, leader of the Mexican revolutionaries, in less flamboyant dress.

2,000,000 men, in the process of which they were coming up against problems and technicalities which were new to the US Army. Among these novelties was the tank, the latest type of fighting machine and one about which few people knew very much. Pershing was being urged to organize a tank corps, and under these circumstances his response to Patton's request was hardly surprising: 'You can have command of an infantry battalion or you can go into the Tank Corps.'

A lust for action is a fine thing, but to offer a dyed-in-the-wool cavalryman an infantry command was bound to make

Below: General Foch and General Pershing pose amicably in June 1918; Pershing's immaculate standard of dress are obvious.

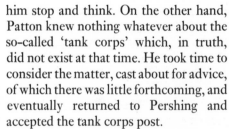

Above: Patton's raw material; draftees from New York City on their way to recruits' camp in 1917.

him stop and think. On the other hand, Patton knew nothing whatever about the so-called 'tank corps' which, in truth, did not exist at that time. He took time to consider the matter, cast about for advice, of which there was little forthcoming, and eventually returned to Pershing and accepted the tank corps post.

As might be expected from the nation which produced Henry Ford and General Motors, the advent of the automobile had not been entirely overlooked by the US Army, though financial restrictions had kept practical applications to a minimum. During the Mexican War there had been a 'mechanized unit' in the expeditionary Force; it had been privately financed by a group of New York businessmen and it was organized as the "1st Armored Motor Battery" of the New York National Guard. Its equipment consisted of three cars, a Locomobile, a White Steamer and a Mack, all armored by Carnegie Steel; two Jeffery trucks, a Locomobile staff car, and 72 Indian motorcycles, some of which towed trailers with steel shields and Colt 'Potato-Digger' machine guns. Whether or not this gave the regular army any ideas is not recorded, but the Mexican affair did release the purse strings slightly and two motorized formations were assembled, one with Jeffery and one with White cars, all armored and carrying Benet-Mercie machine guns in rotating turrets.

It was shortly after the Mexican

expedition had ended that the British unveiled the tank on the battlefield; they had put their handful of existing machines into the Somme battle in the hope of gaining some advantage from the surprise. In this they were disappointed, for the terrain was ill-suited to tank maneuver, but the inspired and usually exaggerated news stories of the day depicted the tank as a war-winner, once

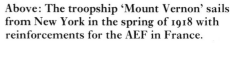

Above: The troopship 'Mount Vernon' sails from New York in the spring of 1918 with reinforcements for the AEF in France.

it got over its teething troubles. The idea caught the imagination of inventors all over the world almost immediately. In the USA several privately sponsored designs of tank were put together, but none of them managed anything more warlike than occasional field days with local National Guard units or appearances for bond-selling drives.

The US Army had observers in France in 1916 and they were instructed to investigate the tanks and submit a report. When this finally appeared it was a distressing catalogue of mechanical shortcomings which entirely ignored the tactical questions raised by the employment of tanks, and the result was that the army felt disinclined to pursue the idea any further. Only after Pershing had set up his headquarters in France and

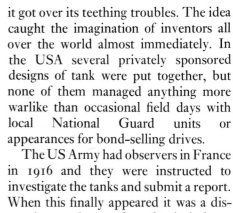

Left: US troops parade through the streets of Paris to celebrate Independence Day 1917.

ordered a closer examination of the tank did any concrete proposals appear. Pershing then reported to the War Department that the tank should be considered an important factor in warfare; that two models, a heavy and a light, should be adopted; and that there should be centralized control over tank affairs. To implement the materiel requirement, the report urged that French two-man Renault and British Mark V heavy tanks should be purchased for use by the American Expeditionary Force until such time as American-built tanks were available. Two technical officers were detailed to liaise with the British and French, a move which later resulted in an agreement for collaborative building of heavy tanks. But in the event this came to nothing. Two other American officers were sent to the French Tank Corps and, after studying the Renault design then in use, entered into negotiations to purchase two tanks and ship them to the United States. There they were to be closely examined and put into manufacture with various modifications incorporated.

Pershing had ordered 600 British Mark VI heavy tanks in September 1917 and was relying on American production to provide him with the necessary light tanks by the following summer, by which time the AEF was to be ready to take the field as a coherent fighting force. It was at this juncture that he offered Patton his chance to join the tank corps. In fact the tank corps as such had not yet been formed. When Patton accepted the posting he didn't *join* the tank corps, he *was* the tank corps. For a career cavalryman to take such a plunge into the unknown, staking his future reputation on a virtually untried weapons system was a jump that required some courage, but that was a commodity of which Patton was never short. He was not a gambler by nature; he weighed the probabilities, considered the type of war that was in progress, saw what the tank offered – in his own words 'A means of inflicting the maximum casualties on the enemy while keeping American casualties at a minimum.' He had sufficient faith in current technology to assume that mechanical improvements would come along, and made his choice accordingly. On 19 November 1917 he was formally ordered to his new assignment. On the following day, like an omen, the British attacked at Cambrai with 479

tanks in a battle which has since been recognized as the first action which really gave an indication of what tanks could do.

The Battle of Cambrai was partially successful because it allowed tanks to attack on ground of their own choosing. This was firm ground which allowed them to roll forward instead of getting stuck in the mud and shell craters which formed much of the more fought-over segments of the Western Front. Moreover, artillery support was restricted to firing at known enemy guns and screening the tanks with smoke and gas, instead of simply shovelling shells haphazardly into the enemy lines, a process which inevitably made the attack more difficult. As a result the tank's attack smashed a hole six miles wide and three miles deep into the German line. When night fell, however, the battle came to a standstill, and the Germans were given sufficient respite to allow them to collect their wits and begin organizing their inevitable counterattack. The Allied High Command had shown little faith in the tank idea and had failed to prepare sufficient reserves to take advantage of any breach which might be made. The only reserves available were tired troops removed from other sectors, who had never worked with tanks before, had no understanding of the tactics involved and were not particularly interested in learning. Once the tanks' strength began to fail, due to mechanical breakdowns or German countermeasures, the infantry were soon evicted from their new positions. German counterattacks followed, and by 7 De-

Above: Replacements disembarking from a truck convoy behind the lines in the Lorraine sector of France.

cember the British line was back where it had started from.

By this time Patton had arrived in England to attend the British Tank School at Bovington where he learned to drive and to command a British Mark VI heavy tank and studied the British tank organization. Having completed this short course, he then returned to France, to the French Tank School at Chaplieu, to learn all about the French system and to master the Renault light tank. The

Below: Back to the armor; a photograph from Patton's own files showing him on his return to 2nd Armored in 1940.

Left: Renault tanks of Patton's force moving forward into action in the Argonne sector in 1918.

Below left: Renault tank of Company C, 327th Tank Battalion, going into action on the first day of the Saint-Mihiel operation, 1918.

Bottom left: Lieutenant Colonel Patton superintending instruction at the Tank Corps School in Langres, July 15th 1918.

initial success of the British attack at Cambrai had also focussed the eyes of the AEF on to the tank once again; Brigadier General S D Rockenbach was appointed chief of the tank corps and sent to France, while Pershing cancelled his earlier order for 600 British Mark VI and asked, instead, for 600 of the later, improved, Mark VIII models. At this time the US-British-French cooperative factory plan was still in the air and it was estimated that deliveries of Mark VIII would commence in April 1918, at a rate of 300 per month, and that American-built Renault light tanks would be delivered at the rate of 100 in April 1918, 300 in May and 600 a month thereafter. Some 23,405 tanks in all were ordered and $175,000,000 approved to pay for them.

The next task was to produce a tank corps ready to man the tanks when they arrived. Patton was promoted major and appointed commanding officer of the US Army Tank Training School, to be set up at Langres in the *département* of Haute-Marne, some 21 miles from the AEF headquarters at Chaumont. This would teach tactics and command, while a second establishment, the 302nd Tank Training Center at Bourg, a village close to Langres, would teach driving and maintenance. Patton was responsible for establishing and organizing both these centers and he rapidly became the American army's tank expert. Equipment for the schools was obtained from the Allies, a mixture of British and French tanks, and a few surplus tanks of obsolescent design were shipped across to the United States to set up further training centers at Camp Colt (commanded by Captain Dwight D Eisenhower), and Camp Tobyhanna, both in Pennsylvania. Recruitment of personnel began, the nucleus being a battalion of engineers. Continuous expansion eventually provided six battalions in

Above: An American patrol, accompanied by a lone tank, runs for cover at the sound of an approaching shell.

Europe and 11 more in the United States. Companies were organized on the basis of 24 tanks each, a command tank for the CO and three platoons each of five tanks, leaving eight tanks to be held as the company reserve. Once the Tank Training Center began operating, Patton gave basic instruction to the first arrivals, and then sent some officers to the French Tank School to learn tactics while others were sent on attachment to French tank companies to gain experience of combat and practical handling of the tanks. Over and above the basic mechanical and technical training imparted, Patton's school soon gained a reputation for strict discipline, immaculate turn out and dress and rigid military deportment which spread throughout the AEF.

The immediate aim was to produce two fully trained battalions by the Spring of 1918. This was achieved but unfortunately, having got his two trained battalions, Patton had no tanks with which to equip them, because the vast and ambitious American tank production program had foundered. In the first place the proposed three-nation venture in building Mark VIII heavy tanks collapsed because the Americans, who were to produce the engines, were unable to do so, while the German April offensive had so drained British stocks that they were unable to produce the necessary raw materials for their side of the task. The light-tank program in the USA had been held up for dozens of minor reasons; the axle manufacturer needed a priority to obtain steel, the steel mill needed a priority to obtain coke, the railroad company needed a priority to obtain cars to deliver the coke, and so on. The French-designed turret was not considered satisfactory and two new designs were drawn up, but after almost four months both were found to be unsuitable and a fresh design was called for. There was also a delay in translating the metric-dimensioned French drawings into American inches. Eventually the first American-built light tanks reached France on 29 November 1918, almost three weeks after the war had ended, and when they were tested it was discovered that their 'armor' was not proof against machine-gun bullets. Of the 23,405 tanks ordered, 64 Renault, 15 Ford Two-Man (basically an improved Renault) and one Mark VIII heavy had been built by the time of the Armistice, and at that point the contracts were ruthlessly slashed. Eventually 100 Mark VIII and 952 light tanks were completed, and these were to form the US Army's entire tank strength for many years to come.

All this, though, was in the future when Patton reported his tank battalions trained and ready for action in early 1918. The AEF were still under the impression that they would be receiving tanks at any moment, so that tank men were left to train and practice while Patton went to watch the French tank units in action at various places on the front. In this period, too, he managed to find time to attend the US General Staff College at Langres. In June 1918 the AEF finally came to realize that they had been fed with optimistic forecasts from the USA rather than with accurate estimates of tank production and delivery, and they therefore turned to the French for assistance. The French provided sufficient light tanks to outfit the two battalions ready at Bourg.

This was not entirely altruistic on the part of the French, who rarely gave anything away for free. They needed the assistance of the AEF and they needed it quickly. Waiting for tanks to arrive from the USA could mean waiting far too long for them to be of any practical use, and if the only way to get the AEF into the war was to give them tanks, then tanks they would have. The spring and summer of 1918 had seen a setback for the Allies on the Western Front. In late 1917 Russia had collapsed, withdrawn from the war and convulsed herself in revolution. Contrary to common belief, the German Army did not immediately withdraw from the Eastern Front and rush back to reinforce the armies in the West; instead, a million Germans rolled forward into Russia and secured some valuable tracts of territory for subsequent use as bargaining counters. Even so, enough troops were withdrawn to give the west a useful reinforcement and, moreover, the amount of supplies needed in the east was considerably reduced. These accretions to his strength in the west were welcomed by Ludendorff, who had calculated that American strength on the Western Front would become available to the Allies in about June or July 1918 – an assessment which was substantially correct. Therefore the Germans had to defeat Britain and France before the weight of the AEF could be brought to bear, and it was this reasoning which had led to the German spring offensive. In this, thanks to sound staff work, the use of 'Storm Troops,' and powerful artillery bombardments, the German armies burst through on the Somme and south of Ypres in April, on the Aisne and Marne in May, and on the Matz in June. In mid-July this terrible advance was finally brought to a halt near Villers-Cotterets, and a few days later the French, assisted by the US 1st and 2nd Divisions, counterattacked with every tank they

Above: In comparative peace, American troops now stream into the Saint-Mihiel Salient after the German retreat in October 1918.

could find. This attack broke the Germans and began their retreat.

Within a week it became apparent to Foch, Pershing and the other Allied commanders that there was now a chance to bring things to a head. The Germans had overstretched their strength and their supply lines in their headlong advances and had left large salients protruding into the Allied lines. The first step, therefore, was to straighten out these bulges, one of which was the Saint-Mihiel Salient, and this task was given to Pershing's First US Army.

The plans for the Saint-Mihiel attack were drawn up by Colonel George C Marshall, Chief of Operations of First Army. Sixteen American divisions were to be used, together with the French II Colonial Corps under US command, a total of about 665,000 troops. The attack was to be supported by 3220 artillery pieces, 1500 aircraft, and 267 Renault light tanks, since no heavy tanks could be spared from other operations. Among this number were the 144 American-crewed tanks making up the 304th US Tank Brigade, composed of the 334th and 345th Tank Battalions and com-

manded by Major George S Patton.

The German commanders in the salient – Generals Gallwitz and Fuchs – recognized that they were going to be attacked sooner or later and their first idea was simply to allow the attack to roll on to the Woevre plain so as to expend its first impetus, and then counterattack. On 9 September it became apparent from troop movements and interrogation of prisoners that the salient was to be attacked on both sides simultaneously, which put a different complexion on the matter. It was then decided to evacuate the salient and fall back to form a new defensive line. On 10 September the

Below: Open warfare at last, and American troops man a defensive line of foxholes in the Saint-Mihiel sector.

Below: American infantry dash through a wire entanglement during the attack on Saint-Mihiel, September 1918.

Left: In the Meuse valley, north of Verdun, American troops occupy a position captured from the Germans during the October retreat.

Below left: Skirmish line of the 103rd Infantry Regiment advancing in open country, near Toncy, in July 1917.

Below: American infantry driving off a German patrol near St Benoit, France.

withdrawal began, heavy artillery and equipment being pulled back first. It was just as this withdrawal was getting under way that the Americans attacked, at dawn on 12 September. They caught the Germans in disarray, since a retiring army finds it difficult to turn about and meet a sudden attack. But even so, the Germans put up a stiff resistance once their initial surprise had evaporated. Some historians have belittled the Saint-Mihiel battle as 'the battle in which the Americans relieved the Germans in the Salient,' but it was not quite as simple as that.

Patton's part in the battle was not particularly significant, but that was not for the want of trying. The whole affair, from his point of view, seems to have been conducted at a full gallop, commencing with the panic-inducing news that with the attack scheduled to begin at 0500 hours his tanks had not arrived at their start point at 0300 hours; indeed,

his last company were off-loaded from their railroad flatcars at 0315 hours. Over 100 of the 267 tanks were bogged down in the mud during the first part of their advance. After watching the first companies move off into the dawn mists, Patton followed in his command tank at 0700 hours.

He was now faced with the dilemma which has frequently been advanced as one of the great problems of World War I: command, control and communication. He could either go forward with his leading tanks and 'lead from the front,' in which case he would have no contact with higher command, his reserves or his supporting artillery or he could set up a static Brigade HQ stay in contact with his superiors and supporters, but lose contact with his forward fighting tanks. Characteristically, he chose the former option, and once his command tank had caught up with the forward elements, Patton rode at the head of his men, urging them forward. At the village of Essey he met another flamboyant member of the US Army, Brigadier General Douglas MacArthur, then commanding an infantry brigade. As Patton later recalled, they stood and conversed for some minutes, but neither was paying much attention to the other, each being more concerned with the shells dropping around them. For some reason, Patton left his tank at this point and walked forward into the fighting zone. Here he came upon a platoon of his tanks which he immediately ordered forward to attack the next village, Pannes. Almost immediately, four of the tanks ran out of fuel, so Patton went ahead with the remaining tank. They reached Pannes and moved on, but Patton now found the pace of the Renault tank too slow and he jumped off and walked ahead. By now he was well forward of the general line of advance and it gradually dawned on him that he was walking forward, all alone, and actually within the German lines. This realization was underlined by bursts of German machine-gun fire which appeared to be getting uncomfortably close, and Patton therefore decided it was time to return to his own lines. He

Below: Men of the 308th Infantry firing rifle grenades in the Argonne Forest sector in October 1918.

Left: Troops of the 23rd Infantry using a 37mm trench cannon during the advance against German positions in October 1918.

walked back, rounded up more of his tanks and directed them forward, then walked to Nonsard and found another 25 tanks stalled for want of fuel. Walking and begging lifts, he got back to a fuel dump and organized a supply for his stalled tanks, then commandeered a motorcycle and rode back to HQ to make his report on the day's activities.

He was not, however, greeted as a conquering hero; Rockenbach, who had been trying to contact him all day to find out what was happening to his tank corps, was furious. He pointed out, in pithy phrases, that Patton's task was to lead his tanks, command his tanks and report their progress periodically, not to go gallivanting off all over the front as his fancy took him. At one stage there was even the threat of relieving Patton of his command. In the face of this, Patton swallowed hard and turned on all his charm and humility, promising never, ever, to stray again, excusing himself on the fairly reasonable grounds that it was the first time his tanks had been in action and he was anxious to see as much as possible. Rockenbach calmed down, made Patton promise to stick to his job in the future, and the matter was closed. It was, however, a portent of things to come.

The Battle of the Saint-Mihiel Salient was over in 24 hours, since the disorganized Germans were rapidly rolled up and the salient secured. On the 14th

Patton went forward again to Nonsard to visit his tanks, and here he found what, to his mind anyway, was an open invitation. The German retirement had fallen back considerably further than the American advance had yet reached, leaving an extremely wide belt of no man's land and to Patton, this was a void itching to be filled. He rallied his tanks and rolled forward on to a broad plain, halting about half a mile in front of the German lines. Seeing a party of Germans moving in front of the line, he ordered 'A' company to drive forward and capture them, but on arriving at the group they were found to be prisoners already, being escorted back to a cage by US troops. Denied the chance to return with a 'bag' of prisoners, Patton now ordered a platoon of tanks forward to attack the German line. Four

Below: US Infantry pass through Varenne after its capture in September 1918.

Left: After the battle, US infantry enjoy German black bread and beer found in a captured dugout.

Below left: Among the many new weapons acquired by the AEF was this Stokes 3-inch trench mortar. The ten-pound bomb had a range of about 800 yards.

tanks, led by Lieutenant McClure, rolled forward, over a rise in the ground and out of sight. After about an hour, sounds of gunfire came from the area, and after another half hour when Patton was beginning to worry about his missing platoon, McClure returned, still with all his tanks, to report that he had charged a German field-artillery battery. To prove it, he presented Patton with a German breechblock. By now the Germans had tired of this gadfly and they began shelling Patton's position. This alerted the rest of the front and while Patton was extricating himself, Rockenbach was informed that his errant tank commander was stirring up trouble once more. He ordered Patton to bring all his tanks back within the American lines and then to report personally.

Considering the promises extracted but two days before, Rockenbach was in no mood to argue; he gave Patton one of the most uncomfortable times of his life, threatened to demote him to captain and to send him back to the USA. Again Patton turned on his charm and humility, but this time he had to accept a formal reprimand which went on to his record. But for the rest of his life, Patton was convinced that the US Army had lost a great chance to finish the war on that front; he maintained ever after that had the American advance continued, it would have burst through the German lines. He was seconded in this opinion by MacArthur who, as Patton was doing his 'reconnaissance in force' in no man's land in tanks, was doing almost the same thing with infantry in the direction of Metz.

As is well known, Pershing bitterly resisted any attempt to dilute American effort by parcelling out US troops to British or French formations. He held to this in the face of every sort of argument, from high political strategy to the simple sneers of Foch, and he eventually got his way. The whole of the AEF would now be used to perform a major offensive, entirely planned, directed and executed by American staffs and forces. On the

Meuse-Argonne front the Germans, with little interruption by the French, had built one of the strongest defensive systems on the whole of the Western Front. It was a 12-mile belt of trenches, wire, tunnels, dugouts, pillboxes and strongpoints, layered off in three main lines of resistance, with a partially completed fourth line along high ground at the rear. Pershing planned a frontal attack on this complex, relying on the weight of over a million men to roll through without losing speed and thus open up the German line so as to permit a war of movement. The attack would punch two corridors through this defensive zone, and Patton's tank brigade was attached to I Corps on the left side, his objectives being the village of Varennes and the Aire Valley.

Patton managed to collect 189 Renault tanks for his force, but due to the short time available he was unable to arrange collective training for the infantry and tank units who were to be working together. After a three-hour artillery barrage the US First Army moved into its attack at dawn on 26 September 1918, whereupon all the careful plans went by the board and the Americans found themselves fighting for their lives in some of the most terrible terrain ever encountered. Rocky, intersected by ravines, wrapped in mist, gloom, smoke and the fog of war, the Ardennes swallowed up the attacking force into a morass which was dominated by German firepower. It was a 'soldier's battle' insofar as it relied entirely on the initiative of individuals, out of the sight and command of their superiors, to take what chances they could.

Patton advanced with his tanks and by 0900 hours had cleared the village of Varennes in accordance with his orders. But the infantry he was supposed to be supporting were nowhere to be seen, and Patton therefore dismounted from his tank, rounded up a collection of infantrymen from other formations, and then led them forward with his tanks towards the village of Chepy. Here they were stopped by German machine guns. Five tanks advanced to the German lines but had to pause there while their crews dismounted to shovel away part of the German trench parapet, a task they performed under continuous fire. Eventually the crews remounted, charged through the breach, and silenced the machine guns. Patton

followed, still on foot, gathering infantrymen as he went, exhorting them forward with that blend of profanity and jocular obscenity which is more effective than patriotic speeches in such circumstances. But his accompanying infantry grew less and less and eventually he was alone with his orderly, Sergeant Angelo. And then the inevitable happened; a machine gun bullet caught him in the hip and, probably luckily, knocked him into the cover of a shell crater. Angelo leapt down alongside him, tried to staunch the flow of blood with a hastily-applied field dressing, and called for stretcher bearers. They carried Patton back to a dressing station, but once he realized that his wound was not serious he was anxious to return to his tanks, in spite of the remonstrations of the medical officer. But since he was too weak to get off the stretcher and walk back, at that point he had little choice in the matter. As soon as he had been loaded into an ambulance he 'pulled rank' on the driver and instead of being driven to hospital he was taken to 35th Division headquarters. There he managed to dictate a report on the day's activities and the situation at the front, after which he passed out and was shipped, uncomplaining this time, back to the base hospital.

While Patton was hospitalized, the battle continued; it was to last 47 days and cost the Americans 26,227 dead and 96,788 wounded. The initial assault had rapidly run out of momentum, due to the extremely difficult terrain, the relative inexperience of most of the attacking

Above: It's all over, over there! General Pershing cheered by French crowds in Paris after the Armistice.

troops, and the greater experience and savage determination of the defenders. Moreover, the distribution of the available tanks (there had been just over 700 in all) was defective – as was the case in most of the battles of World War One – and instead of having a massed thrust of armor, the tanks had been split up into small packets distributed across the front. Add to this the fact that the country was almost impassable for those early tanks, and the difficulties were complete. Nevertheless, by sheer doggedness the attack continued, accompanied by Allied advances elsewhere on the front; the German lines were beginning to crack.

The knowledge that things were coming to a climax while he lay in hospital was enough to upset Patton, but until his wound was sewn up and had begun to heal there was little he could do but lie in bed and fret. Eventually he could stand it no more; he bribed an orderly and, with another officer, broke out of the hospital, 'acquired' an automobile and set out to catch up with the advancing army. They finally reached Verdun, prepared to lie their way back into everybody's good graces and back into the war, but they were too late. It was Patton's birthday, which he felt was bound to be a good omen, but the 11th of November has had a greater significance since then. It was the day of the Armistice and for Patton the war was definitely over.

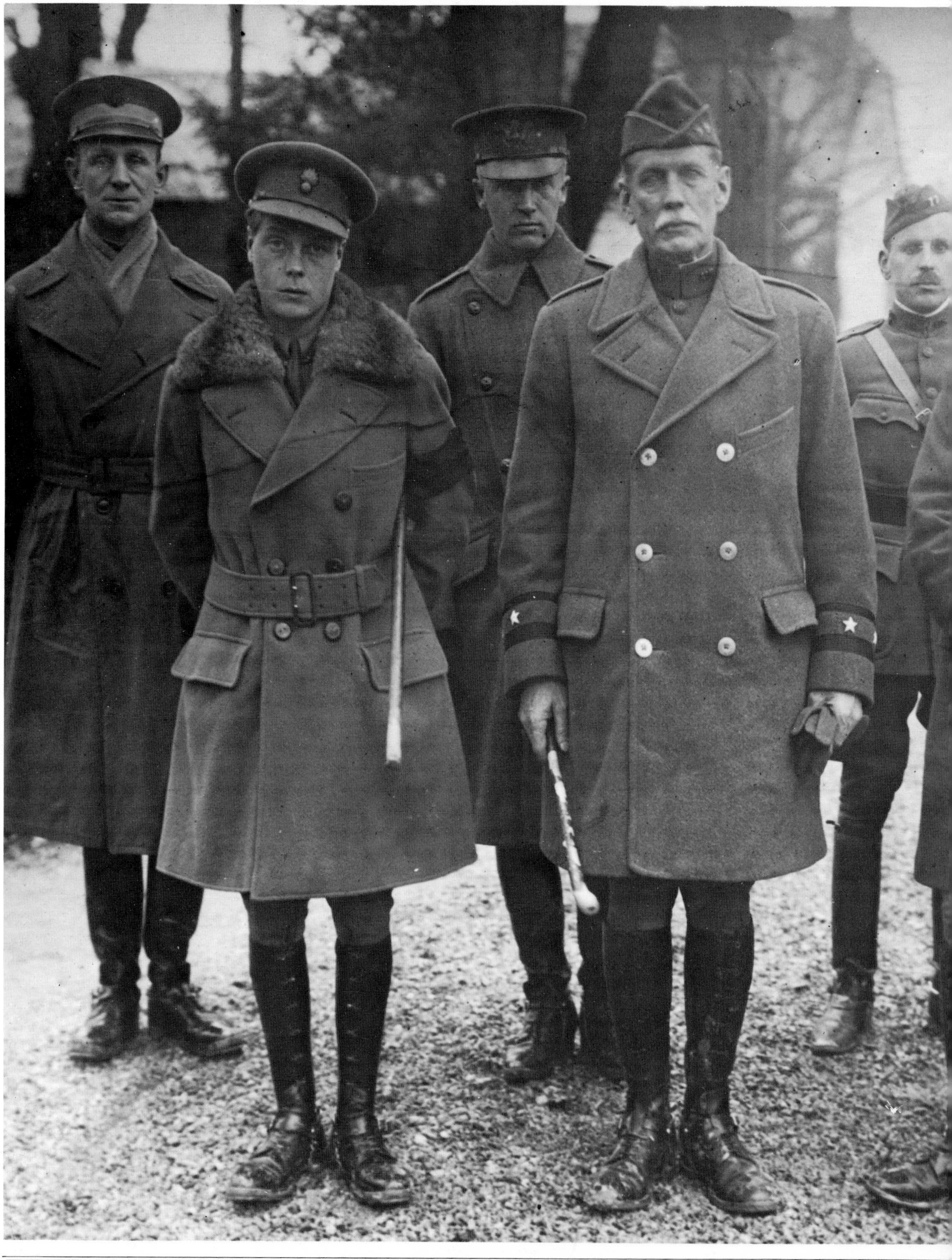

2: BACK TO THE ARMY AGAIN

Now that the pressures of war were off, Patton found himself standing in front of General Rockenbach once again. By this time Patton was a temporary Colonel, but even that didn't save him from Rockenbach's wrath over his break-out from hospital. Patton, however, had taken steps to short-circuit any retribution by seeking a personal interview with Pershing and telling him the whole story, slanting it to look more like a boyish escapade than a breach of discipline. For a man whose exercise of discipline was the strictest in the army and who was renowned throughout the AEF as a stern taskmaster, Patton's views on his own behavior were, to say the least of it, biased; a case of 'do as I say, not as I do.' But Pershing knew his man and smoothed the whole matter over. Patton's next worry was that he would not get the Distinguished Service Cross which he felt was his due, and it looked very much as if Rockenbach had put a spoke in that particular wheel. Seeking out Rockenbach, he taxed him with this, only to be told 'You have your colonelcy – be satisfied with that.' But Patton was not to be satisfied with that, and he lobbied untiringly around GHQ, rounding up acquaintances who could be relied upon to put in a good word with Pershing. Whether or not this campaign was successful, or whether it was even necessary, we will never know, but in any event, on New Year's Day 1919 he received the Distinguished Service Cross from Pershing at a short ceremonial parade in GHQ, with a citation which tied it firmly to his adventure in the Argonne:

'Near Chepy, France, September 16th 1918, he displayed conspicuous courage, coolness, energy and intelligence in directing the advance of his brigade down the valley of the Aire. Later he rallied a force of disorganized infantry and led it forward behind the tanks

Left: Colonel Patton stands behind His Royal Highness the Prince of Wales at 8th Army Corps in 1919.

under heavy machine-gun and artillery fire until he was wounded. Unable to advance further, he continued to direct the operations of his unit until all arrangements for turning over command were completed.'

Shortly after this he was to receive a second decoration, this time the Distinguished Service Medal for his services in organizing the infant Tank Corps:

'By his energy and sound judgment he rendered very valuable services in the organization and direction of the Tank Center at the Army School at Langres. In the employment of the Tank Corps troops in combat he displayed high military attainments, zeal, and a marked adaptability in a form of warfare new to the United States Army.'

And so, in a matter of two and a half years Patton had gone from an untried second lieutenant to a seasoned colonel; he had seen a variety of combat situations, had trained and led the newest technical arm, had been wounded and had been decorated. Now he was confronted with the anticlimax of peacetime soldiering, but he had the reassurance that he would be able to devote his time to perfecting his grasp of tank warfare. Rockenbach called him in and announced that the Tank Corps was to be maintained in the peacetime army, and that Patton, on General Pershing's specific order, was to be offered a post in it. Patton was happy to accept and as a reward he was granted the command of his wartime brigade, with instructions to return it to Fort Meade, Maryland. There it would act as the nucleus for the postwar Tank Corps.

Unfortunately for the Tank Corps and for Patton, other people had different ideas. In the first place the American nation turned away from wars and armies and set about returning to normal; this led to a paring of the military budget to a point where most of the best officers were driven to resign, since their salaries were insufficient to maintain their families. A Congressional report of 1918 pointed out that dockworkers in New York were better paid than were junior military officers. At the same time, the Army was being rapidly run down to its peacetime strength. At the end of the war the Tank Corps had mustered 1,090 officers and 14,780 men; in 1919 General Staff plans reduced this enormous strength to five brigades and a headquarters to suit the reorganized peacetime army of five corps. But before much else could be done a new National Defense Act was passed, and among its other provisions it completely abolished the Tank Corps as an independent arm of the service. Taking into account the supporting role which tanks had played in the war, the Act decreed that a tank was an infantry weapon and that henceforth all tank units were to form part of the infantry, to be known simply as 'Infantry (Tanks).'

In concrete terms this meant that one tank company was allotted to each infantry or cavalry division, a total of 13 separate companies of which only ten were actually activated. There were also five independent tank battalions, for attachment to corps, and a Headquarter 1st Tank Group. These latter formations were based on the wartime Tank Corps and gave some element of continuity and tradition to what remained of the tank spirit.

The reorganization also hit at individuals. Prior to the National Defense Act there had been a massive purge of wartime ranks; Colonel George S Patton was reduced to the rank of captain on 30th June 1919, though he was then promoted to Major, effective 1st July 1919, and he was one of the lucky ones. Nevertheless, he saw little reason for complaint, for he was financially independent, and at least he had his beloved tanks to look after. Then came reductions in scales of supply in the cause of economy. The gasoline allocation for the tank brigade was slashed to 500 gallons per day, scarcely sufficient to permit a useful afternoon's training. Even before this could be fully assimilated the allocation was slashed again; this time to the point where all that could be done was to warm up the motors of the tanks every morning to prevent them seizing solid. The only military activity which could be performed with the tanks was to paint them, and although there was no apparent limit to the amount of paint available, there was a limit to how many times a tank could be painted.

It was at about this time, while the

Tank Corps was still in existence, that Patton met a man who could scarcely fail to appeal to him, another flamboyant character named Walter Christie. Christie was either a brilliant inventor or a dangerous lunatic, depending upon one's point of view; most people held both opinions at various stages of their acquaintance with him. Born in 1866, he became an engineer and mechanical designer, and was involved in the design of naval gun mountings and turrets in the early 1900s. He then grew interested in the automotive field and set up the 'Front Drive Motor Company.' During World War I he was drawn to the possibility of mounting guns on motor chassis, and he developed a series of self-propelled gun mountings. These were greeted with some approval by the US Army, which encouraged him to continue in this line, but in 1918 he abandoned artillery and decided to design a tank. This saw completion in the following year and Christie was invited by the Army Ordnance Department to demonstrate it at Aberdeen Proving Ground. Apparently, it was this demonstration which Patton heard about and, seeking more information, he went to Christie's small factory in Elizabeth, New Jersey, to examine the tank. There is some doubt as to what happened next. According to some legends, Patton told Christie to bring the tank to Camp Meade and demonstrate it

there, and it is said to have made the journey on its own tracks at 30 mph. But the only Christie tank in existence at that time was the M1919 model, and records are abundant to prove that it was difficult to maneuver on its tracks, was insufficiently robust to have travelled from Elizabeth to Camp Meade, Maryland, and could not do more than 7 mph since it was grossly underpowered. In spite of all that it was an impressive design, especially when compared with the wartime tanks. It was low-slung, compact, and once the mechanical problems were ironed out, gave every promise of being a fast and agile machine, a promise which was later realized. Patton is said to have had sufficient faith in it to have lent money to Christie, and there can be little doubt that as combat soldier he would have been keen to give the inventor advice on the practical aspects of design. Whether Christie would have taken any notice of him is another question.

While willing to encourage inventors in a minor way, the US Army was not prepared to back such a complicated device as a tank except by small stages. They bought the M1919 from Christie, tested it for a while, and then sent it back, asking him to make some changes, moving the gun mounting forward and strengthening the suspension. This changed the nomenclature of the tank to

the M1921, and for the original design and the modifications, Christie received $82,000. He now set to work to design an amphibious tank in the hope of interesting the US Marines, and here we can leave him for a while; but we might add at this point that this sudden change from a land tank to an amphibian was entirely in keeping with Christie's character as the Army gradually came to know it. No sooner had an idea been translated into working form than Christie was lusting after something new. When, as often happened, the Army came back to him with a tank and asked for some changes, Christie would refuse, offering instead some totally new and untried concept. Eventually Army Ordnance had enough of Walter Christie, their prime cause for complaint being that over the years they had paid him some $800,000 without ever having received a tank which worked properly.

But Patton believed in Christie's ideas for a fast, highly maneuverable tank which could swoop across the battlefield like the cavalryman of old, upsetting the enemy and cutting lines of communication and supply. But before he could do very much to promote Christie's design or his own barely-formed theories of tank

Below: The Christie T3 tank, which could run on wheels or tracks at high speeds but which never ran well enough for the Army.

employment, the National Defense Act was passed, the axe fell, and Patton's Tank Corps vanished overnight. Though Patton continued to press the need for an integrated tank force and spoke prophetically of a future in which the whole army would roll on tracks and wheels, he was whistling in a graveyard. There was no money for tank development, there was no organization capable of focussing interest on tanks, and, finally very few people were at all interested in tanks. Patton was faced with a choice. Either he could follow his tanks into the limbo of infantry attachment, which would mean transferring to the infantry (an arm in which he was virtually unknown, had no training or background, and precious little interest); or he could make a clean break, get out of the tank business and back into the mainstream of the horse cavalry in which he had been raised.

Patton was an enthusiast, but not a fanatic; he would champion a cause loud and long until the day he realized it was a lost one. Once he saw the futility of a venture he would immediately abandon it and turn to something more profitable or congenial without a second thought. More particularly, he was wise enough to see when pursuit of a course of action was likely to jeopardize his career or his well-being, and at the crucial moment he knew enough to compromise or cut his losses. In this case he had done everything he could to promote the Tank Corps idea, but further advance was effectively stopped by Congress and their National Defense Act. He could do no more good by staying with the tanks, and indeed it was likely that he would do himself a disservice by being shunted off into a backwater and, at the same time, making himself unnecessary enemies by espousing a forlorn hope. There was only one thing to do, and in the summer of 1920 he returned to regimental duty with the cavalry.

He reported for duty to 1st Squadron, 3rd US Cavalry at Fort Myer, Virginia, and soon got back into the routine of peacetime regimental life. Horse shows, hunting, a variety of sports, polo (he captained the Army team) and the social round took up his time, though not entirely. He retained a seat on the Tank Development Board, though there was little tank development to oversee in those days, and he kept up his acquaintance with Christie. He also devoured all

the texts he could find, notably those in European military journals, which discussed armored warfare. He wrote papers for the Cavalry Journal and other military periodicals, expounding on the future of the tank, though it is notable that even there he was hedging his bets; in one paper he advanced the theory that horses and armor could work together in the future, the armor giving the frontal thrust while the horse cavalry swept around the flanks. Odd as this may sound today, it was a popular theory in the 1920s and was seconded by no less than the Chief of Cavalry, Major General Guy Henry, who said, 'In the future we will have two types of cavalry, one with armored motor vehicles giving speed, strategic mobility and the great fighting power of modern machines, the other with horses, armed with the latest automatic firearms for use in tactical roles and for operations in difficult terrain where the horse still gives the greatest mobility.'

In 1923 after his tour of duty with the 3rd Cavalry, Patton was sent to the Command and General Staff School at Fort Leavenworth, graduated, and took posts on the General Staff, first in Boston and then in Hawaii. It was his posting to Hawaii which led to the termination of his attachment to the Tank Development Board, since it was obviously impossible for him to contribute anything to their discussions from his faraway desk. Returning to the USA in 1927 he received a staff post in the Washington office of the Chief of Cavalry, spending most of his time there rewriting the Regulations for the Pistol. Finally, in 1932, his staff tour was over and he returned to his old regiment at Fort Myer, in the post of Executive Officer.

During all this period there had been some slow progress in the American tank world, which had begun when Secretary of War Dwight Davis had visited Britain in 1927 to attend the annual army maneuvers. The focal point of these exercises was the assembly and deployment of an Experimental Armoured Force of tanks, armored cars, truck-borne infantry, self-propelled artillery and mechanized engineers. This force gave a convincing demonstration of the flexibility and speed possible to a fully mechanized force, and Davis was sufficiently impressed as to make him order the US Chief of Staff, General Charles P Summerall, to organize a similar force

from available elements of the US Army.

On 1st July 1928 the Experimental Mechanized Force was assembled at Fort Meade, from a collection of old World War I tanks, truck-borne infantry and engineers, and two batteries of artillery carried on the back of trucks. It sounded impressive, but in reality most of the equipment was on its last legs, and difficulties arose when the Maryland authorities objected to the tanks maneuvering on roads since they were liable to damage the taxpayer's asphalt. One by one the elderly vehicles broke down, no money was available for their repair or replacement, and on 20th September the force was disbanded. Its only achievement was to turn the spotlight on mechanization and start up some profitable discussion within the Army's ranks.

By this time Christie had returned to the tank field and had produced a new design. The M1927 was a light tank which could move on tracks or, with the tracks removed, on wheels to give better road performance and more speed. Propelled by a somewhat unreliable ex-aircraft engine which had been doctored to deliver more horsepower than the

designer ever contemplated, the tank could move at 40 mph on tracks or 70 mph on wheels. It was a grossly unreliable machine, and it had no pretense to fighting ability, but it was fast and nimble and it convinced Major Adna R Chaffee, a cavalryman in that section of the War Department concerned with mechanization, that tank tactics had to be divorced from the infantry-accompanying concept. Chaffee studied the results of the abortive Mechanized Force, considered the Christie tank, and drew up a series of papers for the War Department in which he recommended a four-year development programme. This was 'approved in principle,' but because there was no money available, the approval was hollow.

In due course, however, opinion came around to considering some tank development, if only to keep up with what the rest of the world was doing, and in the appropriations for 1931 the sum of $288,000 was allotted for mechanization, together with an additional $250,000 for the purchase of six Christie tanks. In October 1930 the Mechanized Force was revived and stationed at Fort Eustis, near Lee Hall, Virginia, but immediately ran

Above: Patton the sportsman; as a member of the team which won the Argentine Cup in 1931; the captain, Major Jacob L Devers.

into political problems. Since the National Defense Act had allocated tanks to the infantry, the Chief of Infantry demanded control of the Mechanized Force. Chaffee knew that his visions of an independent tank force would be shattered if the infantry took control. But just at that moment the whole question of the cavalry's future came under review; President Hoover had turned a cold eye on the Army and asked General MacArthur, then Chief of Staff, whether there was any place for horse cavalry in modern war. MacArthur invited the cavalry to present their case, and they began casting around for good military reasons to justify their existence. Chaffee saw his chance in this; he got the ear of the Chief of Cavalry, and eventually the Mechanized Force was assimilated into the cavalry. There remained the semantic problem that tanks were, by definition, infantry equipment. This was evaded by a simple stratagem. If the infantry owned a tank, then it was called a tank; if the cavalry owned a tank, then it was called a

G S Patton Jr
Col. 5 th Cav.

Left: Patton the soldier in his full-dress uniform as Commanding Officer of the 5th Cavalry regiment at Fort Clark.

'combat car.' Honor was satisfied, the Mechanized Force was safe, and the cavalry had a new role.

It was a short-lived victory. In 1931 General MacArthur decided that instead of mechanization becoming the private property of one corps, all the arms and services would 'adopt mechanization as far as is practicable and desirable' and that they could all experiment in whatever direction they felt best suited their role. The Mechanized Force was dissolved once more and MacArthur made it known that 'no separate corps is to be established in the vain hope that through a utilization of machines it can absorb the missions and duplicate the capabilities of others.' In other words, the use of wheels, tracks and armor was open to everybody; there was to be no revival of the Tank Corps.

All this activity had passed Patton by. He knew, of course, what was going on, but he was not directly concerned with it. In 1933, when the 1st Cavalry assembled in Fort Knox, Kentucky to become the first Mechanized Cavalry Regiment, Patton was still Executive Officer of the 3rd Cavalry, which retained its horses. In 1935 he returned to a staff appointment, and in 1937 was appointed to command the 9th Cavalry. By now he was over 50 years old, and his thoughts were beginning to turn towards retirement. He appeared to have failed in his early ambition to make something of armor; he had been content to 'soldier on' in the peacetime cavalry and conform to the norms of regimental life, though since he was never a man to suffer fools gladly, he had trodden on a few toes in his time. He found a pleasant farm in South Hamilton, near Boston, bought it, and made ready to hang up his spurs. The writing on the wall came in 1938 when he was appointed to command the 5th Cavalry at Fort Clark, Texas. It was known throughout the cavalry that this was the green meadow into which old warhorses were turned before retirement, the most quiet and undemanding post in the Army, one from which the Commanding Officer could quietly absent himself for long periods of time while he prepared the ground for his impending retirement.

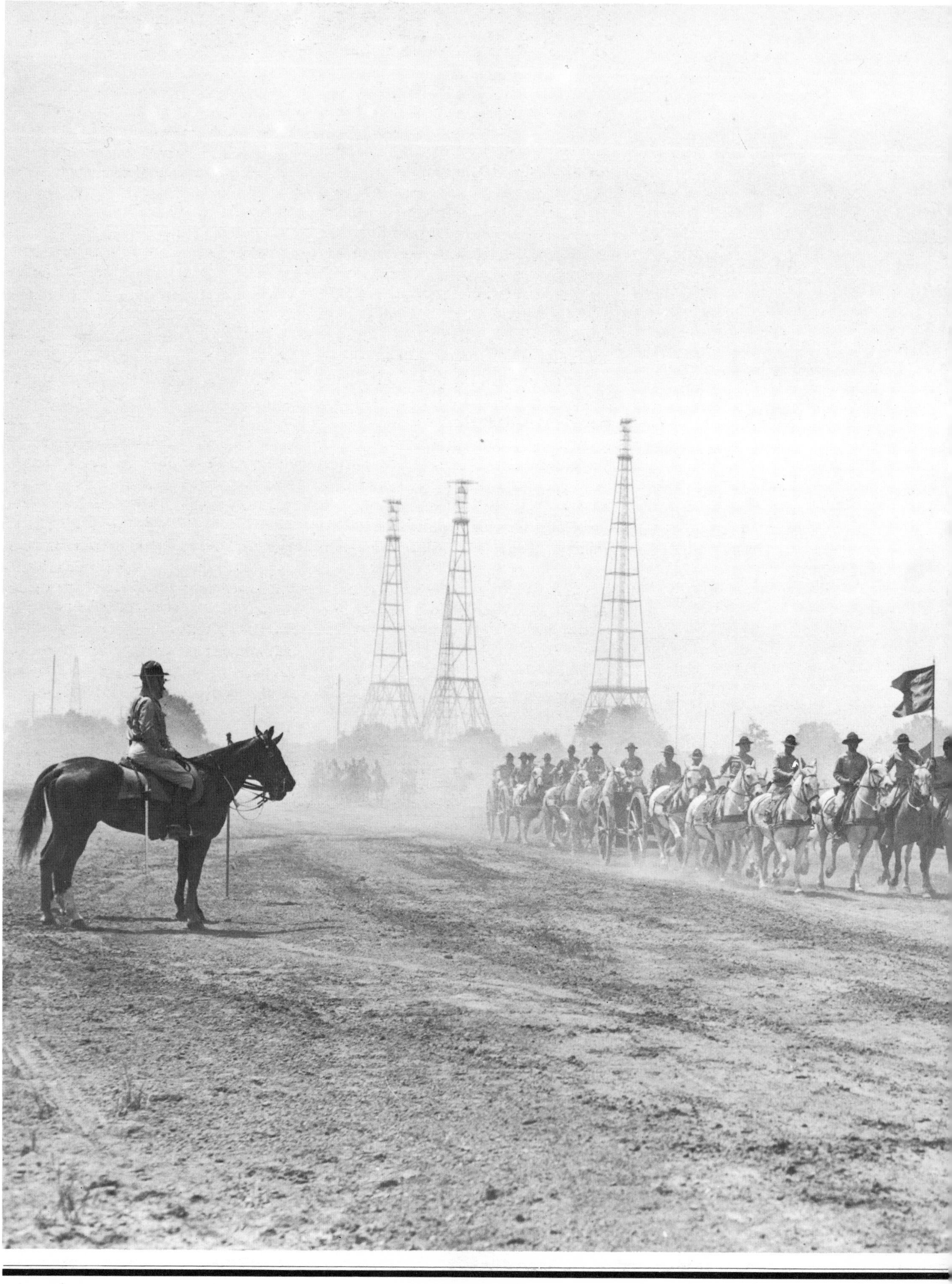

3: THE GREEN HORNET

In 1937 George C Marshall, who had planned the Saint-Mihiel operation that introduced Patton to armored warfare, was appointed Deputy Chief of Staff. Marshall was one of the best and most intelligent soldiers ever produced in America; his grasp of planning and logistics was masterly, he was a shrewd judge of men, and he was loyal to those who deserved loyalty. Although he and Patton were never close friends, they had maintained the acquaintance struck up in France and Marshall had kept an eye on Patton through the quiet years. Now, in 1938, rumblings from Europe convinced Marshall that a war was inevitable and that, sooner or later, America would find herself involved in it. And when that happened there would be a need for fighting soldiers. And so, in spite of the fact that he had ruled that no major command would henceforth go to

any officer over the age of 50, Marshall arranged for Patton to be relieved in command of the 5th Cavalry and given a staff post at Fort Myer so that he would be close to Washington and on hand when Marshall needed him.

On 1st September 1939 the Germans moved against Poland, and on that same day Marshall became Chief of Staff, a post he was to retain throughout the war. Patton had been following events in Europe very closely, and now he devoured every scrap of information which he could find about the German armored thrust, information both in the public press and in the confidential reports flowing in from US military attaches and observers in Europe. At last it seemed that the potential of armor was being realized, though unfortunately by the wrong people. But the rapid advance of the Panzers in Eastern Europe reinforced many of the ideas on independent action with which Patton had been toying since he had been peremptorily pulled back from the Hindenburg Line in 1918. In Patton's view the German Army was now demonstrating that an armored spearhead, given its head and the proper equipment, could cut its way through

Left: The Old Army; 16th Field Artillery passes in review before General Maxwell Murray and Colonel George Patton at Fort Myer, Virginia, 4th June 1940.

Below: General George C Marshall, Chief of Staff, and Henry L Stimson, Secretary of War confer in January 1942.

conventional defenses and change the face of war in an afternoon. He abandoned his desk at Fort Myer and began prowling the corridors of the War Department, haranguing any who would listen and many who would not about the need for an independent armored force in the US Army.

It appeared to have little effect, indeed, so little effect that Patton actually wrote to a friend in the Canadian Army, General McNaughton, asking if a place could be found for him there. McNaughton replied that he could come as a major if he so desired, and Patton was still seriously considering this when in

May 1940 the second phase of Germany's conquest of Europe began and the Panzers rolled once more, this time into Denmark, Norway, the Low Countries and finally France, sweeping all before them. The 'Blitzkrieg' appeared to be so irresistible that even those in the USA who espoused armored warfare began to

wonder whether it might be wiser to keep quiet and not get involved in such a terrible business.

Fortunately, George C Marshall was shockproof; he had seen most of this coming and had long ago begun to plan for it. Now, in an atmosphere of commitment to defense, he began talking about the formation of powerful armies, fleets of bombers, armored divisions, elements of forces which were generally considered to be offensive rather than defensive. In the mood of inertia of the day, Marshall saw his chance and took it; on 10th July 1940 the US Armored Force was brought into being, with General Adna R. Chaffee as its Chief. In fact, because the National Defense Act of 1920 still held good, Marshall's directive to set up the force read 'For the purposes of service test, an Armored Force is created . . .,' a phrasing which circumvented the law and permitted the force to be formed without having to seek Congressional approval or introduce an amendment to the National Defense Act. It is worth noting that when, a few months later, an attempt was made to straighten out this piece of equivocation and formally create the Armored Force as a separate branch of the service, the move was defeated by the combined opposition of the Chiefs of Infantry and Cavalry, and the Armored Force never did achieve independent status. This was to cause considerable problems in postwar years.

Four days before the formation of the Armored Force Patton had written a letter to Chaffee:

'My Dear General,

I was unfortunate in being unable to connect with you . . . while you were here. I did see Scott, who told me that you were good enough to mention me in connection with a command in mechanization. I certainly appreciate your kindness and want to assure you, if it is necessary, which, knowing me, it probably is not, that I am always willing to fight and am enthusiastic in whatever job I have. I will always do my best to give satisfaction should I be fortunate enough to be selected.'

To which Chaffee replied:

'I put you on my preferred list as a brigade commander for an armored

Left: Major General Patton, now commanding 2nd Armored Division, during the Louisiana Manoeuvers, September 1941.

Above: After the manoeuvers, General Patton holds a post-mortem for the officers of 2nd Armored Division at their base in Fort Benning, Georgia.

brigade. I think it is a job which you can do to the queen's taste . . . I hope things work out favorably for you. I shall always be happy to know that you are around close in any capacity where there is fighting to be done.'

Chaffee's preferred list had obviously gone to Marshall for his guidance and approval. No sooner had Marshall ordered the formation of the Armored Force than he ordered Colonel Patton from Fort Myer to Fort Benning,

Georgia to organize and take command of the newly-authorized 2nd Armored Brigade, and shortly afterward promoted him to Brigadier General.

When the Armored Force came into being it inherited about 400 miscellaneous light tanks of various designs, 18 elderly medium tanks, and a handful of armored cars and weapons carriers. For personnel it had a nucleus of trained men from existing tank companies, but for expansion it had to rely upon transfers from other units and, as is always the case, the commanding officers of other units saw this as a heaven-sent opportunity to get rid of all their hard cases, idlers and incorrigible rogues, while carefully blocking any applications from their best men. It was not until September 1940, when conscription came into effect, that the supply of recruits, both in quantity and quality, began to improve. In the meantime Patton had to do what he could with his understrength brigade and their decrepit equipment.

His technique was simple; he drove the men as hard as he could. The tanks were patched and painted – often at Patton's own expense, since spare parts were often unobtainable through the Army's supply channels but could be purchased commercially. He insisted on a high standard of dress and discipline to give the men of his brigade a sense of pride in their outfit, and he played cleverly on this sense of identity by

Left: General Patton addressing troops of the 4th Division at a rally in May 1941.

devising minor distinctions in vehicle markings, dress and tactical maneuvers which effectively marked off 2nd Armored Brigade from the rest of the force and made them instantly recognizable. His supreme gimmick was to design uniforms of unusual color and cut; they were regarded with horror by the upper echelons of the Army and there was never the slightest hope that they would ever become a permitted issue, but Patton wore them, nevertheless. His men became accustomed to seeing him caparisoned in a monstrous golden helmet, green trousers with a black stripe, a green leather jacket of racy cut, and with either his two ivory-handled revolvers (one a Colt .45 Model 1873, the other a Smith & Wesson .357 Magnum) at his waist or with one of them in a shoulder holster

Left: The loneliness of command; Patton ponders his next move during the Louisiana manoeuvers.

surprised. They were treated to rousing tirades couched in language more suited to a drill sergeant than a general officer or to a poolroom rather than a military lecture hall. Four-letter words were common currency, and some of his remarks went into history:

'I hear a lot of crap about what a glorious thing it is to die for your country. It isn't glorious, it's stupid! You don't go into battle to die for your country, you go into battle to make the other bastard die for *his* country . . .'

'You need to grab the enemy by his nose and kick him in the ass . . .'

'War is a killing business. You've got to spill their blood. Rip 'em up the belly or shoot 'em in the guts . . .'

'This war will be won by blood and guts alone . . .'

It was this last phrase which stuck, and earned him the nickname 'Old Blood and Guts' which stuck to him for evermore. Though there is an apocryphal story of a

Below: The General takes a break to study the tactical situation, near Montgomery, Louisiana.

over his jacket. The press, which was beginning to find stories in the expanding army and particularly in the 'glamorous' armored force, discovered that Patton was never too busy to make a few quotable remarks or to make himself available, suitably dressed, for a dramatic picture. His men knew him, from his mode of dress, as 'Flash Gordon,' 'The Man from Mars' or, most often, 'The Green Hornet.' Patton knew that this image sold the Armored Force to the public and it gained him recruits. It even gained him some deserters; men who went absent from other units and surrendered themselves at Fort Benning, happy to exchange a short sentence of detention for a posting to the new Armored Brigade.

His other morale-raising gambit was to have an amphitheater built and there address the troops at frequent intervals. At first, the troops thought they were to be given the usual platitudes about duty, country, church and home, but they were

Left: General Patton with Lieutenant Colonel Mark Clark on a sidewalk in Manchester, Tenn, June 1941.

British battleship. When he appeared before his men he was always immaculately turned-out and, like all experienced officers, he had that uncanny ability to discern where the trouble was and descend on it like the wrath of God. If a truck stalled and held up a convoy, if an artillery battalion occupied the wrong position, if a tank platoon got stuck in a bog, Patton was sure to appear, cursing all, identifying the wrongdoer with unerring accuracy and flaying him with his tongue. But, as many of his men have testified, he was also among the first to strip off his coat and plunge into whatever had to be done, heaving at a bogged truck, coupling a winch rope, shovelling sand from under a track. And then he was off, smelling trouble in some other place. As one sergeant said, 'You're all right if you do exactly what you're told, and you don't have to be too brilliant doing it. But don't ever lay an egg in front of him. He

trooper who left the amphitheater after one such harangue and said 'Yeah . . . his guts, our blood. Big deal.'

Psychologists have been arguing ever since about the pros and cons of Patton's approach to his men, and it is perhaps difficult for a generation accustomed to hearing much the same sort of language on 'family' TV programmes to appreciate the sense of shock with which these speeches were greeted. Senior officers, in those days, simply did not use language of that sort in front of troops. But Patton was unrepentant: 'You cannot change the habits of these boys overnight. . . . You have to shock them out of their ordinary habits and thinking with that kind of language . . .' And whatever the pundits may say, it worked in this case, with those men and at that time. It might not work with the same men today; it probably would not have worked with British, German or French troops. But it worked with Americans. It worked because it gave a spurious air of togetherness, comradeship, all-in-this-together, democracy, Jack's-as-good-as-his-master, which served to break up the civilian image of the Army as a West Point-dominated hierarchy. It was spurious because Patton took good care to distance himself from the men to a greater degree than most other American officers of the period. Not for Patton the bonhomie of meals from a tin plate in the men's mess-

hall; not for Patton the place in the chow line; not for Patton to carry his own bedroll. He lived aloof from the rest of his formation in his own caravan, served by his orderly. As one commentator put it, it was a solitude like the captain of a

Right: General Patton, on his command tank, confers with General Crittenden about the next phase in the manoeuver.

Left: Patton's ivory-handled revolvers. Above is the Smith & Wesson .357 Magnum. Below is the Colt .45 Model 1873.

ficiencies were in junior leaders, in tactical knowledge, and in the soldiers' ability to cope with the hardships of campaigning. Equipment problems were slowly being overcome as the American production machinery slowly got into its stride; in the middle of 1941 Chrysler began producing M3 Medium (General Lee) tanks, while in March 1941 the first M3 Light (Stuart) tanks had left the American Car & Foundry Company's plant. Until these appeared, the Armored Force had relied largely upon the M2 light tank and the relics of previous years until they fell to pieces.

But shortly after the end of the Louisiana Manoeuvers the question of whether or not the US Army would go to war was conveniently settled by the Japanese, and in January 1942 Patton was appointed to command I Armored Corps. He was also assigned the task of finding some location in the southwestern United States which resembled the desert and mountain landscape of North Africa and which had sufficient room to permit large armored formations to manoeuver, practice live firing, and train to a sufficiently high standard to be able to give battle to the German Panzers. For a week Patton and a survey party flew and drove over and through California, Nevada and Arizona until they found a suitable area, a triangle of over 150,000 square miles located between Desert Center, California, Yuma, Arizona, and Searchlight,

don't like it.'

With this sort of driving, 2nd Armored Brigade soon became a crack outfit. At their first major manoeuvers in Tennessee, in September 1941, the Brigade completed its assigned exercises several hours, even in one case a whole day, earlier than the controlling umpires had expected. In the famed Louisiana Manoeuvers in October, the greatest military exercises ever held in the USA to that time, the umpires decided to handicap Patton by presenting him with a scenario which called for him to deliver a frontal attack over ground so soaked with continuous rain as to be impassable. The task was so obviously impossible that, after protests, they allowed him to make a flanking move. He went off on a 100-mile swing into Texas and back which would again have had his Brigade completing their exercise ahead of schedule if the umpires had not imposed some more artificial checks.

Right: A skeptical look as Patton listens to plans for an advance on Montrose, Louisiana during the 1941 manoeuvers.

Even so, the manoeuvers showed up some glaring defects in the training and equipment; the conscripts were morose and thinking only of their return to civilian life, the National Guard were enthusiastic but poorly trained, the regulars enthusiastic and trained but stretched too thin. The principal de-

Nevada. This barren waste, much of which was already public land, became the Desert Training Center, Camp Indio. It was so enormous that two armored divisions could operate, driving up to 400 miles without ever seeing each other. The climate was harsh, a blazing desert sun giving temperatures of 150°F inside the

tanks, and this gave opportunities to test special diets, medical arrangements, tank insulation, tank engine cooling systems, transmissions and every other aspect of equipment, while the men of I Armored Corps, driven unrelentingly by Patton, learned to fight and survive in the most hostile type of environment short of actual war.

On 30th July 1942 Patton's part in all this activity was abruptly halted by a telephone call from Washington. General Marshall wished to see General Patton as soon as possible; General Patton was to be prepared for a long absence from Camp Indio; indeed, General Patton was not to be surprised if he never saw Indio again. Like a warhorse smelling the battle, Patton was galvanized into activity, rounded up his personal aircraft and set out for Washington without delay. Here, at last, was the call to action.

The call came because in July 1942 things were looking black in all directions. The Japanese were victorious throughout the 'Greater East Asian Co-Prosperity Sphere;' the Germans were storming across the USSR taking

Left: Field Marshal Erwin Rommel, the 'Desert Fox' who was destined to give Patton his chance to demonstrate American armor.

Above: While America manoeuvered, Germany advanced; German Afrika Korps troops in the Libyan Desert.

prisoners by the tens of thousands, and Rommel had chased the British Eighth Army all the way across the Western Desert of Libya to Alamein, a bare 80 miles from Cairo. Stalin was demanding that Britain and America immediately launch a Second Front against Germany, and the American Chiefs of Staff, with little appreciation of the immense difficulties involved, also favored this course of action. The British for very good reasons did not. They pointed out that a premature attack on Hitler's *Festung Europa* would undoubtedly end in disaster and that there were not sufficient men, guns, tanks, landing craft or anything else to perform anything better than a major raid, which would be thrown straight back into the sea. The British alternative was to make a landing in North Africa which would re-open the Mediterranean to Allied shipping, threaten Rommel's supply lines, and, possibly, bring the French in Morocco and Algeria into the war on the Allied side.

This idea had been argued back and forth for some time, but Rommel's push across the Western Desert brought matters to a head. Two alternatives now presented themselves: either the despatch of US troops to Egypt to fight alongside the British, under British command, or a landing in Morocco and Algeria under American command. And bearing in mind Pershing's rigorous defense of all-American operations in 1918, it is obvious which of these courses would have had more appeal to the US Chiefs of Staff. On the 25th July they agreed to 'Operation Torch,' the North African landing under the command of General Eisenhower. But at this point the precise details were far from agreed upon; the British wanted to see a landing well inside the Mediterranean, followed by a rapid advance into Tunisia so as to cut Rommel's supplies and pose an immediate threat to his operations. The Americans wanted a landing on the Atlantic coast of Morocco so as to secure an Atlantic port in case the Germans retaliated by thrusting down through Spain and Gibraltar to cut off the Mediterranean landing force. Both points

of view were sensible, and whatever else was decided, the Moroccan landing was definitely part of the plan. There were, though, some aspects of this landing which looked as if they might cause difficulties – things like surf with 15-foot waves, the questionable attitude of the French garrisons, and the need to make very rapid moves to secure airfields – all of which pointed to the need for an aggressive commander not afraid to take chances. Hence the call to Patton.

On arriving in Washington, Patton was given a short briefing on the broad plan, much as outlined above; he was also told by Marshall to go and consult with the Planning Staffs about the more detailed aspects of his part in the operation; he was also told, in no uncertain terms, that he was to make his plans with the troops and equipment which the Planning Staffs would allot him.

Patton went off to the War College, met the Planners, heard their appreciation of the operation, and was told what troops he would have available. Neither their outline plans nor the troop alloca-

tion satisfied him, and within a very short time he was on the telephone to Marshall's deputy, General Joseph T McNarney, to tell him exactly what he thought about it all. 'I need more men and more ships to be able to do the job,' said Patton. McNarney promised to tell Marshall and rang off. He did tell Marshall who ordered Patton back to Indio forthwith, without even seeing him again.

This was a reaction which Patton had not expected. He returned to Indio, spent some time thinking things over, and came to the conclusion that if he was to get into the war at all, then he would have to eat humble pie. After all, the combat command of the first American troops to go into offensive action was an honor not to be lightly passed over and Patton had been breathing fire and demanding the chance to go to war for years. Now that the chance was there it would be unwise

Below: General Bernard Montgomery, with General Horrocks behind, makes his plans for the Battle of Alamein in 1942.

Right: Field Marshal Rommel with the Italian C-in-C Marshal Cavallero (centre) and General Bastico of the Italian Corps.

to pass it up for the sake of a few men and ships; he might not get a second chance at his age and there were a lot of young men pressing on his heels. Anyway, his own experiences in trying to form 2nd Armored Brigade and 1st Armored Division had shown him that America *was* having problems producing all the equipment needed by her vast armies. Maybe the plans were less unappealing than he had thought. He telephoned Marshall, but was told that he was at a conference; after several more abortive attempts to reach him, he finally rang McNarney. 'I've been doing some thinking . . . maybe I could do the job after all, even with the force your stupid Planning Staff are willing to give me . . .' McNarney reported this to Marshall; 'Fine,' said Marshall, 'Order him back. You see? That's the way to handle Georgie Patton!'

The planning for Torch, the first major Anglo-American operation, was bedevilled by hesitation, disputation, argument and plain misunderstanding before it was all sorted out. The involved course followed by the debate – which was later, and with some justification, called 'The Great Transatlantic Essay Competition' – need not be followed here in great detail. It is enough to say that overlying all else were two prime considerations: first, that pressure had to be put on the Germans before they could react, and second, that the possible reactions of the French carried a great deal of weight in any proposed plan. The American planners put more emphasis on the latter point; one reason for their insistence on American overall command was that they were sure that the French would be less likely to put up an armed resistance to an American force than they would to a British one. This was in spite of Churchill's observation that 'he did not wholly share the American view that either they were so beloved by Vichy or we so hated as to make the difference between fighting and submission.'

The eventual plan was for three forces to strike simultaneously; the Eastern Task Force under General Ryder would land at Algiers, the Center Task Force under General Fredendall at Oran, and the Western Task Force, under General Patton, at Casablanca. (These were broadly-defined targets; in fact the ports, presumed to be well-defended, were not the actual targets – the landings took place on their flanks.) The Eastern and Central forces sailed from Great Britain, using British transport and escorted by the Royal Navy. The Western force sailed from Norfolk, Virginia, with 35,000 men, in American transports and escorted by the US Navy. It was truly a remarkable feat to lift 35,000 men across 3,000 miles of U-Boat infested ocean and

Left: Major General Dwight D Eisenhower, then chief of the Operations Section of the General Staff, in January 1942.

odds of approximately five to one against them.

His military intelligence was scanty, but the political intelligence given to Patton was very misleading. In the hope of persuading the French to accept the forthcoming American invasion, various secret agencies and missions were flitting about North Africa, each sounding out their own contacts and coming to conclusions which, almost without exception, were erroneous. Patton was given a 'political advisor,' Paul F Culbert, whose views were idiosyncratic to the point of idiocy and who filled Patton's head with garbled tales of ethnic strife between Moslems and Moroccan Jews, the dangers of starting a *Jihad* or holy war.

All this political activity, though, meant that all sorts of restraints were laid on Patton's actions. He had to avoid any activity in the vicinity of the 'sacred cities' of Rabat and Sale, he had to be prepared to adopt various courses of action depending upon which way the local political wind blew or whether the stealthy 'missions' discerned some possible advantageous alliance, and so on. And as well as the possibility of dissention in the ranks of those about to be invaded, there was a good deal of it in the ranks of the invaders. At the very first planning

deposit them on a potentially hostile shore in concert with two other forces landing several hundred miles away in a different sea. Patton's directive was 'To secure the port of Casablanca and adjacent airfields and, in conjunction with the Center Task Force at Oran, establish and maintain communications between Casablanca and Oran. Also to build up land and air striking forces capable of securing Spanish Morocco, if that action should become necessary.' Intelligence sources estimated that there were between 60,000 and 100,000 French troops in Morocco, while the Spanish were assumed to have about 100,000 troops in thier area, so that at worst reckoning Patton's forces would have

Below: Field Marshal Rommel and General der Artillerie Karl Boettcher discuss the progress of the battle for Africa.

Left: German reconnaissance troops use a motorcycle combination during a routine patrol in North Africa.

Below: A German Panzer III Ausf L tank with long 75mm gun passing a collection of captured South African vehicles late in 1942.

Right: British prisoners near Tobruk, being escorted by a German guard in a captured American truck.

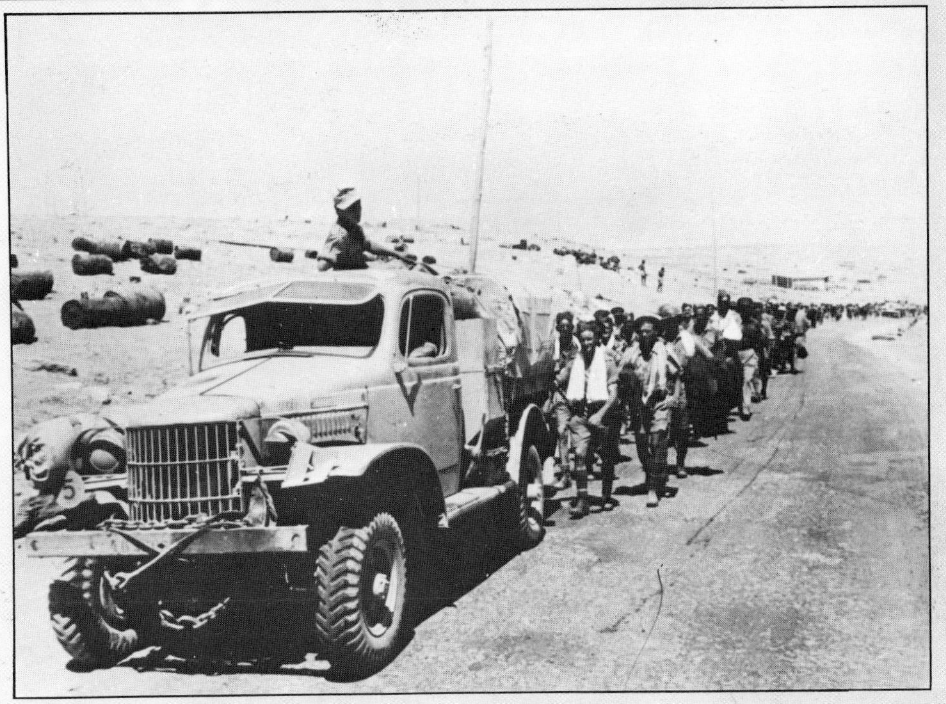

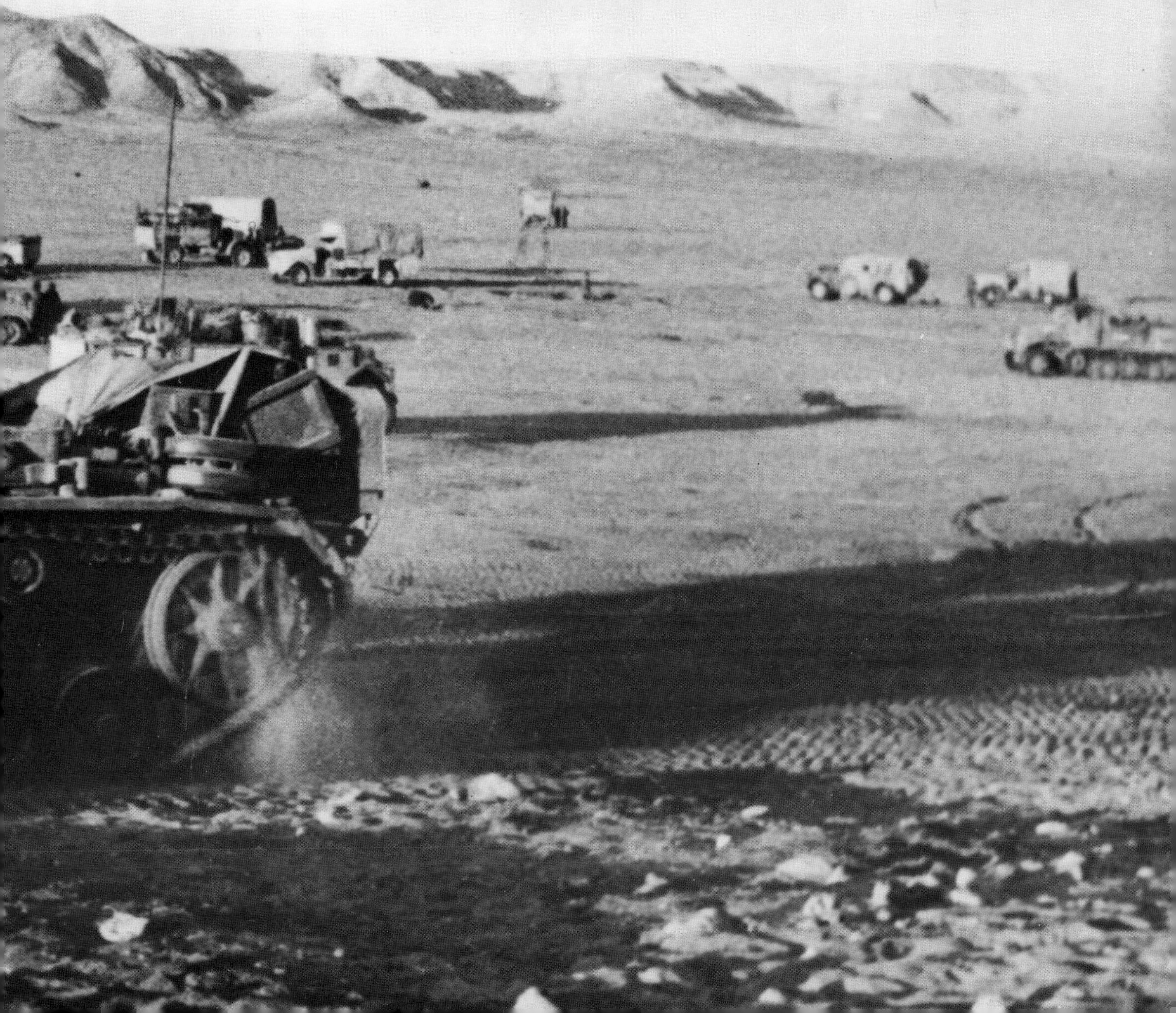

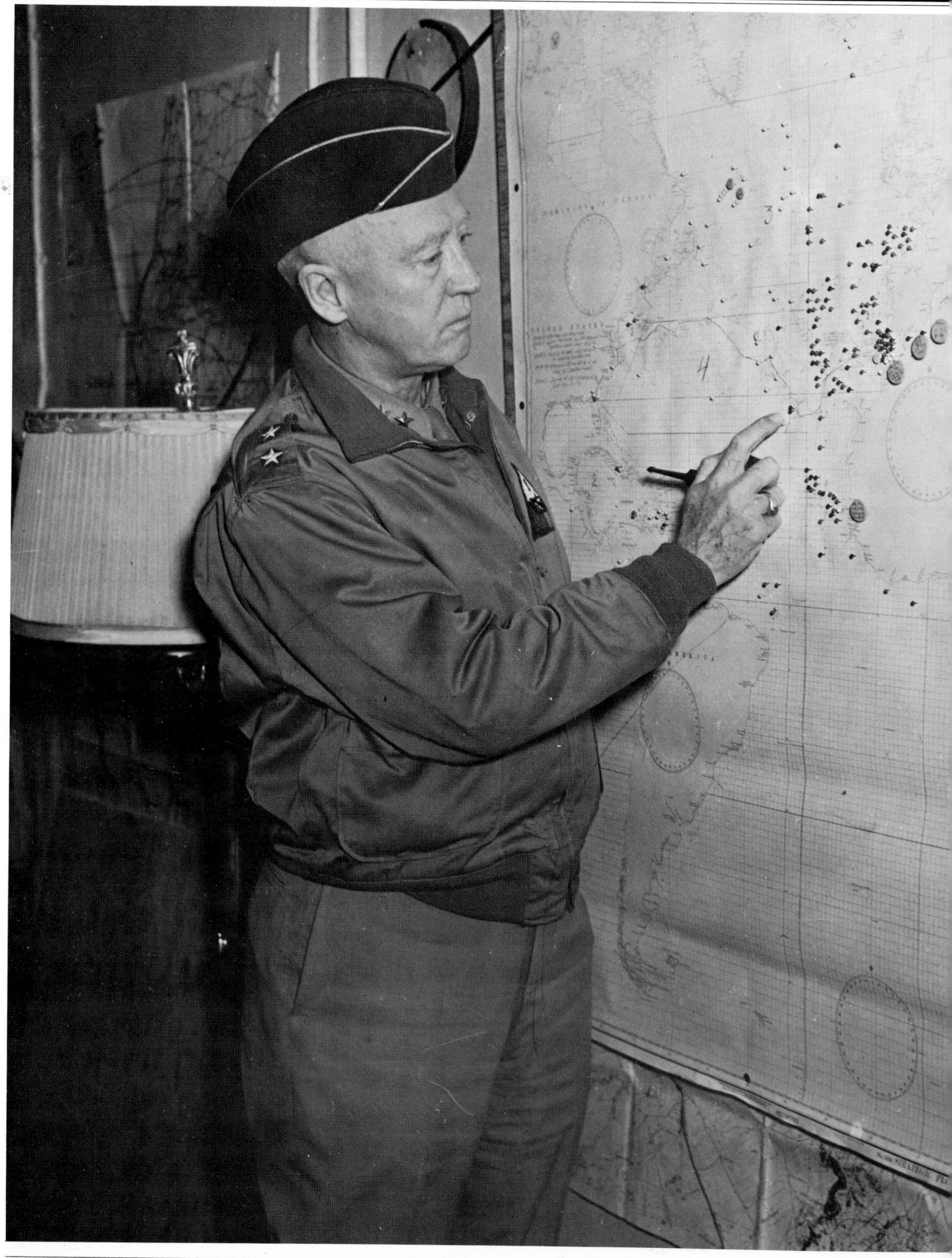

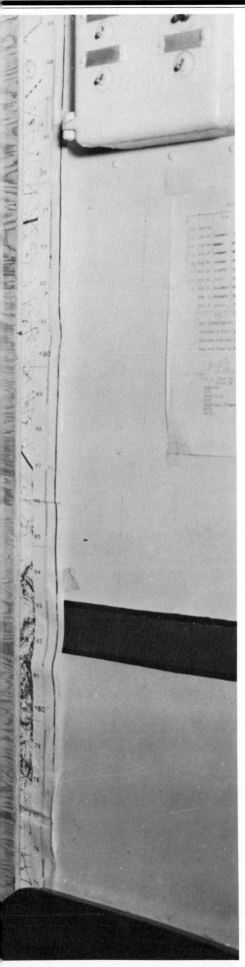

Above: The deck of the USS *Massachusetts* as it approached Casablanca during Operation Torch in 1942.

session Patton and Rear-Admiral Hewitt, commanding the Naval Task Force, fell foul of each other. Hewitt in all seriousness reported back to his superior Admiral King that either Patton be removed from the operation or the US Navy should remove itself, since it was obvious that the two would never agree. Though how he thought Patton would reach Casablanca if the Navy withdrew was something he did not explain. Eventually their differences were smoothed over and by the end of the operation they were even moderately good friends, although Patton almost opened the rift again when on the final briefing, he announced 'Never in recorded history has the navy put the army ashore at the planned time and place. But if you manage to land me anywhere anywhere within 50 miles of Fedala and a week of D-Day, I'll go in and win!'

Fedala was one of the selected landing beaches a few miles north of Casablanca; others were at Rabat, further north, and at Safi, about 100 miles south. But in deference to his political advisers, Patton changed the plan. To avoid religious troubles he decided against Rabat and, instead, moved his third beach-head to Port Lyautey about 100 miles north of Casablanca. As the assault fleet approached the coast of Africa, Patton gave out his first Order of the Day:

Left: General Patton tracing the track of the convoy to North Africa, aboard the USS *Augusta*.

'Soldiers:
We are now on our way to force a landing on the coast of Northwest Africa. We are to be congratulated because we have been chosen as the units of the United States Army to take part in this great American effort.
Our mission is threefold. First to capture a beachhead, second to capture the city of Casablanca, third to move against the German wherever he may be and destroy him. We may be opposed by a limited number of Germans. It is not known whether the French Army will contest our landing. It is regrettable to contemplate the necessity of fighting the gallant French, who are at heart sympathetic, but all resistance, by whomever offered, must be destroyed.
When the great day of battle comes, remember your training and remember that speed and vigor of attack are the sure roads to success. And you must succeed, for to retreat is as cowardly as it is fatal. Americans do not surrender. During the first days and nights after you get ashore you must work unceasingly, regardless of sleep, regardless of food. A pint of sweat will save a gallon of blood.
The eyes of the world are watching us . . . God is with us . . . We will surely win.'

G S Patton, Jr

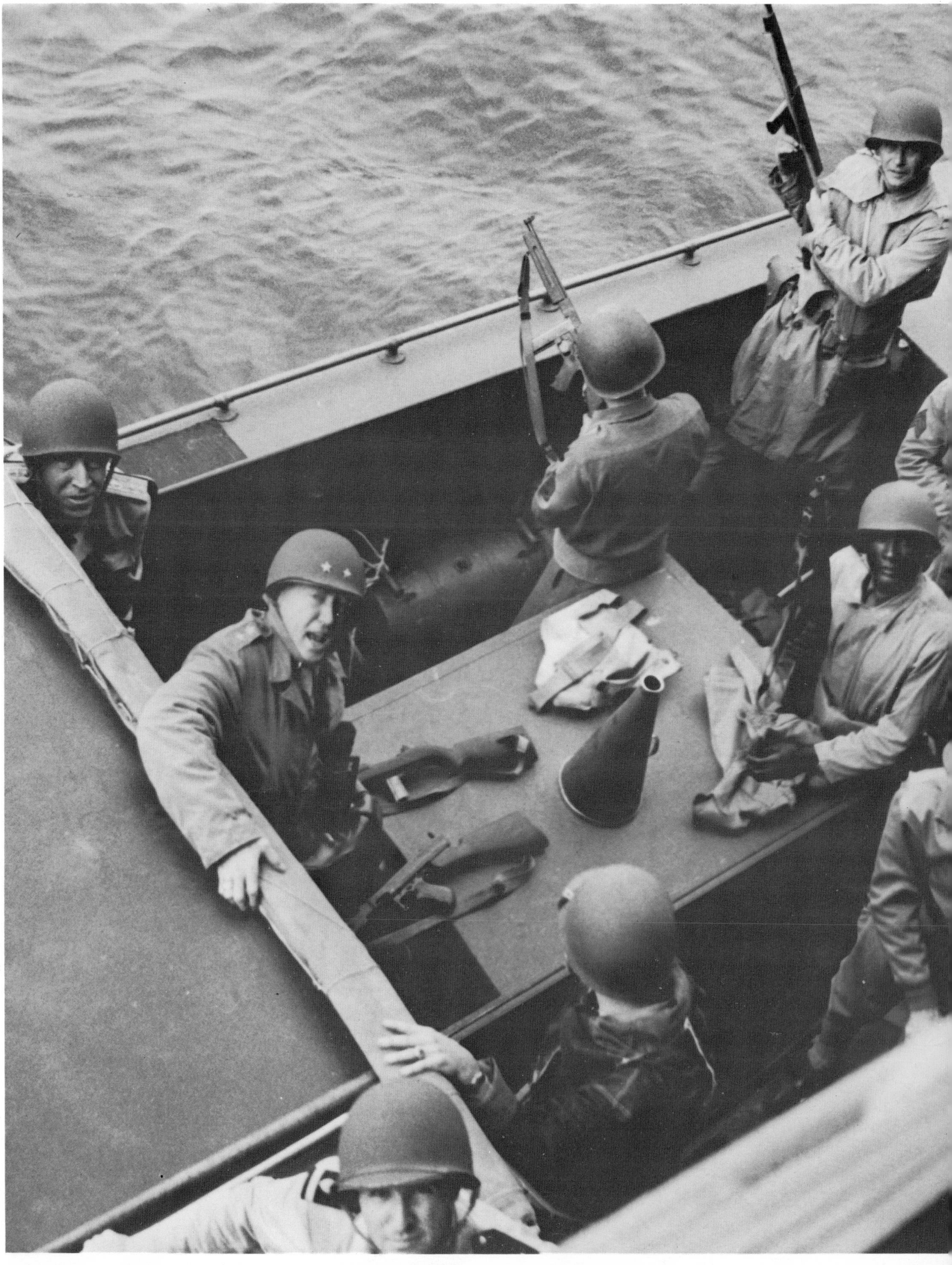

4:NORTH AFRICA

Within Morocco the military and political scene had assumed Byzantine complexity. The American political experts had made contact with at least three separate groups of French officers who were believed to be sympathetic to the Allied cause, and it was hoped that they would be able to exert sufficient influence to prevent an armed clash when the American troops came ashore.

The French Resident-General at Rabat, the *de facto* governor of Morocco, was General Noguès. It was held fairly certain that he would remain loyal to the Vichy government, since he was known to be as anti-Semitic as any Nazi and an admirer of Hitler on those grounds alone. But the military commander of the Casablanca district was General Béthouart, and he, it was understood, was definitely Pro-Allied and ready to assist. Unfortunately, the military organization within Morocco was such that Béthouart had less practical influence than the Allies believed. His superior officer was Admiral Michelier, who had overall responsibility for the defense of the coastline; Bethouart merely controlled the Casablanca sector, while two other Generals, Martin and Dody, commanded the sectors around Safi and Port Lyautey. Finally, between Admiral Michelier and the Resident-General was General Lascroux, General Officer Commanding Morocco. So that all Béthouart actually controlled were the troops in the vicinity of Casablanca.

Although they were willing to let Béthouart into the secret that a landing was about to take place, the American agents appear to have been reluctant to tell him much more, and it was not until Patton's force was closing up to the coast (amazingly, undetected by French naval or air patrols) that Béthouart was finally told that the landing would take place at 0200 hours on the following morning, 8 November. Even then, he was not told where. Making what was a reasonably accurate appreciation under the circumstances, Béthouart concluded that the

Left: Having regained his composure, if not his baggage, Patton leaves the USS *Augusta* for the beach at Fedala on 9th November.

assault would take place on the undefended beach of Rabat. He therefore despatched a force of troops to the beach to act as guides for the Americans, then surrounded the Army HQ at Rabat and arrested General Lascroux, telephoned Noguès and Michelier and told them that a landing was about to take place and that he was henceforth in command in Morocco until General Giraud arrived to take control.

The French Army have a long-standing tradition of going off half-cocked, and Béthouart continued this. Had he been better informed he might have done a better job. What he failed to do was to isolate Noguès, who had his own lines of communication and was able to speak directly with the other commanders. Meanwhile the French soldiers on the beach at Rabat waited well beyond the appointed time without seeing any signs of an invasion.

In Casablanca Admiral Michelier checked with his naval and air headquarters for reports of any approaching invasion force and found none; to this day nobody has satisfactorily accounted for this failure to detect the American fleet. Michelier therefore assumed that Béthouart was playing some devious game of his own, had him arrested, and reported this to Noguès. Shortly afterwards, when the first reports of landings came in, Michelier assumed them to be minor nuisance raids and ignored them. And with Béthouart's disappearance from the scene went any hopes of unopposed landings.

The invasion force, however, knew nothing of all this. Their principal worry had been the weather, which blew up a small storm and threatened to disrupt the landings. But this moved away, the wind and seas abated, and as the transports hove to shortly after midnight the troops began to clamber down the scrambler nets and into their landing craft. Although they had performed a few rehearsals in Chesapeake Bay before leaving the USA the operation itself turned out to be rather different. Now they were burdened with some 90 pounds of equipment, climbing in darkness down a slippery net to drop into tiny craft bobbing up and down in the Atlantic swell. It was a slow business and the assault fell behind schedule even before it had begun.

The northern force assaulting Port Lyautey and Mehdia lost formation as it neared the coast, another delaying factor, and the invasion fleet was detected by a French coastal vessel. This passed the alarm to the shore, and at 0430 hours the local coast defense guns opened fire, thus announcing that whatever the secret agents had been arranging was ineffective and that the invasion force was going to have to fight its way ashore. The landing parties were late, scattered, soaked to the skin with spray, and greeted with rifle and machine-gun fire when they finally reached the beach. While they were still

gathering their wits the dawn broke and brought French aircraft to machine-gun and bomb the beaches. The daylight also aided the coast guns, and their fire now became so accurate that the transport ships some 15 miles from the shore up-anchored and pulled away, leaving the US Navy to reply to the shellfire.

Once the force was ashore, two officers were despatched with a white flag to the French HQ to deliver an ultimatum to the commander there. One envoy was shot dead and the other made prisoner, which made the Americans somewhat dubious about the value of white flags and emissaries thereafter. Brigadier General Lucian K Truscott, commanding this northern force, was supposed to secure Port Lyautey and Mehdia, then move inland to take the nearby airfield, the only one in Morocco with concrete runways, so that P-40 fighters waiting at Gibraltar and on the US escort carrier *Chenango*

could fly in.

In the south, at Safi, Major General Ernest K Harmon's 2nd Armored Division had an easier time. Because he had no Tank Landing Ships capable of dropping the armor directly on to the beach, his orders were to land his infantry on the beach, sieze the port, then sail the transports in and unload his armor on the dockside. After this he was to hold off any French reinforcements which might appear from Marrakech and then move north to join in the attack on Casablanca. Thanks to little or no opposition, this plan went very smoothly and by 0900 hours the tanks were being unloaded onto the dockside.

Patton's central force, however, was having difficulties. Batteries of coast

Below: Troops laying netting across the soft beach to give the incoming transport a firm foothold on Africa.

Right: Aircraft of the carrier USS *Chenango* are prepared for launching in order to cover the North African landings.

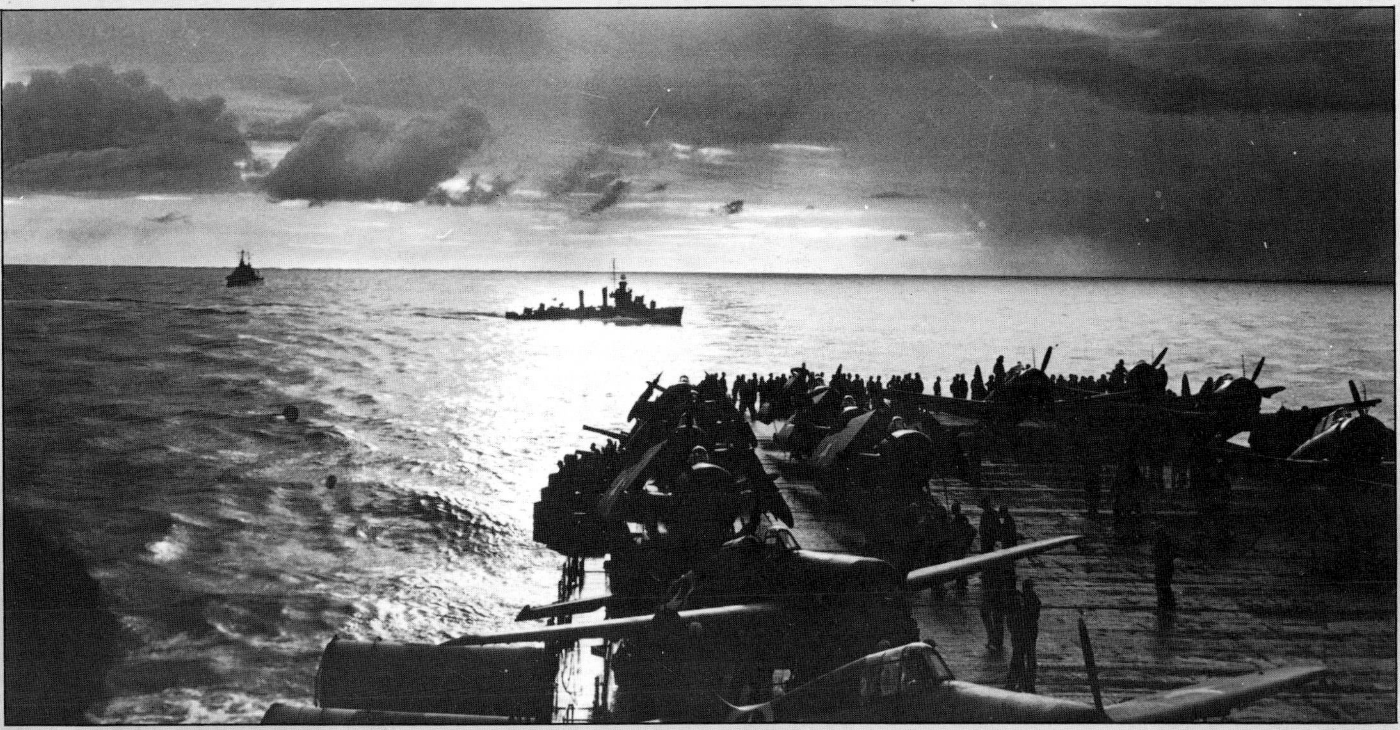

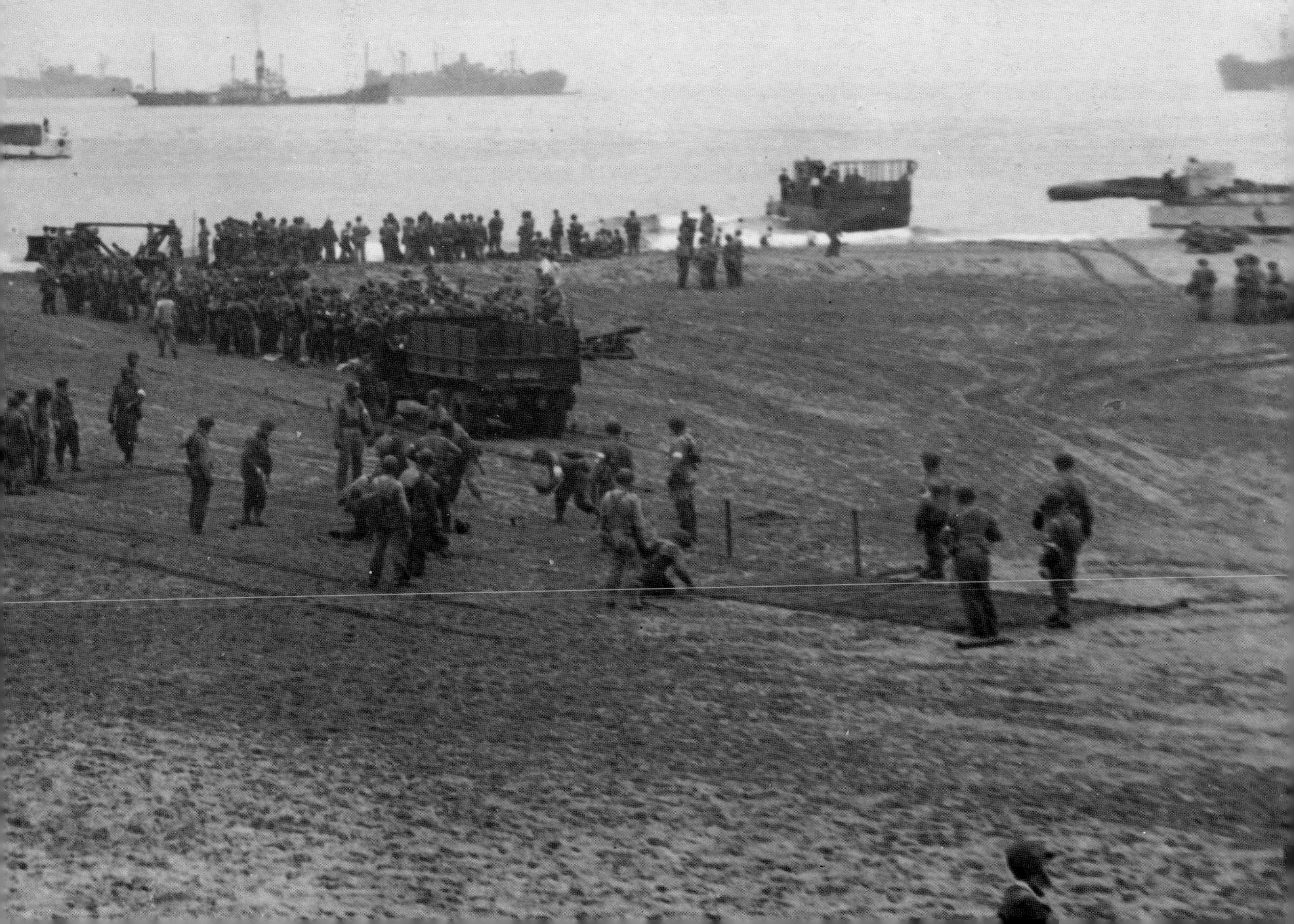

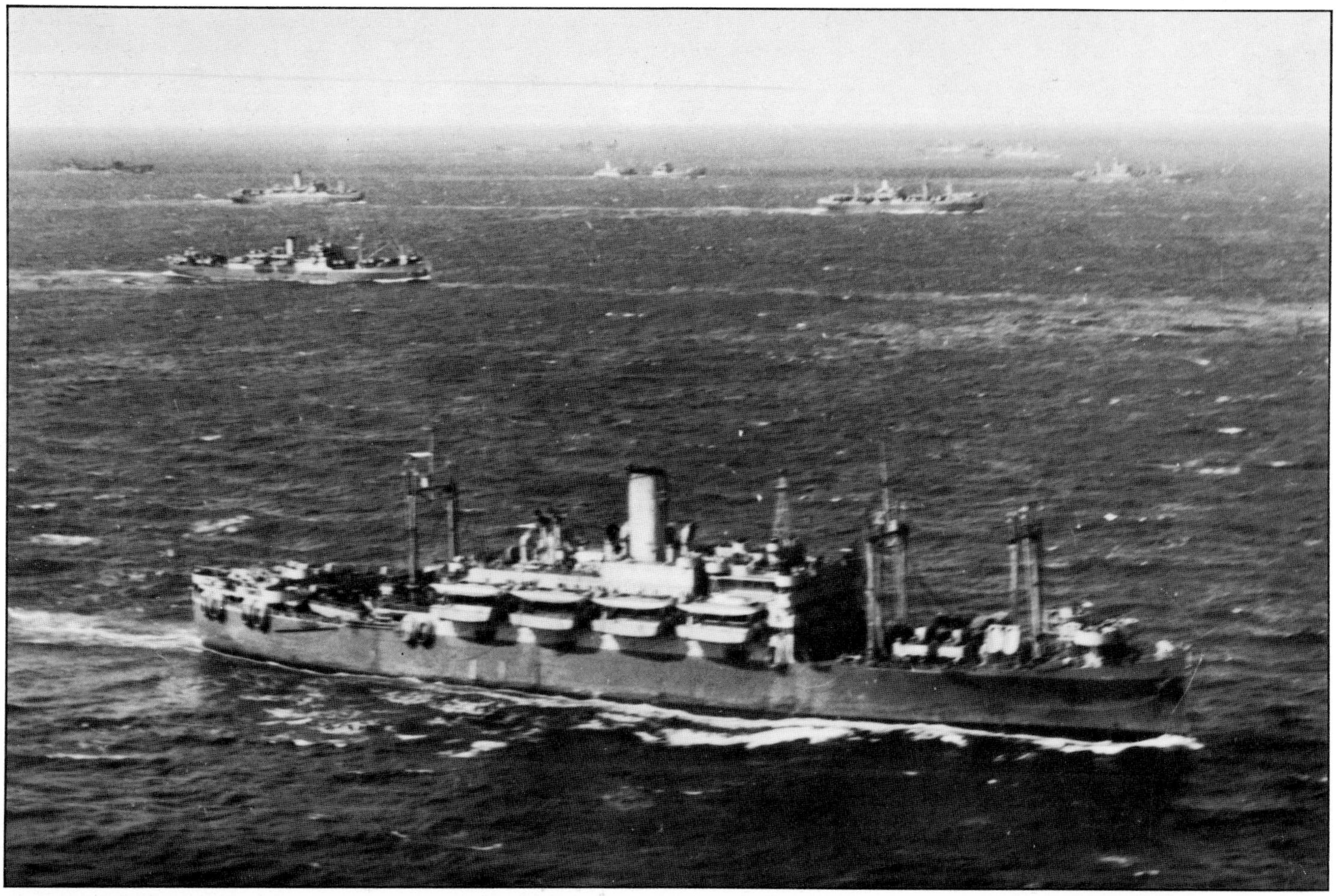

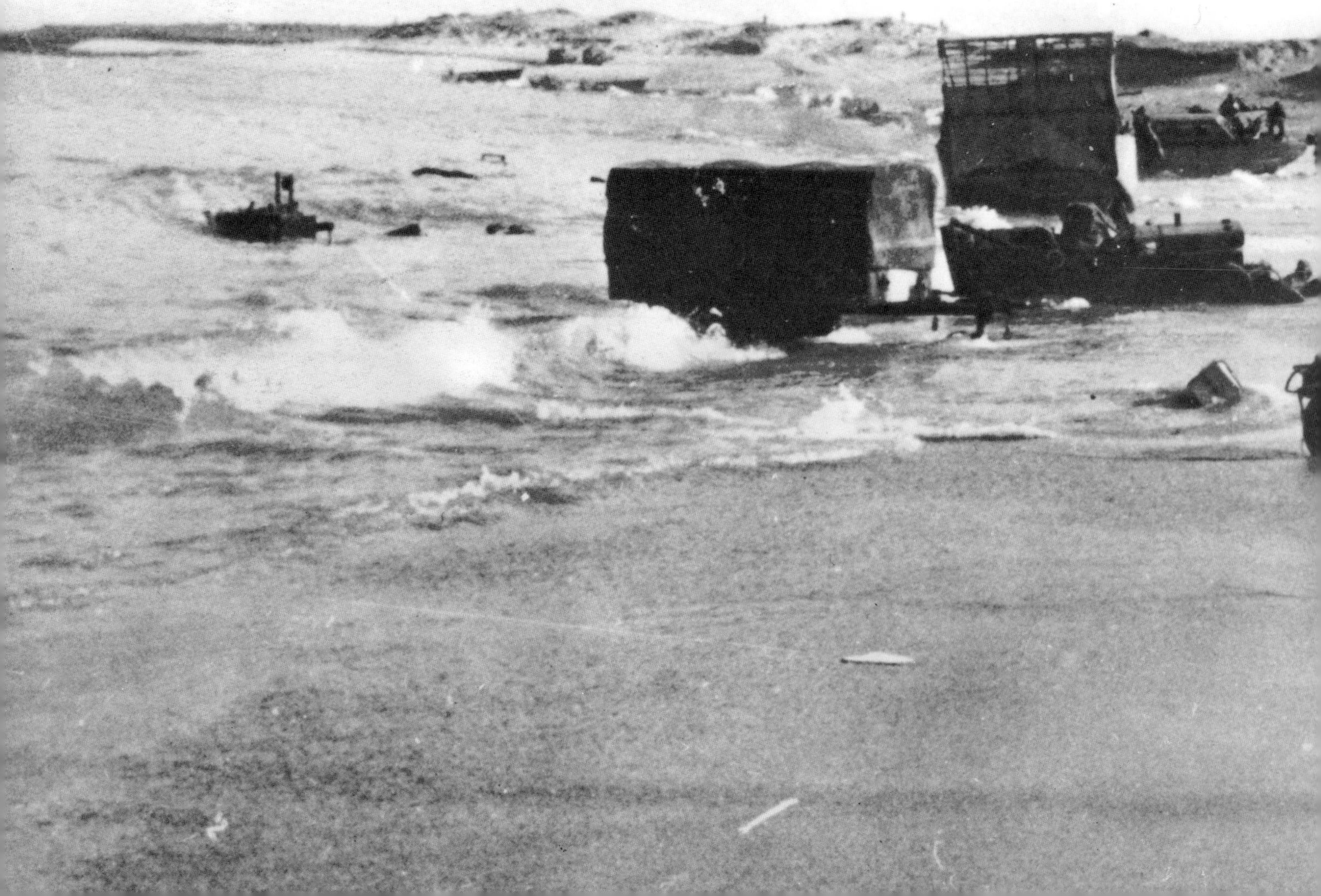

defense guns enfiladed the chosen beaches, while the French battleship *Jean Bart* with 15-inch guns, and several other well-armed warships were inside Casablanca harbor. There were several thousand infantry and field artillery troops around Casablanca, and more infantry and some tanks were stationed at nearby Meknes.

The invasion force neared the shore shortly after midnight and the troops began embarking into their landing craft. It was then discovered that an un-suspected coastal current had made for faulty navigation and the fleet was actually about six miles from its proper position, which meant that the run-in to the beaches took much longer than planned. The surf, too, was deeper than anticipated, and many landing craft were swamped during the run-in, their heavily-burdened occupants being thrown into the sea to drown. Scores of men landed in the wrong places, and when the beaches were finally reached they were found to be under constant

Left: The transport convoy bearing Patton's invasion force, photographed 'somewhere in the Atlantic Ocean'.

machine-gun and artillery fire. The coast defense guns and the *Jean Bart* opened fire on the invasion fleet and the USS *Massachusetts* and other ships of the escort returned the fire. With the coming of daylight the troops eventually got their bearings and began to move, and by 0600 Fedala was secured.

Patton had arranged to go ashore from the flagship, USS *Augusta* at 0800 hours, by which time the first objectives would be taken and his command post in opera-tion, ready to receive him. His landing craft was slung on davits and his personal kit loaded. But the Navy suddenly found itself occupied in an artillery duel with the French shore guns and it looked as if Patton would have to wait for a short time. Immaculate as ever, the only things lacking were his pistols, which were packed in his shore-going baggage, and he sent Sergeant Meeks, his orderly, to fetch them from the landing craft. No sooner had Meeks returned and Patton buckled on the two pistols than seven French destroyers came out of Fedala harbor and headed for the American task force at full speed. As alarm bells clanged and the *Augusta* leapt to 20 knots, so its guns opened fire on the French attack.

The blast from the aft turret guns blew Patton's landing craft straight over the ship's side, complete with all his baggage.

From then on, Patton was a captive aboard the *Augusta* as she went into action, giving him a grandstand view of a naval battle but one which he willingly would have foregone. So long as the battle continued, landing Patton ashore was the last thing the Navy thought about, while due to communications failures he had absolutely no information about what was happening ashore. It was not until 1320 hours that the naval action ceased and Hewitt was able to sail back towards the shore, lower a replacement boat and send Patton and his staff to the beach.

Upon reaching the beach at last, Patton was greatly displeased to find that very little appeared to be happening. The assault waves had gone through and were advancing well enough, but the support-ing troops, who were supposed to be unloading landing craft, sending them back for more supplies, and forwarding supplies to the front line, had abandoned

Below: The waste of war; Red Beach, Fedala, and the abandoned and neglected equipment which greeted Patton when he arrived.

this and were solely concerned with digging themselves foxholes. So instead of going forward himself, the commanding general stormed up and down the beach, cursing and threatening, until the startled soldiers and sailors began unloading the several landing barges which were crashing up and down in the surf. Only when this was organized to his satisfaction did Patton leave the beach and seek his headquarters which had been set up in a hotel in Fedala. Here he finally received information on the progress of the other landings; Harman had secured Safi and was moving towards Casablanca, while Truscott had Port Lyautey under control and had also captured the vital airfield.

The next morning Patton descended on the invasion beaches like an avenging deity, intent upon getting the supply line operating. He had discovered that barely one-fifth of the planned supplies had actually got ashore the previous day and

he was determined that this particular bottleneck be eliminated. Returning to his HQ in the early afternoon he found that radio communication with Eisenhower at Gibraltar, upon which he was relying for information on the progress of the other parts of Torch, was still erratic. The 3rd Division reported that they had managed to advance toward Casablanca, in spite of being short of transport and heavy weapons, while Harmon, reported from Safi that his troops had suffered a sharp air attack from the French, although a French column approaching from Marrakech did not appear to be keen to engage. He therefore proposed to throw out an armored squadron as a screen and let the main body of his force advance on Casablanca as quickly as he could. Truscott reported from the north that he had been attacked by a French force accompanied by 18 ageing Renault tanks; this ran into an American force with

Above: In high spirits, and led by Old Glory, US infantry move off inland after the landings.

seven M3 Light tanks and thus precipitated the first American tank-to-tank battle. It ended in outright victory for the Americans; the French tank fire was ineffective against the American armor, while the American 37mm guns set four tanks aflame and put the accompanying infantry to rout.

In fact, although Patton had no coherent information, the remainder of Torch had progressed very well. At Algiers the landings had gone smoothly, the local French commander not being disposed to argue overmuch, and there had been little resistance. At Oran French resistance had also been lacklustre. By the evening of 9 November both these objectives were more or less secured. On the 10th, radio communication improved sufficiently for Eisenhower to send Patton a message urging him to speed up the operation. 'The only tough nut left is in your hands. Algiers in bag for two days. Oran now in. Crack it open quickly and ask for what you want.'

The implied criticism was a little harsh on Patton, who needed no urging and was in fact doing all that any reasonable person could expect. His political advisors suggested that it might be possible to treat with certain French officers, and Patton was mindful of instructions he had received both to avoid unnecessary casualties and damaging Casablanca by bombardment if at all possible. He therefore allowed truce parties to pass back and forth through the lines, and by the evening of the 10th it seemed that while the French Army were satisfied that they had done their duty and could now honorably surrender to a superior force, the French Navy, obsessed with vanity and glory, was resolved to fight to the bitter end, using the guns of their warships to bombard the approaching Americans.

Despairing of ever being able to talk sense into these people, Patton decided on an all-out attack timed for 0730 on the 11th. The original suggestion was for a traditional dawn attack, but Patton was dubious of his troops' ability to conduct operations in the half-light and moved the time up so as to have daylight for the assault. Plans were drawn up and troops briefed, artillery emplaced and targets allotted, and then, in the night hours, emissaries appeared from General Noguès, under a flag of truce. Escorted to Patton's HQ at Fedala, they agreed to an armistice, and at H-Hour minus 40 minutes the ceasefire orders went out, the Armistice took effect, and the brief campaign for Casablanca was over.

Patton was well satisfied with this outcome; indeed, it made a fine present for his 57th birthday. He ordered the 3rd Infantry Division to move into the town and to be prepared to fight if any resistance was offered. None was, but Patton later wrote that 'The hours from 0730 to 1100 were the longest in my life.' At noon 3rd Division reached the French HQ and accepted the surrender of the Casablanca garrison, and US troops moved in to take over key positions in the city.

At 1500 hours General Noguès arrived at the Hotel Miramar, where Patton had set up his HQ, to be met by General Keyes and an Honor Guard. After inspecting the guard Noguès was taken to meet Patton, who made a short speech congratulating the French on their gallant resistance. He then ordered the armistice terms to be read out, preparatory to being signed. In fact, two sets of terms had been drafted before the operation began; one assumed token French resistance and its terms were relatively mild. The other, and obviously the version now appropriate, had been drawn up assuming stiffer French resistance followed by their capitulation, and this was much harsher, prescribing total disarmament and disbandment of all French forces. On hearing these terms Noguès, whose political acumen was far keener than Patton's, countered by demanding to know who, if the French were disarmed, was going to keep order among the native population of some 8,000,000 Arabs, Berbers and Jews. Who was to defend the border with Spanish Morocco and who was to protect the Allied lines of communication? These tasks, said Nogues, were obviously beyond the capacity of the limited American forces, and disbandment of the French control structure would inevitably lead to bloody insurrection.

Thus, entirely without warning and with no sort of briefing except for the

Below: Patton explains his plans to Eisenhower on the day before the attack on Gafsa, 16th March 1943.

broad-brush (and largely inaccurate) treatment given by his political advisor, Patton was flung into the morass of French colonial politics. Being a non-political man, his reaction was predictable – as, no doubt, Noguès had gambled. His response was that of the bluff and hearty soldier; he and Noguès would henceforth have a 'gentleman's agreement' in which the US forces would take over only what was necessary for their prosecution of the war, while the French forces would retain their positions and their arms. It was a snap decision which was to cause immense trouble in the future.

To put it bluntly, Patton had been out-maneuvered by Noguès. While professing brotherhood-in-arms, allied cooperation and Franco-American amity, and while mounting spectacular parades and ceremonials for Patton's enjoyment, there is little room for doubt that Noguès was secretly maintaining communication with the Vichy Government in France and possibly even with the Germans. Meanwhile those officers and soldiers who had given any overt assistance to the Americans during the invasion were quietly removed from their posts and thrown in jail, and Béthouart came very close to being shot for treason by Noguès' order. Thousands of Jews and Arabs were being whisked away into concentration camps in the south, well away from American eyes, and there were widespread arrests of Gaullists, radicals and even of Republican Spaniards. Little of this was even suspected by Patton, though he did get to hear of Béthouart's predicament and managed to have him removed from jail and flown in an American aircraft to Algiers. Even though various people tried to point out what was happening, Patton could see no alternative to allowing Noguès his head; in

Above: Still at the Casablanca conference, the Commander in Chief stops to chat with one of his generals.

Patton's view the American task was simply to get on with the war against the Axis forces in North Africa and leave civil administration to the French. The fact that most of them were pro-Vichy, anti-Semitic, and as rabidly Fascist as Hitler himself held no interest for him.

But in promoting the progress of the war, Patton moved with indisputable vigor. He established his staffs in the Shell Oil Company's modern office buildings, and from there they rapidly transformed Casablanca into a thriving military base. The port was cleared of wrecked ships, dockside cranes and installations were repaired, railroad tracks laid, airfields modernized and extended, and the logistic back-up for the army placed on a sound footing. The combat troops went into intensive training in order to rectify the mistakes which Patton had observed during the short campaign. At a meeting with his officers he tabulated some of those mistakes in his own manner:

'Mistakes were made. We should not have fallen into ambushes. Some of the troops were too slow. Too many of them want to sit on their asses and stick their heads in holes. . . .'

One day in the week was spent in the field, without sleep; strict discipline was enforced, particularly in the matter of dress – Patton's love of a smartly turned out soldier surfaced again and orders went forth that shoes were to be shined, hel-

Below: January 1943, and Patton meets Churchill at the Casablanca conference.

mets and neckties worn, leggings to be properly laced, salutes to be made punctiliously. Patton never stopped telling his men that what lay in front of them was going to be a damned sight harder than fighting a half-hearted French colonial garrison. Their time would come. In fact, it came even faster than Patton expected.

Away to the north, in Tunisia, the Allied invasion had bogged down. One reason for this had been the extremely rapid reaction of the Germans under Field Marshal Kesselring, commander of Luftflotte II and overall chief of the German forces in the Mediterranean theater, a reaction which took the Allies by surprise. This in spite of the fact that by now they were reading most of the German coded radio traffic. The operation made considerable use of Ultra, the code-breaking coup in which the British intelligence services had managed to unravel many of the allegedly unbreakable Enigma machine codes used by the German High Command, and an Ultra detatchment had gone to Gibraltar accompanying Eisenhower. At this stage of the proceedings the list of people allowed to know about Ultra was a short one. Eisenhower, some of his senior staff officers, and the British General Anderson, commanding the British First Army were among the few privy to the existence of Ultra and being fed the information it collected. Intercepts had shown that Kesselring was definitely alert to the possibility of invasion somewhere in the Mediterranean area, and he had asked Hitler for more troops. These had been refused, so Kesselring had issued his own orders, concentrating such troops as he could muster in the south of Italy, together with whatever transport aircraft he could acquire. Next came a signal from Rommel to Kesselring, after the Allied victory at El Alamein, that Rommel would fall back to El Agheila in view of the Allied landings in Algeria and Tunisia which had by then taken place. No sooner were those landings reported to Kesselring than he was ordering the collected troops in Italy to be flown into Tunis and ordering fighter aircraft to be flown across to occupy Tunis and Bizerta airfields. This build-up continued at a speed which totally surprised Eisenhower and which had not been anticipated when the plans were drawn up for the westerly landings.

By February 1943 a stalemate had set in. The Germans had established a ring of defenses along the chain of mountains which formed the border with Algeria, and the Allies, hampered by tenuous lines of communication, poor and congested roads, slow build-up of supplies, a shortage of airfields near the front, and, above all, by particularly severe winter

Below: General Patton, leading from the front, in his personal armored scout car during the attack on Gafsa, March 1943.

Above: A 105mm howitzer of Battery 'B', 33rd Field Artillery Battalion, firing in defence of the Kasserine Pass, February 1943.

Above right: A Ranger battalion practising forced marches through the rocky Algerian hills near Arzew.

Right: 2nd Bn, 16th US Infantry, marching through the Kasserine Pass, scene of Rommel's breakthrough.

weather, were merely standing facing this line without having much effect on it. The French political imbroglio was taking far too much of Eisenhower's time and energy, to little effect, and he had more or less deputed command of the battle to an advanced HQ under Truscott at Constantine. But even this was 200 miles behind the front and its duties and responsibilities were ill-defined. Montgomery, in late January, had arrived at Tripoli intending to use that town as a supply base, but he found the port and its facilities had been utterly ruined by the retreating Germans; he was, therefore, in no position to go forward until he had built up some reserves, mostly by trucking or flying them in from Egypt, a very long way. Von Arnim, now commanding the German troops in Tunisia was getting restive, making probing attacks, and it looked as if Rommel would soon make contact with him, a threatening prospect.

It was at about this time that Patton was initiated into the Ultra secret. Some reports aver that Patton was not privy to this until late 1944, because Eisenhower refused to trust him with such sensitive knowledge, but F W Winterbotham,

Chief of the Air Department of the British Secret Intelligence Service, the man who was responsible for the security of the Ultra operation, actually went to Algiers early in 1943 to brief Patton. According to Winterbotham (in his book *The Ultra Secret*)

'He was delighted at the idea of reading the enemy's signals, but when I got on

to the security angle he stopped me after a few minutes. "You know, young man," he said, "I think you had better tell all this to my intelligence staff. I don't go much on this sort of thing myself. You see, I just like fighting."'

From that time onward, Patton was fully aware of the Ultra network and was constantly appraised of the enemy's

movements, so far as they were known. At the beginning of February 1943 the Allied strength in North Africa was a variable factor; the British First Army, in fact consisted of no more than two infantry divisions and a parachute brigade; this force held the northern flank of the Allied line, between Bou Arada and the sea. From Bou Arada to Fondouk was the French XIX Corps; then the US II Corps, under General Fredendall, held a 100 mile sector to El Guettar. This Corps consisted of 1st US Armored Division and a French division. The 1st Armored mustered 15,000 men with 390 tanks, 100 armored cars and 730 half-tracks, plus artillery, and it was designed to operate as two balanced sub-units, Combat Command A (CCA) and Combat Command B (CCB). The only drawback was that Fredendall was a useless commander; he had set up his command post in caves some 60 miles behind the line, in an area notorious for poor radio reception. He was ill-tempered and overbearing, full of animosity toward the British and French, and he barely con-

Above: A less-than-pleased Patton photographed during his visit to 1st Armored Division near El Guettar.

cealed his dislike of General Ward, commanding 1st Armored Division. Indeed, he virtually took control of 1st Armored, over Ward's head, issuing orders down to each individual sub-unit, ignoring Ward, and positioning the various components of the division in badly-selected locations. By this time German and Italian reinforcements to Tunisia totalled nearly 30,000 men and over 100 tanks, and Rommel and Von Arnim had joined forces and combined as the Army Group Africa under Rommel. In the face of such a threat, Fredendall's dispositions were suicidal.

The blow fell on 14 February when Von Arnim, with 10 and 21 Panzer Divisions, attacked at Sidi Bou Zid, while Rommel with his Afrika Korps attacked towards Fériana and the airfield at Thélepte, by way of El Guettar and Gafsa. Their plan was to link up near Kasserine, head then for Tebéssa, and then cut north to either Constantine or Bone, thus slicing off the Allied front line from its rear elements. It was a classic maneuver, and it was to come close to success.

Just before the attack Allied intelligence learned (and not through Ultra) of a proposed German attack towards Fondouk, cutting through the French line so as to take the British First Army in the flank. It was a reasonable plan, in the circumstances, but there is still considerable mystery as to its source; there is reason to suspect that it may have been a piece of deliberate misinformation by the Germans, intended to set the Allies looking in the wrong direction. Whatever the source, it was given sufficient credence that General Anderson of First Army was alerted; his response was to prepare to 'roll with the punch' and he suggested that Koeltz, the French commander, and Fredendall should prepare to fall back, allow the intervening country to soak up the attack, and set up a fresh defensive line on the Western Dorsale, a

Below: Not all North Africa is sand; a German staff car slithers through the mud in Tunisia.

second line of mountains some 60 miles behind the existing line. This would have exposed the German flanks and left them open to a counterstroke, but Koeltz, a typical French officer of his generation, scorned the very idea of falling back before the Germans, while Fredendall considered that Anderson's reaction was excessive and that he could hold any German attack. Neither moved.

Thus, when the German attack did come, in a different area to that predicted and, providentially, concealed by a sandstorm, it quickly cut off some 2,000 men and destroyed a large number of American guns and vehicles. From this promising start it progressed well, setting off a minor rout among some units of II US Corps. In the middle of this critical period, Fredendall decided to uproot his headquarters and move further back, so

Above: US infantry march through the Kasserine Pass in high spirits – before Rommel's attack took place.

that for several hours there was no communication with him; no information flowed up and no orders flowed down. At the very moment that the front was crumbling, the commanding general was incommunicado and totally unable to direct operations.

By 17 February Rommel, having reached Fériana, paused to regroup and take stock; at the same time Von Arnim's Panzers had reached Sbeitila. Rommel was keen to move on rapidly while the Allies were still wrong-footed, but Von Arnim was proposing to move one of his Panzer divisions northward against the French and, at the same time, dismissed his Italian division and sent it back to reinforce the line at Mareth, facing Montgomery's approaching Eighth Army. This pause gave the Allies time to reorganize, but Rommel appealed to

Kesselring, obtained some measure of agreement with Von Arnim, and the two turned inwards to perform a pincer movement to take the Kasserine Pass and debouch into the valley beyond. The result of this combined attack, on 20th February, could fairly be described as a rout; General Harmon, who had been sent up to assist Fredendall, reported later to Eisenhower that:

'It was the first – and only – time I ever saw an American Army in rout. Jeeps, trucks, wheeled vehicles of every imaginable sort streamed up the road toward us, sometimes jammed two and even three abreast. It was obvious that there was only one thing in the minds of the panic-stricken drivers – to get away from the front, to escape to some place where there was no shooting. . . .'
One result of this setback was a public

outcry in the USA and a rapid search for scapegoats; the American public had been conditioned since Pearl Harbor with constant propaganda about the superiority of American troops and equipment, and now those troops had suffered a defeat; obviously, somebody must be to blame. The first excuse was that it had all been the fault of the British, notably Anderson, who had split up II US Corps and spread them all over the place under French and British command in 'penny packets,' but there was no truth in this whatever. The dispersion of II US Corps was entirely within their own area and was due to Fredendall's poor appreciation of possible threats and

Right: An armored troop carrier of the Afrika Korps hurries through the dust of Tunisia as the end approaches.

his poor tactical dispositions. Moreover the general public rather overlooked the fact that most of the American troops were seeing combat for the first time and were up against a highly professional enemy who had been fighting for nearly three years. Nevertheless, after Eisenhower had visited II US Corps and talked to the various unit commanders, Fredendall was dismissed, to return to the USA and take up a training post. Eisenhower's initial choice to replace him was Harmon, but Harmon refused,

Right: Paratroops waiting for their heavy equipment to be dropped, during training for the Sicily landings, June 1943.

because he felt that it would look as if he had intrigued in order to obtain Fredendall's post. Harmon, in his turn, suggested that since it looked like being an armored war once the line was broken, Eisenhower really ought to get hold of Patton. And so on 5 March 1943 Patton was sent for, to report to Maison Blanche airfield near Algiers to be briefed.

Eisenhower's briefing of Patton was short and to the point. Patton's prime task was to restore American prestige by restoring II US Corps' faith in itself. Such tactical matters as mine clearance and antitank defence had to be drilled into the troops, but more vital was to restore their belief in their own abilities. Furthermore, Patton was advised, he was to remember that he was commanding an American formation within an Army Group under the orders of the British General Alexander. And finally, Ike concluded, 'I want you as a Corps Commander, not as a casualty...'

On the following day, as Patton was moving up to take over his new command, Rommel attacked Montgomery at Medenine with the 10th, 15th and 21st Panzer divisions. Unfortunately for Rommel, all his signal communications with Germany were being read by the Ultra team, and a most revealing interchange of information had been picked up. In the first place there had been orders from Hitler to Rommel for him to hold the Mareth Line against Montgomery. Then, by way of

Above: German troops, accompanied by an Arab guide, reconnoitring Allied positions in Tunisia.

reply, Rommel's staff had obligingly transmitted a full breakdown of the Mareth Line defences, position by position and gun by gun. Then came orders to Rommel to make a spoiling attack against the British. Finally Rommel signalled to Kesselring with his outline plan of action, indicating when and where his attacks would fall. With all that information available to him, Montgomery merely had to distribute his troops accordingly, sit tight, and let events take their course. Four times Rommel threw in his Panzers, four times they were repulsed, and in the end they had lost 52 of their precious tanks.

Alexander had already indicated that he expected Patton to be ready to move against Gafsa on 17th March, which left just 11 days for Patton to get II US Corps back into fighting trim. Wasting no time the new Commanding General roared round his Corps area and visited every sub-unit 'like Moses descending from Mount Ararat.' His hearers were left in no doubt about what was wanted. Discipline was tightened overnight, dress regulations were enforced, saluting reappeared. Mail was speeded up, field kitchens were pushed forward so that troops had hot meals whenever possible, instead of existing on K-Rations, recreation facilities, concert parties and entertainments appeared. At the same time, training was concentrated on the defects

which the previous weeks had uncovered. Patton was promoted to Lieutenant General.

He was, of course, burning to take his corps into action and prove that American troops could fight the famed Afrika Korps as well as could the British. He was quite

confident that once he was given the word he would dash forward, sweeping all before him, and drive Rommel into the sea. Unfortunately, not everyone shared this confidence. Nobody doubted Patton's drive or his ability to command; what they doubted was the ability of the lower-level commanders and of the soldiers themselves. Alexander, therefore, was reluctant to allow Patton too much rope; if he did, and Patton succeeded, well and good, but if Patton, or his men failed, the consequences were too terrible to contemplate. The military consequences could be recovered, but the blow to American confidence and self-esteem, particularly in the eyes of the folks at home, would be fatal. So, irksome as it was to all concerned, Patton had to be kept on a tight leash until it was clear that II Corps was a sound fighting machine once again. Omar Bradley, who had been appointed as Patton's Deputy Corps Commander, played a valuable role here, as he exercised all his diplomacy and tact, working in close concert with Alexander's staff to ensure that the orders which went out to Patton were

phrased so as not to upset his dignity.

The plan of attack for 17 March revolved around Montgomery. He was to attack and smash the Mareth Line, and then break through into the coastal plain beyond to pursue Rommel back to Tunis. Patton was to support this manoeuver by making threatening moves against the flank which would draw off German and Italian formations from the Mareth defences. These moves were to take the form of recapturing lost airfields and striking towards Gafsa, there to set up a forward base from which the British Eighth Army would be able to collect supplies during its advance. Patton's attack on the 17th would take place three days before Montgomery moved, so that as many Axis troops as possible would be drawn toward him.

The II US Corps now consisted of 1st Armored, 1st, 9th and 34th Infantry Divisions, and 13th Field Artillery Brigade. The 1st Infantry Division moved

Below: Heading for the chow line as the mud dries out; a camp close to Bizerta in November 1943.

Above: The gun they hated, the celebrated German '88' AA gun deployed in an anti-tank position in Tunisia.

off in pouring rain, marched 45 miles through the night and took Gafsa with relatively little trouble. The next day 1st Ranger Battalion pushed ahead to take El Guettar. By this time the unusually heavy rainfall had so swollen the streams and soaked the ground that cross-country movement on wheels was almost impossible, and it was not until the 20th that 1st Armored was able to get under way, capturing Station de Sened on 21 March. By this time Montgomery had begun his attack, but even though he had full knowledge of the Mareth Line defences, the combination of foul weather, rough country and solid fortifications proved so difficult that his plan to send the New Zealand Corps and X British Corps around the left flank of the line would take some time to get into effect. Montgomery suggested to Alexander that Patton be brought in to help by making a direct thrust to the sea, so cutting the German supply lines and trapping Rommel's troops in a pocket. Indeed Patton had already proposed this same manoeuver and was anxious to make a start on it, but Alexander was still fearful of the consequences of any American setback. He therefore modified the plan, ordering Patton to go forward to the Eastern Dorsale range of mountains and there capture a pass east of Maknassy, then use this pass to push through a light armored column to disrupt airfields and raid supply lines and dumps.

On 22 March 1st Armored Division moved off on this mission and captured Maknassy, still in pouring rain. The next objective was the pass, but instead of pushing forward as hard as possible and relying on surprise, General Ward, commanding 1st Armored, halted his force and set about preparing a formal attack, preceded by long reconnaissance and accompanied by an artillery bombardment. The delay was fatal. By the time Ward finally made his move, he found that *Kampfgruppe Lang* of the Fifth Panzer Army had forestalled him and had siezed and fortified the vital pass.

Patton, meanwhile, had moved east of El Guettar with 1st Infantry Division, trailing his coat in front of 10th Panzer Division. Keen to repeat their success of the Kasserine battle, they willingly obliged, and on 23 March they attacked with 'a huge hollow square of tanks and self-propelled guns interspersed with carrier-borne infantry' which carried everything before it. Two American field artillery battalions and some infantry were overrun, but the remainder of the American force stood firm; two tank destroyer battalions caused heavy casualties among the Panzers, setting 30 tanks ablaze, and 10th Panzer Division fell back. They regrouped and returned, and once again they were severely mauled and driven off. The 1st US Infantry Division had proved their masters and they did not return for a third try.

Delighted at 1st Infantry's prowess, on

the next day Patton went across to see how 1st Armored was getting along; he was incensed to discover their lack of progress. Ward's tanks were stalled and his infantry had gone to ground. In no uncertain terms he instructed Ward to get his division moving and to launch an attack on the pass in the morning, and, further, that Ward was to make sure he led it in person. Ward did, was wounded for his pains, but had no success. The Germans had an almost impregnable position in the mountain massif, from which they could see and shoot at every

Below: General George C Marshall visits with General Mark Clark and George Patton after the victory in North Africa.

move the Americans could make. Patton strained every nerve for three weeks to try and force a way through this line; he was everywhere in the forward areas, arguing, ordering, cursing, persuading and browbeating his troops. When a task force stalled at a minefield, Patton appeared, fired the commander, and led them forward through the mines. But for all his efforts, 1st Armored was a broken reed, and finally Patton had to take the extreme step and replace its commander, relieving Ward and replacing him with Harmon.

However, throughout this period and in spite of not achieving any tangible results, Patton was doing precisely what was required; drawing Axis troops away

from Montgomery's advance. In fact he had drawn almost two Panzer divisions on to his sector. He continued to argue that had he been given a free hand, and relieved of Alexander's control, he would have charged across the mountains and cut through to the sea, but the cold facts argue against this. He was unable to break through the mountain chain even to put in the armored column, as we have seen, and there is no reason for believing that he could have done any better had he been independent. If Ward had moved faster after taking Maknassy, it might have been a different story, but he did not. Even so, it seems that Alexander, anxious to 'blood' the Americans gradually, entirely failed to appreciate the im-

portance which the US Commanders placed upon public relations and public opinion. Alexander was a professional soldier in the British tradition, a completely non-political man whose sole concern was to get on with the war in the most efficient manner. He did not care about press or public opinion, and he found the American attitude quite strange. In some respects it might have been better had he given Patton his head and allowed his troops to take a bloody nose trying to take the pass; the result would have been the same, but Patton

Below: March 7 1943 and the new commander of 1st Armored with his Deputy, General Wilbur.

would have had his precious independence. Much the same sort of problem was now to arise when, as the German forces moved back toward Tunis, Patton discovered that II US Corps were to be given what he considered to be a minor role in the closing stages of the campaign, then being planned. There were sound logistic reasons for this decision; to put the US forces where Patton wanted them, would involve moving them across the British lines of supply, the sort of maneuver that causes staff officers to lie awake at night in a cold sweat. Nonetheless Patton went to Eisenhower, and Eisenhower spoke with Alexander, and in spite of the difficulties the change was made in the cause of Allied amity and so

that the US forces should be seen to have a major part in the final victory in North Africa.

That rearrangement was to be Patton's only contribution to the final phases of the campaign. He had taken over II US Corps on the firm understanding that it was to be a temporary command; now he had to go back to Rabat, where his staff were busy planning for the next campaign, 'Operation Husky', the invasion of Sicily. This was due to take place on 10 June, a bare seven weeks ahead, and there was much work yet to be done. And so on 15 April Patton handed over II US Corps to Bradley and departed. He was moving up; he had handed over a corps and was now to command an army.

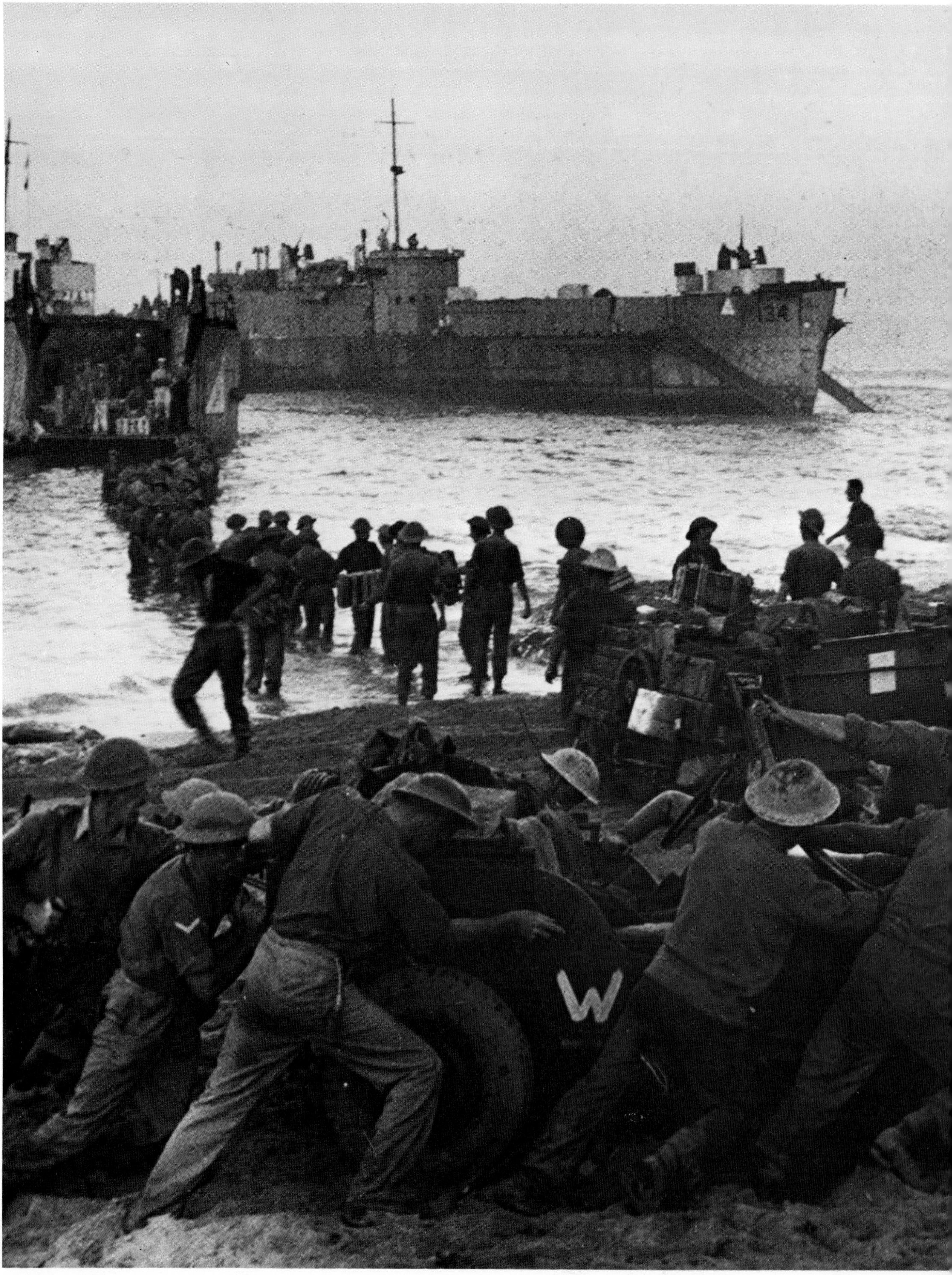
134
W

5: SICILY

Operation Husky, the invasion of Sicily, was the first major amphibious landing to be undertaken by the Allies, and it served two purposes. First, and most obviously, it gained a foothold on what Churchill, optimistically, called 'the soft underbelly of Europe.' Secondly it acted as a dress rehearsal for the landing on the mainland of western Europe already being planned, giving the Allies an opportunity to perfect their techniques and make their mistakes. There were mistakes in plenty, but fortunately they were largely counterbalanced by the detailed knowledge which the Allies had of the German and Italian forces on the island and their disposition.

When Patton arrived back at his HQ in Rabat to see how his planners were progressing, they had reached their fifth or sixth version. What might appear to the layman to be a fairly simple proposition was being complicated by the demands which various interested factions were making. The supply people wanted some ports rapidly captured, because they were apprehensive about supplying the invasion forces across open beaches. The aviation experts wanted airfields taken rapidly, since they would otherwise have to fly their air support from airfields in North Africa, leaving them little time or fuel over the target area for useful work. The soldiers wanted to be landed where there were few defences but from where they would be able to move and exploit the road network. The sailors wanted the plans altered so as to simplify their task and take advantage of currents and sea conditions. Somehow all these conflicting demands were shuffled and cut until something practical emerged, but even so, there was still room for differences of opinion. Patton favoured a plan which contained an element of risk; he visualized two widely separated landings, the British coming ashore on the southeast coast near Catania and the Americans on the northwest coast near Palermo. The two forces would then strike out on a

diagonal so as to cut the island in two, with the object of preventing the Germans setting up a defensive line. The British plan, on the other hand, argued for a more safe and sure advance by landing both the American and British forces on the southeast corner of the island, slightly separated, after which both forces would swing over and aim for Messina, the object being to get there in time to prevent the embarkation and escape of any German troops.

The background to this was the Allied knowledge of enemy plans which had been extracted from Ultra intercepts. After the Tunisian campaign was finished, it was fairly reasonable to assume that the next Allied move would be against Sicily or Italy, and therefore some stocktaking had been done by the Germans. Kesselring sent a long signal to Hitler detailing the complete set-up of German and Italian defences in Sicily. This revealed that he had stationed part of 15th Panzer Grenadier Division at Palermo, together with two Italian divisions. The rest of 15th Panzer Grenadier Division, together with the *Hermann Goering* Panzer Division, was divided into three battle groups placed in the centre of the island ready to move in any threatened direction. In addition there were four field and two coast defense divisions of the Italian Army distributed around the island. Analysis of the positioning of these troops strengthened the arguments for the British plan – Patton would have been badly mauled had he tried to come ashore in the face of 15th Panzer Grenadier Division, for example – and it also gave assurance that the proposed landings would meet with little opposition and that some strategically-placed airborne troops could block the roads to the coast and prevent the Panzer battle groups from acting too promptly.

The final plan called for the British Eighth Army to land on a 30 mile front with two Corps, XIII Corps (General Dempsey) south of Syracuse, and XXX Corps (General Leese) astride the Pachino peninsula with the aim of quickly capturing the airfield there. The US Seventh Army, under Patton, would land

Left: British troops heaving equipment through the soft sand of the Sicily beachhead as the build-up of stores begins.

Above: General Patton inspecting a guard detail during one of his visits to units during the Sicily campaign.

on a 70 mile front; on the right flank was Bradley's II Corps with 45th Infantry Division at Scoglitti and 1st Infantry Division at Gela, whilst on the left the 3rd Infantry Division would land at Licata. In reserve Patton had 2nd Armored Division and part of 9th Infantry Division. The landings would be preceded by airborne assaults; by the British 1st Airborne Division in gliders and by the US 82nd Airborne Division by parachute. The remarkable thing about this plan was that it more or less left open the question of what this force was going to do when it got ashore. Alexander seems to have had the general idea of leaving Montgomery to make his own way up the eastern coast towards Messina while Patton protected his flank. With two *prima donnas* like Montgomery and Patton ashore alongside each other, this was a highly optimistic point of view. On the other hand it might have been

that Alexander was relying upon Ultra information to give him his strategy once ashore, so that he could move to confound any enemy manoeuver; in which case he was backing a loser, because over the short distances involved in Sicily, telephone and short-range radio were the means of communication, and the high-powered Enigma network was not called into play and Alexander was therefore to remain ignorant of Italian and German counter measures.

Nothing on the scale of the Sicily landings had previously happened in the history of war; 2760 ships and landing craft were making their way towards the island, and among them was the *Monrovia*, Admiral Hewitt's flagship, which carried Patton and his headquarters. For the many on board the ships who regarded the Mediterranean as a placid sort of oversized lake, there was an unpleasant surprise in store. As the fleet closed with its objective on 9 July 1943, so the weather deteriorated; the morning was calm and hot, but by mid-afternoon the wind had freshened, and by evening

it was blowing a Force 7 gale. Most of the soldiers in the smaller landing craft were seasick and soaked to the skin by the time they arrived at the beaches. The wind had also played havoc with the airborne plans. Many gliders, released too soon, smashed into the cliffs, scores of parachutists were blown away from their scheduled drop zones and many aircraft finished in the wrong place. Of the 134 gliders which set out, less than a score reached their objectives, and only about 200 parachutists from the 82nd Airborne Division managed to reach their principal target, the plateau of Piano Lupo. The remainder were scattered all over southeastern Sicily but, with infinite resourcefulness, banded together in small groups and roamed about the countryside, cutting communications and performing hit and run raids against any Italian post they happened to find.

The British Eighth Army got ashore relatively quietly in sheltered water. The Americans, apart from 45th division which was an hour late due to the high seas, also had an uneventful landing, wet and miserable as most of them were. The 3rd Division, at Licata, was the first ashore and by 0630 artillery and tanks were passing across the beach. Coastal artillery units at Gela opened up against 1st Division but were rapidly silenced by naval counterbattery fire, and at Scoglitti the 45th Division landed with minimal opposition. By mid-morning 1st Division had linked with the 82nd Airborne at Piano Lupo to hold the road junction there, and had siezed Gela with its airfield; 3rd Division had Licata and some eight miles of coastline; 45th Division was five miles inland and going well. However, by midday the island garrison had reacted; 15th Panzer Grenadier Division was ordered to move toward Enna, in the center of the island, to stand by as a mobile reserve, while the *Hermann Goering* Panzer Division and

the Italian *Livorno* Division were ordered to attack Gela. There was a mix-up in the orders which resulted in the Italians mounting a half-hearted attack which was driven off. Then the *Hermann Goering* Division mounted another, more serious, attack accompanied by artillery bombardment and air strikes on the crowded beaches but the short notice and confused orders led to a confused attack which was also beaten off. Next came another attack using Tiger tanks but this too failed, and the battle line degenerated into a string of minor and confusing firefights.

Patton foresaw that the following day would see the Germans in possession of their wits once again and mounting some serious counterattacks, and so during the afternoon of the first day he cancelled the planned schedules and ordered 2nd

Above: A jovial Patton, camera at the ready, during one of his pep talks to his soldiers in Sicily.

Left: Italian troops with an improvized white flag surrender to troops of Montgomery's Eighth Army in Sicily.

Armored Division ashore. By evening the tanks were landing, and their disembarkation continued throughout the night. At 0900 the next morning Patton himself went ashore, amid sporadic German artillery fire, and then drove off to see 1st Division at Gela. On the way he saw the Rangers command post and decided to visit with them which was just as well, since had he continued on the Gela road he would have run into a German tank troop. The *Hermann Goering* Division had thrust in, during the dawn, and had separated the Rangers from 1st Division. Now Patton was tied down in the Rangers CP while a battle ranged in the streets outside between the Rangers and the Italian *Livorno* Division troops. In the nick of time 10 Sherman tanks, which had landed with 2nd Armored and driven straight from Licata into battle, came to tip the balance in the American favour, and shells from the 6-inch guns of the USS *Savannah* added the final touch. The enemy were driven back and Patton continued his journey to 1st Division.

They were under considerable pressure; the *Hermann Goering* Division had attacked them with 60 tanks, hoping

Above: A C-47 Dakota laden with paratroops and with heavy stores lashed underneath, on its way to Sicily.

Left: An M3 105mm airborne howitzer being loaded into a Waco glider in North Africa ready for its flight to Sicily.

to drive the Americans back into the sea, and 1st Division had only two tanks with them. The 32nd Field Artillery Battalion, disembarking their 105mm howitzers from DUKWs on the beach, went straight into action and opened fire on the German panzers over open sights; soon the plain around Gela was littered with burning tanks. Naval gunfire added to the toll, and then the tanks of 2nd Armored came thundering into the battle, forcing the panzers to retire. Had Patton not had the forethought to bring forward 2nd Armored's disembarkation, it is doubtful whether the battle would have gone in the Allies' favour.

By the evening of 12 July, Montgomery had captured Augusta and was about to begin an advance on a four-division front into the Plain of Catania. Patton had linked up with him and was some 20 miles inland. Meanwhile the German and Italian forces had rallied, and reinforcements from XIV Panzer Corps were filling up in front of the British. It was time for Alexander to make up his mind as to the next phase of the invasion. If, as appeared likely, the weight of the German defenses was being placed in front of Montgomery, then it seemed to Patton that the logical course of action was to allow him to cut straight across the island to the north coast, then turn outwards and gradually envelop the rest of it. But before Alexander could make up his mind, Montgomery, stalled with two Panzer Grenadier regiments and two regiments of German parachute troops in front of him, decided (without, apparently, informing Alexander) to sidestep left around the foot of Mount Etna and outflank them. This move, however, brought him over the agreed American Corps boundary and gave him possession of Route 124; of the three good roads running north, he now had two. Alexander, faced with a *fait accompli*, regularized the position by sending out orders allotting Montgomery the main effort against Messina, driving northward on both sides of Mount Etna.

This was too much for Patton to stomach; he took off for Tunis and pressed for his plan to drive on Palermo, rather than simply keep in step with Montgomery, protecting his flanks. Alexander, for his part, appears to have finally comprehended the American point of view; not the tactical point of view, but the public relations point of view, that American troops had to be seen to be excelling wherever they appeared. By this time he had begun to appreciate the fighting qualities of Patton and of his troops. And, moreover, he had at last received some hard information from Ultra which indicated that the mass of the enemy resistance was facing Montgomery. To the Germans, the British Eighth Army was a known quantity and a tough one; on the other hand, they knew little of the Americans and, because of this, they tended not to have a high opinion of their fighting abilities. Alexander now, therefore, gave Patton his head.

Back in Sicily, and released from the confines of the original plan, Patton burst loose and headed for Palermo like a rocket. A Provisional Corps, under Major General Keyes, his Chief of Staff, and composed of 3rd Infantry and 82nd Divisions and 2nd Armored was to make for Palermo from the south, while Bradley's II Corps struck north to cut the coast road. In a lightning six-day advance Keyes' corps, with the infantry hitching rides on the tanks, roared forward 100 miles and took 53,000 prisoners. On 22 July Patton, with 2nd

Armored Division, entered Palermo to the cheers of the inhabitants and set up his HQ in the Royal Palace. The next day Bradley's force cut the coast road and reached the sea at Termini Imerese. The Americans had a deepwater port, and several thousand Italians had their dreams fulfilled with a free trip to the USA.

After the war there were attempts to detract from Patton's dash by ascribing it all to the Mafia influence. This is, of course, nonsense, but there are grounds for suspecting that this was put up semi-officially as a red herring in order to keep prying eyes away from the secret of Ultra. Patton's advance was not, as it appeared at the time, a carefree drive into unknown odds; he knew very well that there were few serious enemy forces in front of him, because he was in possession of the

Above: US Paratroopers mounting their C-47 Dakota for the assault on Sicily.

German order of battle. But Ultra was to remain a secret until 1973, and in the immediate postwar years it was thought better to ascribe his success to the Mafia than to admit the existence of Ultra.

The fact remains, though, that while Patton's dash was a spectacular tactical move, it was of little strategic value, in that while he was concentrating on Palermo, he took the weight off the Germans in the Mount Etna area and they, while holding Montgomery with one hand, occupied the other in building up some formidable defensive lines against Patton's next move. As a result, when he turned back in late July to begin moving towards Messina, the Germans

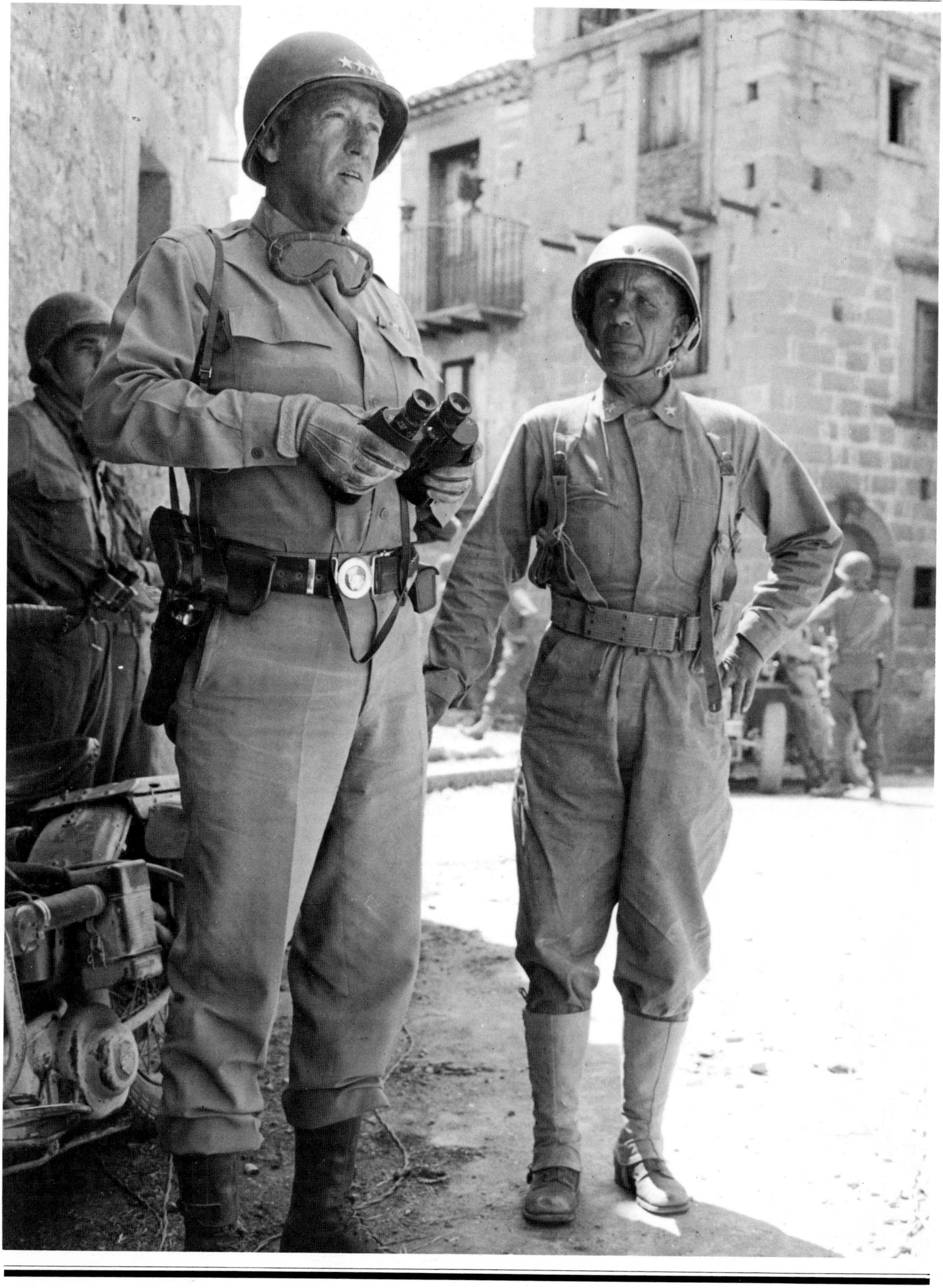

Left: General Patton, with General
Roosevelt at an observation post in a small
Sicilian village.

were well dug in and had built ample
field fortifications.

The combined Anglo-American attack
toward Messina moved very slowly. The
British were in the south, moving against
Catania, Canadians were in the center at
Regalbuto, the 1st US Infantry Division
further north attacked Troina, and the
45th US Infantry Division tried to move
along the northern coast road from
Termini. All ran into severe opposition
from well-trained troops in sound
positions.

The Mount Troina area was particularly severe, a mountainous region
against which the 1st Infantry battered
for four days, leaving the mountainside
strewn with their dead. The divisional
commander, General Terry Allen,
openly wept as he saw the carnage, but
this was not the sort of reaction which
appealed to Patton, who drove the
division relentlessly into the attack again
and again. The men of 1st Division began
to feel that they were being asked to do
more than their share, and few of the men
who served in this battle have anything
good to say of Patton, especially since,
after the mountain was taken, he fired
both Allen and his deputy commander.

In an endeavour to break the deadlock
Patton now called for an amphibious
'left hook' along the northern coast, to
drop an assault party behind the German
lines in order to cut their communications
and generally raise havoc. A first attempt
was aborted for various reasons; a second
try on 8 August put a raiding force ashore
east of Sant' Agata. This managed to
ambush German reinforcements moving
up and rout them, then moved west to
join up with the slowly advancing main
force. This minor raid had one very
useful result in that it secured a vital road
tunnel and also secured the heights
around a gorge in which an equally vital
road bridge had been destroyed, which
allowed US engineers to repair the bridge

Right: General Patton, unusually wearing
a shoulder holstered pistol, with General
Eisenhower at Palermo airport.

Above right: General Patton meets Bob
Hope and Frances Langford after a USO
show for the troops in Sicily.

without coming under fire. It was claimed, at the time, that this was worth 24 hours to the Americans; unfortunately they lost the time because the Germans held their next positions rather more obstinately. Another amphibious landing was mounted on the 16 August, of larger size, but this was a blow into thin air because the German forces had already fallen back beyond the landing area and

Below: Patton says farewell to the staff of 1st Division, leaving Sicily. Generals Huebner, Andrews, Gaffey and Gay with Col Wyman.

were in a position to put down heavy artillery fire on the landing beaches.

By the 16th Patton was no longer worried about the effect of the landing; German resistance had finally cracked and Messina was within his reach. The one driving force which had obsessed him throughout the campaign was to get to Messina before Montgomery. On the morning of 17 August Patton stood on a ridge overlooking Messina but he didn't stand long. 'What the hell are you all waiting for?' he roared at his retinue, then jumped into his scout car and took

off for the prize. The movie story of Montgomery arriving shortly afterwards is untrue; the British force which arrived was a party from 40 Royal Marine Commando who had made an amphibious landing near Scaletta during the night but who had been delayed due to demolitions and booby-traps en route.

The Sicilian Campaign came to a successful conclusion after 38 days of combat. Approximately 113,000 German and Italian troops had been taken, 256 tanks destroyed, 2324 vehicles wrecked and 1,162 pieces of artillery either

smashed or captured. More to the point, Patton had fought his first victorious campaign, one in which US troops had shown themselves capable of equalling the feats of their allies or their enemies. He was lauded as one of the new generation of lively, forceful, mobile commanders and the American press corps were beginning to build him up as the man of the future. Then, just as his reputation seemed to have reached its height, his unpredictable temper got the better of him and flung him into the depths from which he very nearly did not

return. This paragon, this disciplinarian, this man to whom regulations were like Holy Writ, did something which any second lieutenant two days out from officer school knew was fatal. He struck a soldier. Worse than that; he struck a *sick* soldier, in, of all places, a hospital.

It was on 3rd August, while the battle of Troina raged, that Patton, frustrated by the deadlock, had taken off on a cruise around the front in order, as he put it, 'To do some ass-kicking.' The delays and difficulties with 1st Division at Troina undoubtedly put him into a foul temper, but after visiting various units and chewing out a few unfortunates he seemed to mellow a little. Then more or less by chance, he stopped by the 15th Evacuation Hospital. Patton did not really *like* visiting field hospitals and talking to the wounded men. It depressed him to see young lives mangled, but he respected the wounded and, overcoming his dislike, made it his duty to go and see how the soldiers were being looked after, award them medals and cheer them up in his bluff and forthright way. This visit to the 15th began that way, but then he came to a bed upon which lay a private from 1st Division. When asked what ailed him, the boy unwisely replied 'I guess I can't take it, sir.' This, to Patton, was like a red rag to a bull, and it got more or less the same response. Patton cursed him up hill and down dale and closed his oration by smacking the boy across the face with his gloves. Then he stormed out of the hospital, cursing malingerers, idlers, cowards and 'battle fatigue' cases in general.

There the matter might have rested; everybody knew what Patton was like,

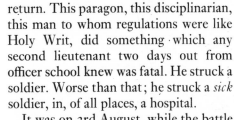

Above: A tight fit as a jeep is slowly backed into a Waco glider ready for the airborne assault upon Sicily.

the soldier should have known better than to give such an answer, and anyway, shortly afterwards he was examined and found to be suffering from malaria and dysentery. As a matter of record these complaints had reached near-epidemic level in Seventh Army and, when the final records were compiled, it was discovered that the number of malaria cases evacuated from Sicily exceeded the number of battle casualties by 1500. In any event, Patton sent out a stinging memorandum to all commanders that evening:

'It has come to my attention that a very small number of soldiers are going to hospital on the pretext that they are nervously incapable of combat. Such men are cowards and bring discredit to the Army and disgrace to their comrades who they heartlessly leave to endure the danger of a battle while they themselves use the hospital as a means of escaping. You will take measures to see that such cases are not sent to hospital but are dealt with in their units. Those who are not willing to fight will be tried by Court-Martial for cowardice in the face of the enemy.'

On 10 August Patton was clouded with the cares of office; he had just issued orders for the mounting of an amphibious attack, and he was faced with the unpleasant task of firing the commander and deputy commander of 1st Division. He set off for Bradley's HQ and, en route, saw the signs indicating 93rd Evacuation Hospital. On a sudden whim he ordered

Above: The men he respected – Patton talks to wounded GIs awaiting evacuation from a Sicilian airfield.

his driver to pull in and stop; he would defer his unpleasant duty a little longer while he inspected the hospital. He found that 15 casualties had just come in, and walked down the line of beds, speaking kindly to the men. Then he came to a young soldier seated on his bed and still wearing his helmet. Patton stopped and asked him what was wrong with him; the man replied 'It's my nerves' and began to sob. Patton, enraged, roared 'What did you say?' and the soldier replied 'I can hear the shells come over but I can't hear them burst.'

Patton, mistrusting his ears, turned to Major Charles B Etter, the hospital receiving officer, and asked 'What's this man talking about? What's wrong with him, if anything?' Before the doctor

could answer, Patton turned back to the soldier and shouted 'Your nerves, Hell, you're just a Goddamned coward, you yellow son of a bitch. You're a disgrace to the Army and you're going back to the front to fight, though that's too good for you. You ought to be lined up against a wall and shot. In fact I ought to shoot you myself right now, Goddam you!' And with that Patton drew one of his pistols and waved it in the man's face. Then, with his free hand, he slapped the man sharply across the face and began cursing him again. By this time Colonel Currier, the CO of the Hospital had entered the ward; Patton, seeing him for the first time, shouted 'I want you to get this man out of here right away. I'll not have these other brave boys see such a bastard babied!'

Without waiting for Currier to reply, Patton reholstered his pistol, turned, and began to storm out of the ward. Then he

turned back suddenly and saw that the soldier was weeping. Rushing back, Patton struck him again, this time with such force that he knocked the man's helmet across the ward. By now Currier had overcome his initial shock and moved rapidly to place himself between the man and Patton, who turned and began to leave the tent once more. Currier followed him out to his car, and as he prepared to leave Patton said to Currier 'I meant what I said about getting that coward out of there. I won't have these cowardly bastards hanging around our hospitals. We'll probably have to shoot them some time anyway, or we'll raise a breed of morons.' He later added 'These cowards who claim they're suffering from psychoneurosis; they shouldn't be allowed in the same hospital as brave wounded men.'

Patton drove off and soon afterwards arrived at Bradley's headquarters. 'Sorry to be late, Brad,' he said; 'Stopped off at a hospital on the way; there were a couple of malingerers there; I slapped one of them to put some fight back in him.' And that, for George Patton, was that. Quick to strike but slow to wound, he had acted on the spur of the moment and considered the affair was now closed.

Others, though, did not; two days later Bradley was astounded when his Chief of Staff, accompanied by the Corps Surgeon, presented him with a neatly typed report of the whole incident, submitted by Colonel Currier. Once he read it, it was obvious that there was more here than a mere slap. Patton had struck the man at least twice, threatened him with a firearm, and abused him roundly in the presence of a score of witnesses, none of whom, it seemed, would be reluctant to come forward and testify at Patton's court-martial. 'Has anybody else seen this?' asked Bradley. On being told that no one had, he ordered his CoS to lock it in a safe and keep quiet about it. Bradley was in an unpleasant spot; by all the regulations he should have forwarded the report to Eisenhower, but his loyalty to Patton over-rode his duty in this case and he kept quiet.

But to keep such a thing quiet on a combat zone, with soldiers avid for any gossip or rumor, was patently impossible. Within hours of the affair it had reached the ears of press correspondents, and some went to the hospital to question

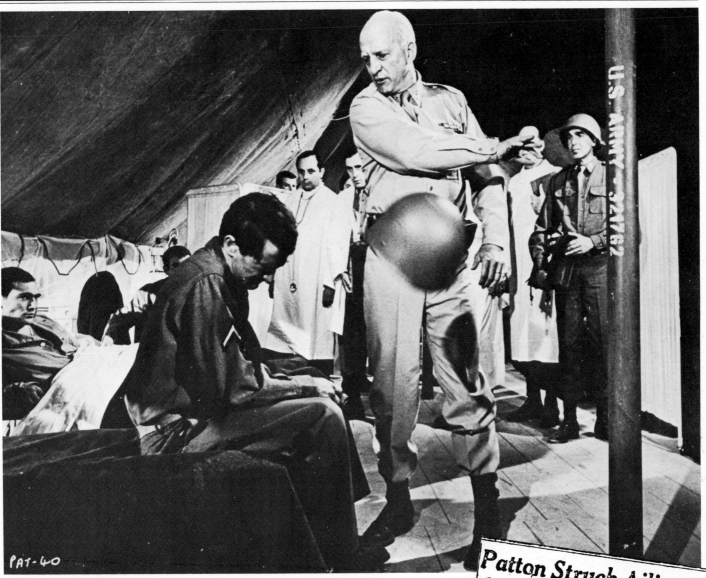

PAT-40

Above: The man he assaulted – a fictionalised 'slapping incident' from the movie 'Patton' with George C Scott playing the General.

Below: The American press had a field-day over the slapping incident, and Patton's career was in jeopardy.

THE NEW YORK TIMES, WEDNESDA

Patton Struck Ailing Soldier Apologized to Him and Army

By MILTON BRACKER
By Wireless to The New York Times.

ALGIERS, Nov. 23—Lieut. Gen. George S. Patton Jr. struck and insulted a shell-shocked American soldier in an evacuation hospital in Sicily last August and ordered the patient to return to the front lines, it was officially revealed today. Gen. Dwight D. Eisenhower denounced the conduct of the commander of the American Seventh Army as "despicable" and threatened to break him unless he made amends at once. General Patton thereupon apologized to the soldier, to the officers and patients who had witnessed the incident and to the Seventh Army.

Although there were at least fifteen witnesses to the incident, none was a professional reporter. The first two reporters to check on the episode arrived at the hospital about twenty-four hours later. One of them was Merrill Mueller of the National Broadcasting Company, who gave his version today in the

Continued on Page Six

Patton Struck Shell-Shocked Soldier

HE SLAPPED

Continued From Page One

resence and with the explicit approval of a high member of General Eisenhower's staff. The other man was Demaree Bess of The Saturday Evening Post, who is now in the United States.

On Aug. 10, General Patton made one of his periodic visits to the evacuation hospital at Sant' Agata di Militello, southwest of Cape Orlando and about two-thirds of the way from Palermo to Messina. The colonel commanding the hospital was a native of General Patton's home town. He walked alongside the General down the central aisle of the admission tent, a typical large brown canvas installation with accommodations for possibly twenty-five men. There were at least fifteen patients in the cots.

The soldier whom the General struck was a regular Army man only 21 years old, with considerable pre-Pearl Harbor experience

knew, emphasizing the issue of the rights of the American private soldier.

General Eisenhower promptly showed Mr. Mueller that he was completely informed of the case and had taken the steps that he felt necessary. At no time, however, was General Patton "disciplined" in any of the three ways open in the Army—court-martial, reprimand or admonition. His official record, according to a source close to the Allied command, bears no evidence of the incident.

[General Eisenhower "ripped the hide off" General Patton, a high staff officer told The United Press. It was explained that General Patton had been continued in his command only because he was considered "necessary and valuable" to Allied operations.]

The result of the incident was a series of apologies unprecedented in the annals of the American Army. General Patton apologized not only to the soldier but to the colonel who headed the hospital and its staff, including the nurse whom he had made hysterical.

Indi
O

M
—T
Her
clo
fro
be
G
c

the pa
probably won't go through, don't know' Just forget about in your letter."

In his letter Private Kuhl, w is slight of build, said that he h been shell-shocked in the landi in Sicily, but that his superior of cers had not believed that he w seriously hurt. He was ordered

RUSSIANS RETREAT TOWARD KIEV AGAIN

Germans Win Several Towns at High Cost, but Red Army Gains on Other Fronts

By The United Press.

LONDON, Wednesday, Nov. 24 —German forces, driving back toward Kiev and the Dnieper line without regard for prodigious losses, yesterday reached the vicinity of Brusilov, less than fifty miles from the Ukraine capital, Moscow acknowledged today.

The Soviet operational and supplementary communiqués reported that the Red Army had abandoned several towns and villages north f Zhitomir, in the area of Charyakhov, and east of the rail

Above: General Patton and General Mark Clark at a Sicilian airport, awaiting the arrival of General Eisenhower.

Right: US paratroops check each other's equipment as they prepare to emplane for the assault on Sicily.

staff and patients. Within another day newsmen had carried it to North Africa, and by 16 August Eisenhower had a full report, prepared by the Surgeon-General's staff, of both incidents.

Eisenhower had no choice in the matter by this time. Too many people knew that Patton had done *something* and unless he took action, rumor would magnify whatever it could find. So he wrote a formal letter to Patton, asking for a report in writing, giving his reasons for his actions. Eisenhower's letter was coldly official:

'I am well aware of the necessity for hardness and toughness on the battlefield. . . . I clearly understand that firm and drastic measures are at all times necessary in order to secure desired objectives. But this does not excuse brutality, abuse of the sick, nor exhibition of uncontrollable temper in front of subordinates. . . . I will not tolerate conduct of the sort described in this report by anyone, no matter how high his rank . . .'

Eisenhower then assembled the press corps, told them of the contents of the report and of the action he had taken, told them that he was sending a special envoy to Sicily to get to the root of the affair, and left it at that. The press, with commendable restraint, voluntarily agreed to keep the affair quiet, in view of the delicate military situation and the impact it was likely to have on morale.

Eisenhower's next move was to send John Lucas, one of his corps commanders, to see Patton and read the riot act to him. He also sent the Inspector-General for North Africa to conduct a 'survey of morale,' which was a high-sounding euphemism for a fishing expedition around the men of Seventh Army to find out what the troops thought about the whole affair and about Patton in particular. He also insisted that Patton was to make a public apology to the staff of the 93rd Evacuation Hospital.

This apology duly took place; 'You have all been witnesses of an incident that has turned out to be unfortunate . . .' Patton began, and then launched into an involved story about a World War I friend of his who had committed suicide in a fit of depression. 'If someone had been rough with him, and slapped some sense into him, his life would have been saved.' After this Patton drove around

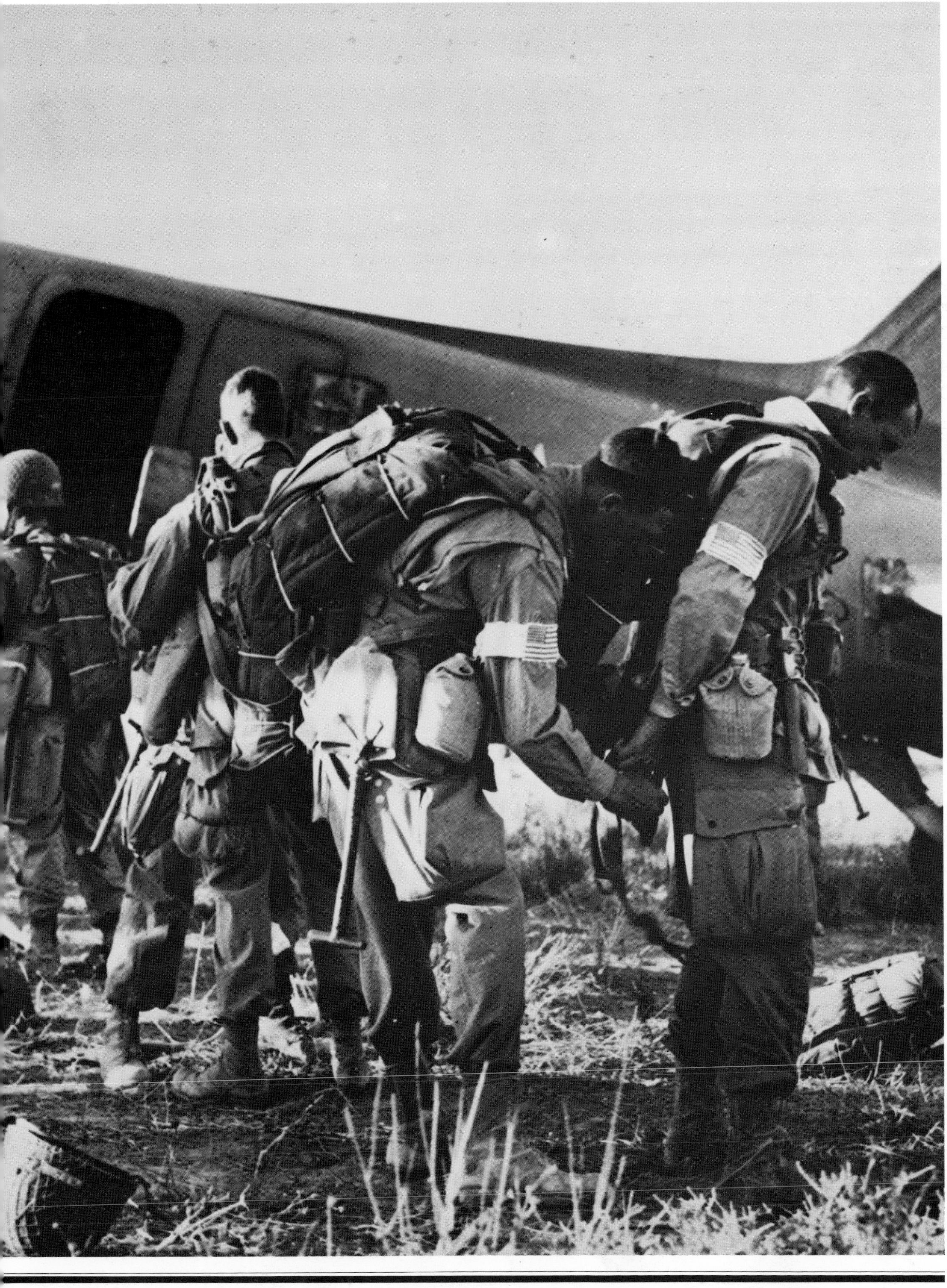

Right: The British monitor HMS *Abercrombie* begins a night bombardment with her 18in guns off the coast of Sicily.

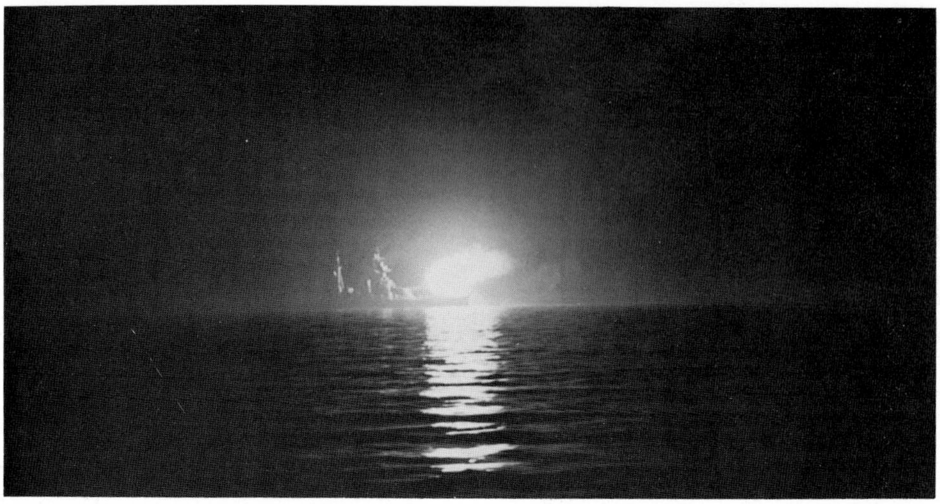

the Seventh Army area and delivered a general apology to each division. Even so, there is little doubt that he felt badly done by. He wrote in his diary 'It is rather a commentary on justice when an Army Commander has to soft-soap a skulker to placate the timidity of those above.'

The simple answer to all this was that Patton simply could not understand what all the fuss was about. He had come to maturity in World War I, in the days when matters were seen in an extremely simple light; either a man was a man and took what the enemy threw at him, or he was a coward and ran. It was as simple as that. The gradual development of psychiatric studies, the realization that battle fatigue was a genuine complaint which would in time affect every man irrespective of his degree of courage or lack of it, the dawning understanding of the delicate knife-edge between sanity and neurosis under combat conditions, had completely passed Patton by. His reactions he therefore considered those of a normal soldier; as he once wrote,

'The greatest weapon against the so-called battle fatigue is ridicule. If soldiers would realise that a large pro-

Below: Tank Landing Ships putting transport and stores ashore at Licata in support of Patton's drive through Sicily.

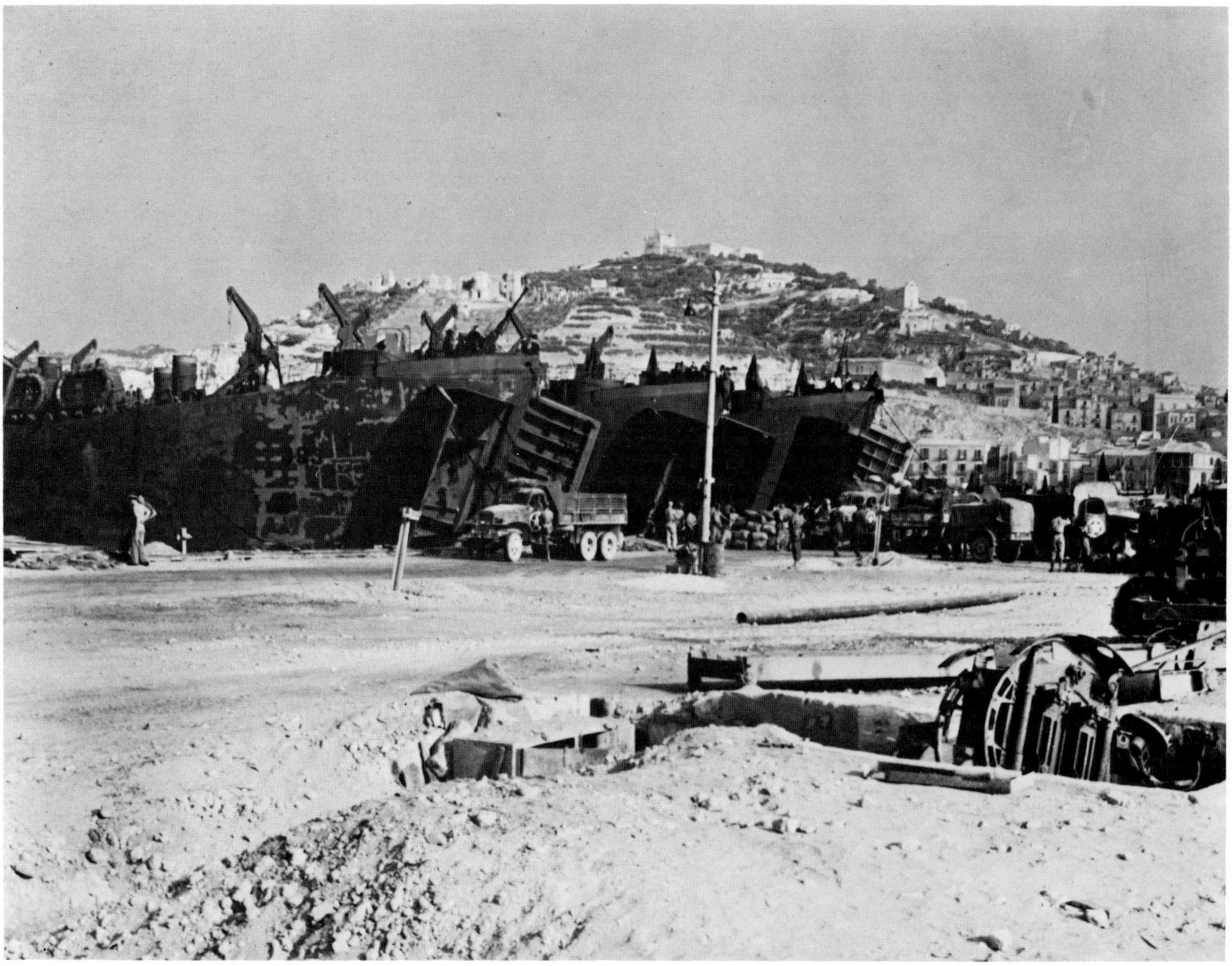

Above: Patton confers with Lt Col Lyle Bernard, commanding 30th Landing Regiment, near Messina.

portion of men allegedly suffering from battle fatigue are really using an easy way out, they would be less sympathetic. Any man who says he has battle fatigue is avoiding danger and forcing those who have more hardihood than himself the obligation of meeting it...'
It might also be pointed out that, at that time, Patton was far from being alone in his view. Many of his contemporaries, both officers and men, also regarded battle fatigue with some degree of suspicion.

His next task was to make formal reply to Eisenhower's formal letter of enquiry, and in this he claimed that he had never intended to be either harsh or cruel in his treatment of the two men, but to 'try and realise in them a just appreciation of their obligations as men and soldiers.' Eisenhower was now in something of a dilemma, as neither he nor anyone else in the theater had sufficient rank to try Patton by court-martial. The choices were either to send Patton back to the USA to be tried, demote him to his

permanent rank of colonel and try him in North Africa, or forget the whole affair. After a great deal of thought he chose the latter course, on the grounds that while Patton had undoubtedly acted in a stupid manner, his value as the best combat general available outweighed his shortcomings.

This might have been the end of the matter but, as was inevitable, the story leaked and in November it broke in the USA when Drew Pearson, the noted columnist, retailed the affair in a radio broadcast. The newspapers took it up, radio reporters embroidered it, and even German radio stations were soon busy spreading the tale, adding the hopeful falsehood that Patton had been relieved of his command. General McNarney, the Deputy Chief of Staff, demanded full details from Eisenhower, and the uproar was most chastening for Patton. Through it all, though, Eisenhower stood by his decision and his subordinate. In a letter to General Marshall he stressed that though Patton had his faults, and some of them were sizable, he was a sound combat commander and worth retaining on that score alone:

'I believe that he is cured, not only

because of his great personal loyalty... but because fundamentally he is so avid of recognition as a great military commander that he will ruthlessly repress any habit that would tend to jeopardize it...'
However, for all his willingness to retain Patton, Eisenhower now realized that he had reached the limit of his abilities. In a later letter to Marshall, Eisenhower noted that 'In no event will I ever advance Patton beyond Army Commander.' Future events were now casting strong shadows before themselves and, like several other generals, Patton was speculating on his likely role in the forthcoming invasion of Europe. Surely, with the brilliance of the Sicily campaign behind him he was a natural choice to command the American invasion force? It was not to be. If there had been any discussion among the Chiefs of Staff about Patton's eligibility to command in Europe, it stopped abruptly once the news of the 'slapping incident' broke. Five minutes of anger had very nearly cost Patton his career; it had certainly ensured that he would be carefully watched from now on, and that he had reached his military ceiling.

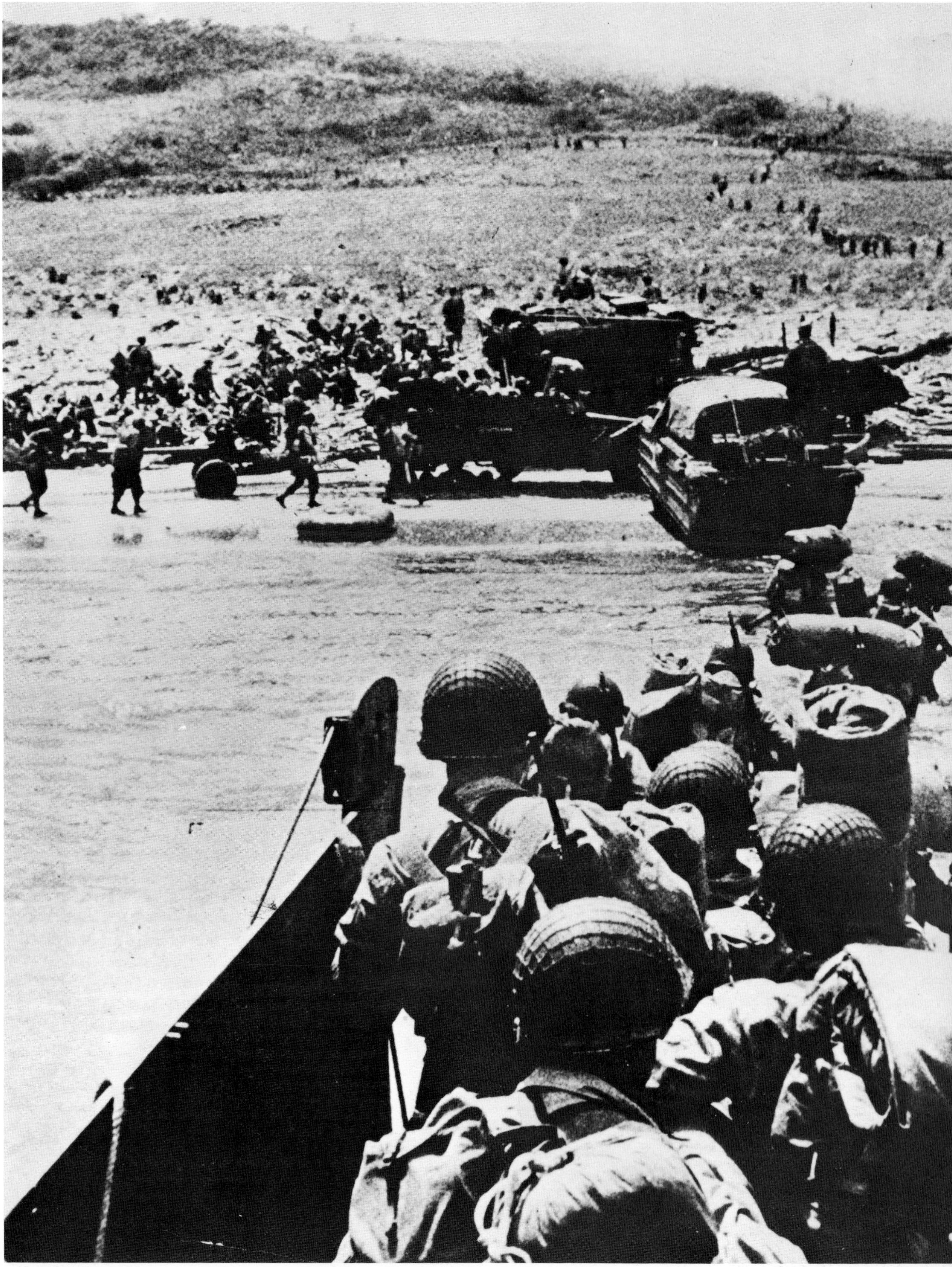

6: INTO EUROPE

In March 1943 Lieutenant General Morgan, of the British Army, had set up a planning headquarters to work on the proposed invasion of Europe. By August 1943 he had made sufficient progress to be able to present an outline plan at the Quebec Conference, but it was not until November that Roosevelt and Churchill agreed on the command structure, when they met in Cairo after the Teheran Conference. There was some vacillating by Roosevelt over his choice of commander. His first preference was General Marshall, but coupled with this was the desire to have Marshall command not only in Europe but throughout the Mediterranean and North Africa as well. Roosevelt's motives were complicated. It was partly because he was in considerable awe of Marshall and felt that only a 'supremo' position was worthy of him; partly because he was anxious to get as much power in American hands as possible; and, it would seem, partly because he simply had no idea of the magnitude of the task he was proposing and how impossibly difficult it would have been for any one man. In the event, Churchill refused to consider the idea, because of its political implications in the Mediterranean area, and he insisted that American command was to be confined to 'Overlord,' the code-name for the invasion. Roosevelt was intelligent enough to back down, but in doing so he began to have second thoughts about his choice of Marshall because, in his view, the Overlord post was beneath Marshall's dignity. Moreover he also realised that if Marshall received a field command, then his replacement as Chief of Staff would have to be Eisenhower, and Roosevelt was dubious of Ike's ability to control the political side of the business and also of his near-total ignorance of the nuances of the Pacific War.

Even so, the generals themselves were of the opinion that Marshall was the man for the job, and Eisenhower was already contemplating his move back to Washington, though not with any great degree of enthusiasm. But on 5 December, in Cairo, Roosevelt finally made his decision. On the 7th he flew to Tunis, where he was met by Eisenhower and gave him the news of his forthcoming appointment. Eisenhower then went to Sicily to talk with General Mark Clark about the prospective Italian campaign, and also saw Patton, giving him the news that he would be commanding an army in the invasion. He was elated by this, convinced that Seventh Army would be withdrawn from Sicily and sent to Britain to train. This sustained him for a month, but early in January he was relieved of command of Seventh Army, and on 26 January 1944 he landed in Scotland, wondering what the future held for him.

On reporting to Eisenhower's headquarters he was told that he was to command the Third US Army . . . but not yet. He was to have no part in planning for the invasion, nor would he actually participate in it. The Third Army was to be held back for action after the invasion had succeeded. In the meantime he could train his army, but, more important than that, he was to act as one of the principal characters in a piece of play-acting. He was to star in 'Operation Fortitude.'

The invasion plan, as it stood when Patton arrived in Britain, called for an initial assault with three divisions and two airborne brigades, followed up by three corps leapfrogging forward through the divisions. However, the landings in Sicily had taught people a few lessons, and Montgomery (who had also returned to Britain for the invasion), with Eisenhower's approval, made some radical changes. He turned down the idea of leapfrogging troops through the divisions on shore as being far too prone to go wrong. He insisted in the initial landings being made with larger forces, which meant expanding the proposed beachheads, and he wanted the western flank secured by more airborne landings. Once the initial beaches were taken and the landings stabilized, then Patton's army was to cross the Channel, clear the Brittany peninsula, and, together with Bradley's (later Hodges') First US Army,

Left: The second wave of US infantry disembark from a landing craft on a French beach. Anti-tank guns and a command post are already ashore.

make the breakout which would take the Allies across France. Patton was, at first, disappointed not to be in the initial assault force, but, on mature consideration, he perhaps realised that by taking on the breakout role he would have the chance to apply his particular talent for mobile action and, more to his liking, he would avoid the frustration and uproar which came to be the lot of the commanders of the actual assault parties as they jockeyed for landing craft and wrote and rewrote their loading schedules.

What had to be borne in mind, of course, was that the invasion was not a

Above: An aerial view of Omaha beach, showing landing craft and vehicles stranded in the surf.

one-sided affair; there were many thousand armed German troops on the other side of the water who had been preparing for such an event for some time. While the Allies were fairly confident that they could get ashore, there was less certainty about staying ashore. The German Army was renowned for its rapid response to threats and the speed with which it could produce a counter-attack. To mislead the German High Command about where the landings would take place, and keep them misled as long as possible would create a considerable advantage. If they could be persuaded, if only for a few days, that the Normandy landings were a feint, and the real weight would fall somewhere else, they would be reluctant to commit their reserves until they could see where the major blow was going to fall.

'Operation Fortitude' was a deception operation with the object of convincing the German High Command that the major invasion objective was the Pas de Calais, that it would be made by an army of 12 divisions which would rapidly be reinforced to 50 divisions, and that any landings elsewhere were in the nature of diversionary raids. This, in fact, accorded well with German logic and thinking; they recalled the abortive Dieppe raid of 1942 and were always convinced that this had been a dress rehearsal. From Kent to the Pas de Calais was the shortest distance by sea and fighters based in southern England could quickly cross the Channel to protect the beaches. A landing near Calais also put the invasion force poised for a rapid strike to the Ruhr, Germany's vulnerable manufacturing heartland.

All this theory of the Germans needed was some confirming evidence, and it was given this in a variety of ways, all forming part of the 'Fortitude' deception plan. The Royal Air Force and US Army Air Force bombed more targets in the Pas de Calais than they did in Normandy, and all major inland bombing attacks concentrated on the rail and road links north and east of the River Seine. Dummy military headquarters were set up in Kent, together with dummy camps, dummy embarkation points with dummy

Below: The USS *Texas* off Cherbourg, June 22nd 1944, opens fire on the German 'Batterie Hamburg' group of coast defense guns.

landing craft, and dummy airfields with dummy transport aircraft and gliders. Highly-trained radio operators with intricate equipment spent their days and nights sending dummy messages of the sort normally associated with an army in training and preparation, generating the traffic the German intercept stations expected to hear. As the invasion loomed closer, military units were drafted into Kent, however, at night they were moved elsewhere for embarkation, and actually put to use in the Normandy landings. Again, a skeleton radio network assumed their place and kept up traffic as if they had never moved.

All the Germans needed for final conviction was a commander with some status to head all this. Judicious hints were dropped here and there, through the press and through diplomatic channels, and eventually the Germans knew that George Patton was in Britain and was commanding this enormous force, a force which they logically christened *Armeegruppe Patton.*

Patton himself, of course, had little or nothing to do with 'Fortitude,' merely lending it his name. He had his headquarters at Peover Hall, near Knutsford in Cheshire and he occupied his time with administering the training of his new Third Army. This force had spent its previous two and one half years as a training army in the USA, based on Fort Sam Houston, Texas, and with its constituent units scattered across the western states. Its first commander had been General Krueger, universally acclaimed as a brilliant trainer of troops. It had then been taken over by General Hodges and brought to a fine pitch of perfection. Whereupon its staffs sailed, to be greeted by the news that they were now to be commanded by Patton and not by Hodges. The second shock came when the senior staff officers were informed that their services would not be required by the new army commander, since he was replacing them with members of his staffs from North Africa and Sicily, principally from 2nd Armored Division. This was something of an innovation among the Americans, though it was

Above: Now commanding Third Army,
Patton addresses troops on a visit to
Northern Ireland.

standard practice in the British Army for a general to take his senior staff elements from post to post. Patton's Chief of Staff was Brigadier General Hugh J Gaffey, a highly-skilled staff officer and an expert on armored warfare; he later departed to command a division, and later a corps, of his own, and was replaced with Brigadier General Hobart R Gay, an equally competent cavalryman. Below the heads-of-section level Patton made few changes. As he once said to Eisenhower 'I don't need a brilliant staff, I just want a loyal one,' and that was what he got.

Even though Patton was doing his best to 'keep a low profile,' events conspired to catch up with him. During the Sicily campaign there had been some unfortunate incidents of German prisoners being shot by American troops. One such incident involved a captain who, having

Below: General Patton on a tour of inspection of the 10th Infantry Regiment near Hilltown, Northern Ireland in March 1944.

Below: Troops of the 175th Infantry practise the techniques of beach landings at Slapton Sands, Devon, in August 1943.

Left: Patton, accompanied by General Robertson, D Division Commander, salutes as the 2nd Division pass in review, April 1944.

captured 43 German soldiers, lined them up against a wall and shot them down with machine guns. General Bradley, the corps commander concerned, was horrified and went to report the matter to Patton. Patton considered that the tale was probably exaggerated, but was sufficiently concerned to consider its impact if the press got hold of the tale. He told Bradley to instruct the captain to maintain that the captured troops were all snipers, or had attempted to escape. Bradley, though, was not happy with this line of argument and placed the whole matter under investigation, and eventually the captain and another officer were arraigned for court martial. In their defense they quoted a speech by Patton in which, they claimed, he had instructed them to kill prisoners.

Unfortunately there is no record of exactly what Patton did say in this speech, which was one of his many off-the-cuff exhortations to the invasion troops shortly before they sailed for Sicily, but, knowing Patton, we can have little doubt that he uttered a variety of bloodthirsty sentiments. What is surprising is that two officers should have actually considered such an exhortation in the nature of orders. It is more likely

that they were grasping at any straw to help them in the court martial. And so in March 1944, months after the affair had taken place, an officer from the Adjutant General's office arrived at Peover to ask Patton whether he had, in fact, ordered his men to kill prisoners. Patton denied any such statement, and since no records existed, that was that. That particular line of defense failed, the two officers

Above: Reviewing the 2nd Division in their training area at Armagh, Northern Ireland, April 1944.

were found guilty, but were returned to their units for the duration of the war, their cases to be reconsidered when the war ended. In the event their cases were never brought up again, since they were both killed in action.

vided that he could be assured that his remarks would be unofficial and not reported in the press.

For all the assurances, when he arrived at the club, on 25 April, he found the press were in attendance and he was photographed as he got out of his car. Mrs Constantine-Smith, introducing the General, emphasised to the assembled audience, with particular reference to the press, that the General was attending quite unofficially and that 'he will be speaking to you in a purely friendly way and nothing he will say must be quoted.' Patton then stood up and adlibbed a short speech:

'The only welcoming I've been doing for some time is welcoming Germans and Italians into hell. I've done quite a lot in that direction, and I've got about 177,000 of them there so far. I agree with Mr Bernard Shaw that the English and American peoples are separated by a common language. We certainly have some difficulty in understanding each other. The idea of these clubs could not be better, because it is undoubtedly our destiny to rule the world, we British, American, and, of course, Russian people, and the more we know each other the better it will be. It is very fine for our men to meet English people and to find that in spite of this unjumpable wall of language that we are very nearly the same sort of people. The sooner our soldiers write home and say how truly lovely the English ladies are, the more jealous the American dames will become and thus force the war to a successful conclusion. Then I can have a chance to go and kill the Japanese.'

Patton sat down to prolonged applause, doubtless feeling that he had done a reasonable job in the circumstances; but the press reported his speech and the fat was in the fire. Although reported with meticulous accuracy in British newspapers, when the text appeared in the USA the vital words 'and, of course, Russian' were omitted – whether by mischance or design no-one can now say. In consequence, the American press headlined the fact that 'British and American people will rule the world.' The New York Sun said that Patton

However, the case had brought Patton into the official limelight once again, which he could well do without. Far better to be seen industriously attending to the welfare of his men. So when a local women's organisation asked him to 'say a few words' at the opening of a soldier's canteen he was happy to oblige.

The troops of Third Army had made a good impression on the local inhabitants of Cheshire. Compared to some US troops to be seen in other parts of Britain, those in Cheshire were clean, smartly dressed, saluted punctiliously, were correct and polite in their dealings with the natives and, in general, were well liked. (The author can personally vouch for this since he was living within Third Army's area at that time). As a result the local population responded with offers of hospitality, and one such move was to establish a 'Welcome Club' for American officers. It was felt that there were plenty of clubs for soldiers, and one for officers would be a welcome innovation. Mrs M Constantine-Smith, leader of the Knutsford Women's Voluntary Service, asked General Patton if he would be kind enough to open the club. Patton replied that he would be happy to do so, pro-

had 'blundered' and that he 'has again demonstrated his unhappy faculty for getting himself and others into hot water. His speech is the latest essay in imprudence.' Senator Harlan Bushfield, a Republican, said 'The General has stepped out of bounds. This is another barrier to his promotion. His job is to carry out military assignments without discussing civilian arrangements.' A Washington newspaper referred to Patton as 'Big Chief Foot-in-Mouth.' Left wing organisations went berserk at the implied sneer at Russia, while Republican politicians read all sorts of devious meanings vis-a-vis the Roosevelt administration into his words. But so far as the Army were concerned, the very worst feature about the incident was that the Senate was about to rubber stamp a batch of promotions to permanent rank for the senior US officers, Patton among them, and with this latest uproar confronting them they simply rejected them all for the time being. Marshall sent a priority cable to Eisenhower asking him to investigate and pointing out 'We were just about to get confirmation of the permanent makes; this, I fear, has killed them all.' This was very bad news around Eisenhower's HQ, since Bedell Smith, Eisenhower's Chief of Staff, was among those up for promotion, as were several others. He is reputed to have telephoned directly to Patton and up-

braided him, saying that his stupid remarks had cost them their promotions. Eisenhower was extremely angry and cabled Marshall that he was beginning to have doubts about retaining Patton in a command position, in spite of his acknowledged skills. Marshall, however, reminded Eisenhower that Patton 'is the only available Army Commander for his present assignment who has had actual experience in fighting Rommel and in extensive landing operations . . .' Eisenhower sent for Patton, sat him down, and this time read the riot act in person. He then sent him back to Cheshire to stew for a few days before sending him a telegram: 'I have decided to keep you. Go ahead and train your army.' Privately, he had put it more succinctly: 'George,' he said, 'You talk too much.'

George kept on talking, but now he kept it 'in the family,' delivering speeches to his troops:

'I am not supposed to be commanding this Army; I am not even supposed to be in England. Let the first bastards to find out be the Goddam Germans. Some day I want them to raise on their hind legs and howl: "Jesus Christ, it's that Goddam Third Army and that son-of-a-bitch Patton. . . ."'

Eventually the waiting was over; the invasion was launched, the grand strategy was about to be played.

Reduced to its basics, the strategy

followed in Normandy was very simple: Montgomery with the British 21st Army Group was to make threatening movements in the direction of Caen, to the north of the landing area. This would draw the maximum German armored strength against him, reducing the resistance in the southeastern area of the landings and allowing the Americans to spread west and cut off the Cotentin peninsula, so gaining the port of Cherbourg as a supply port. Once this was done the Americans would strike out, with Montgomery still holding the German main strength, and advance across France. Put this way it sounds simple, and it was simple, but it seems to have been too simple for many people to grasp. Patton, strangely, was among them. Interviewed by Basil Liddell Hart, a prominent English military writer and critic, in late June, he said 'American forces have penetrated much deeper than the British at every stage, and around Caen the British have failed to gain any of their objectives, while the Americans are over-running the Cherbourg Peninsula.' He went on to say that there were more German divisions facing the Americans than were facing the British, which was quite incorrect. It is possible

Below: Mail call and Corporal Al Franczaki passes out the welcome letters in a barn near St Lô.

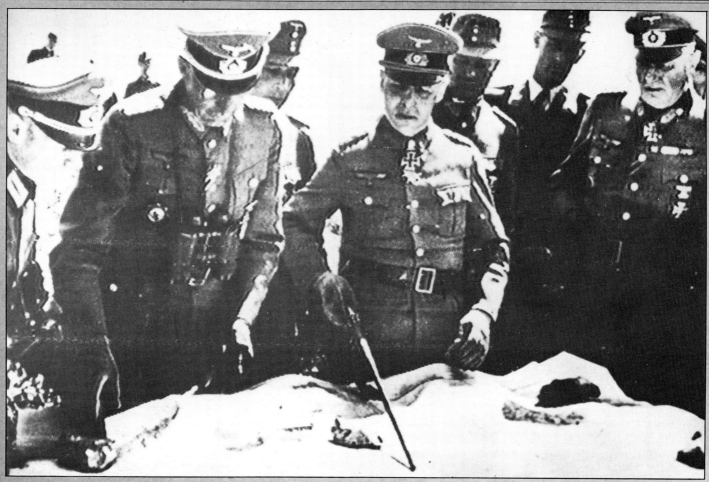

Below: A landing craft, struck by gunfire and burning as it heads towards Omaha Beach on D-Day.

Left: Field Marshal Erwin Rommel (second from left) studies a sand-table model at his invasion headquarters.

Above: Field Marshal Rommel, accompanied by General der Pioniere Wilhelm Meise, inspects beach obstacles forming part of the Atlantic Wall, shortly before the Allied Invasion.

Right: Rommel and Guderian, the Panzer General, discuss tactics at Rommel's headquarters in France.

Above: Patton with his Chief of Staff Major-General Gaffey, studying the battle map prior to the crossing of the Seine.

and Montgomery, Patton returned to his new location. From here, every day, he would drive out to visit the various American HQs and keep up with the latest situation reports. The first task which came his way was the planning of an amphibious landing by Third Army in the Morlaix area of Brittany, a proposal which came about because of the slow progress which the Allies were making.

Montgomery, after attracting as much of the German armor as he could reasonably expect, mounted 'Operation Goodwood' on 18 July. This was aimed at threatening Falaise and drawing even more German armor away from the area of the intended breakout further west. Three armored divisions supported by 776 pieces of artillery and 2000 medium and heavy bombers formed the bulk of this attack, and the preliminary bombard-

Below: A fine portrait of General Patton together with his Chief of Staff General Hugh J Gaffey, in July 1944.

that at this time he was not being fed with up-to-date Ultra information which had precise figures of the German dispositions. It was known that there were three Panzer Divisions facing Montgomery, plus two more *en route* from the Russian front and the 1st SS Panzer Division coming from Belgium. The 2nd SS Panzer Division, facing the Americans at St Lô was being withdrawn to Caen to strengthen the front there.

He soon had the chance to see for himself when on 9 July he took off in a Dakota transport and was flown to Bradley's HQ near Isigny. Because he was still supposed to be heading an invasion army in Kent, his presence in Normandy had to be kept quiet, but it was impossible to conceal his tall figure as it stalked around the 1st Army HQ accompanied by his white bull terrier. Bradley's intelligence officer, Colonel Monk Dickson, realized the dangers and acted promptly. He called a press conference and, when all the pressmen attached to the HQ were present and accounted for, addressed them briefly: 'Gentlemen, I don't know whether any of you have seen what you took to be General Patton around here with his dog. You were mistaken. Good morning,

gentlemen.' The press took the hint and Patton's presence was never mentioned.

Meanwhile his Chief of Staff and an advance party had crossed the Channel and had set up Third Army's headquarters in an orchard near Bricquebec in the Cotentin peninsula, and after visiting with Bradley, Hodges, Collins

Left: General Patton visits a divisional headquarters in the field, August 1944.

Below left: A worried-looking Patton prepares to take to the air in a light observation plane in August 1944. Notice the plate with his three stars prominenently displayed.

by yard, hedgerow by hedgerow, cost 40,000 US casualties. All this delay prompted Eisenhower to look for some alternative line of attack, and he suggested that Third Army outflank the deadlock by making an amphibious landing some 100 miles west of Cherbourg. The planning was passed across to Patton, and he quickly came up with a proposal to land one armored and two infantry divisions near Morlaix which would then drive eastward via Dinan to swing north and strike the Germans, facing First US Army, in the rear. Once this was dealt with, First and Third Armies could then set off east towards Alençon, Argentan and Chartres. Put as simply as that it sounds an impressive scheme, and post-war commentators have suggested that had Patton been given his head to perform this operation much of First Army's hedgerow battles would have been eliminated and the advance across France would have been done much sooner. This is doubtful; the naval staffs were quick to point out that the selected invasion point was in an area with strong coast defenses, appalling navigational problems, and close proximity to several German U-Boat bases from which rapid and lethal naval countermeasures would have been mounted. The air staffs also pointed out that air support would have been extremely difficult due to the distance of the proposed landing point from the principal Allied airfields.

But the Morlaix landing was not to be. On 11 July Bradley went to Eisenhower with a plan he called 'Operation Cobra.' This called for Collins, of VII US Corps, supported by a powerful aerial bombardment, to break through on a narrow front in the middle of First US Army and drive a mass of armor towards Coutances. This would be followed by another thrust to take Avranches, at the base of the Cotentin peninsula, a major road junction and valuable strategic location. Avranches was a bottleneck, but whoever held it commanded the rest of Brittany, and once it was taken Bradley proposed pouring Third Army through to take the

ment overcame the German forward defences so that the leading tanks were able to drive through their lines for some 4000 yards until they met a second line of resistance. The Germans were well aware that the British Second Army contained a high proportion of armor and they had concentrated as much antitank artillery into this second line as they could find. Even the antiaircraft guns emplaced for the defence of Caen depressed their barrels and took part in this role. This halted the British advance and, as usual, counterattacks began to develop. Finally some unseasonable heavy rain

began to fall on 20 July and Goodwood came to a standstill, having gained little more than 10,000 yards.

The First US Army's operations in Normandy had begun with the near-disaster of Omaha Beach, then a variety of setbacks in the advance to Cherbourg, and finally settled in to the extremely expensive pattern of hedgerow battles in which every field became a separate battleground. St Lô, which was expected to fall by 11 June, was not cleared until 18 July and although in US hands was still under intense shellfire. The battles around Vire, taking the countryside yard

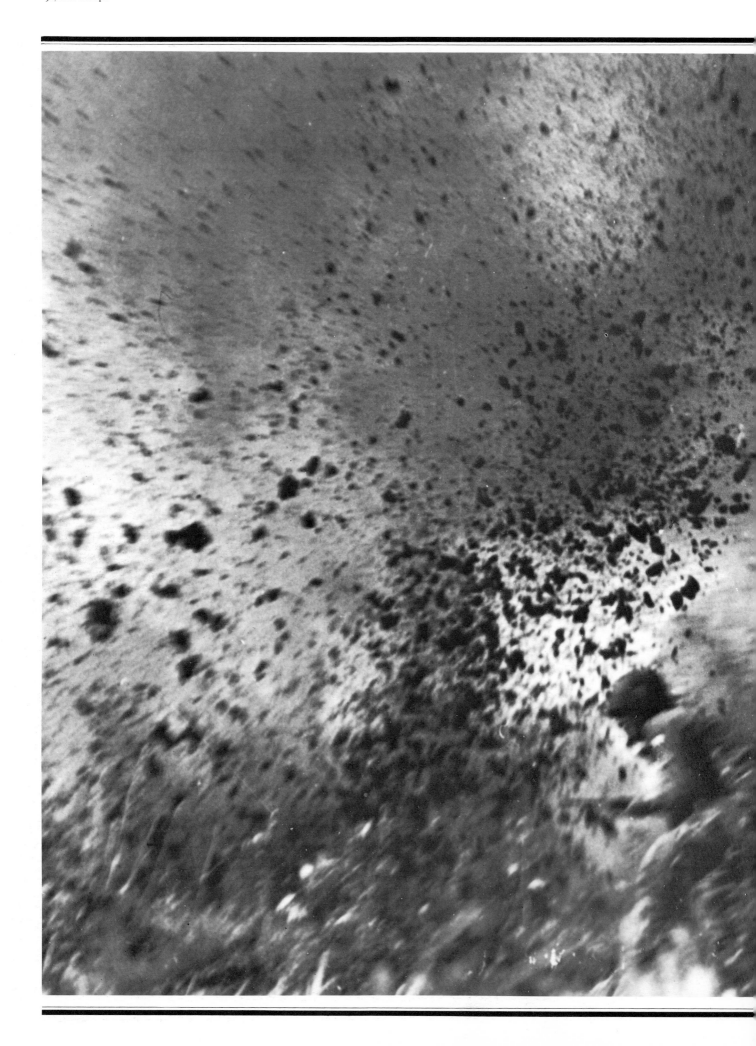

Top: Tank landing ships at half-tide
discharging their cargoes on to a
Normandy beach.

Above: A US Navy beach control post
calling in supply craft to the beaches, on
D-Day plus five.

Left: The hazards of war; a US
paratrooper dashes through the dirt and
smoke of a close mortar-bomb burst.

whole of Brittany, set up a supply port in Quiberon Bay, then turn east and head for Alençon.

Given this broad outline, Patton proceeded to place his own interpretation on it. While the SHAEF staffs had put a lot of emphasis on setting up a supply port and base, to be capable of sustaining 100 divisions, Patton was less than enthusiastic about that part of the plan. He had his eye firmly fixed on the east and on the destruction of as much of the German Army as possible. Old soldier that he was, he never lost sight of the fundamental strategic truth, that the purpose of battle is *to destroy the enemy's forces*. Once that is achieved, everything

Below: Lines of infantry landing craft, crewed by US Coastguards, carrying the assault troops on D-Day.

else follows, and theoretical discussions about areas of influence, economic warfare and so forth left him unmoved. As soon as the German Army in France was annihilated, the remaining problems would virtually sort themselves out. His plan, therefore, was first to head for Quiberon Bay with the intention of cutting off the base of the Brest peninsula and isolating the German forces therein, after which they could be 'rolled up' at leisure. At the same time 6th Armored Division would strike out for Brest, clearing a large area of central Brittany and, again, isolating large numbers of German troops from the main battle area and leaving them to be dealt with by an infantry force. Finally a special 'Task Force A' would sieze the main railroad line, capturing the bridges before they could be destroyed, so as to secure a

Above left: An aerial view of a Normandy beach, with tanks and landing craft moving ashore.

Above: US Infantry, forming part of the first assault wave, in their landing craft and preparing for the final run in to the beaches on D-Day.

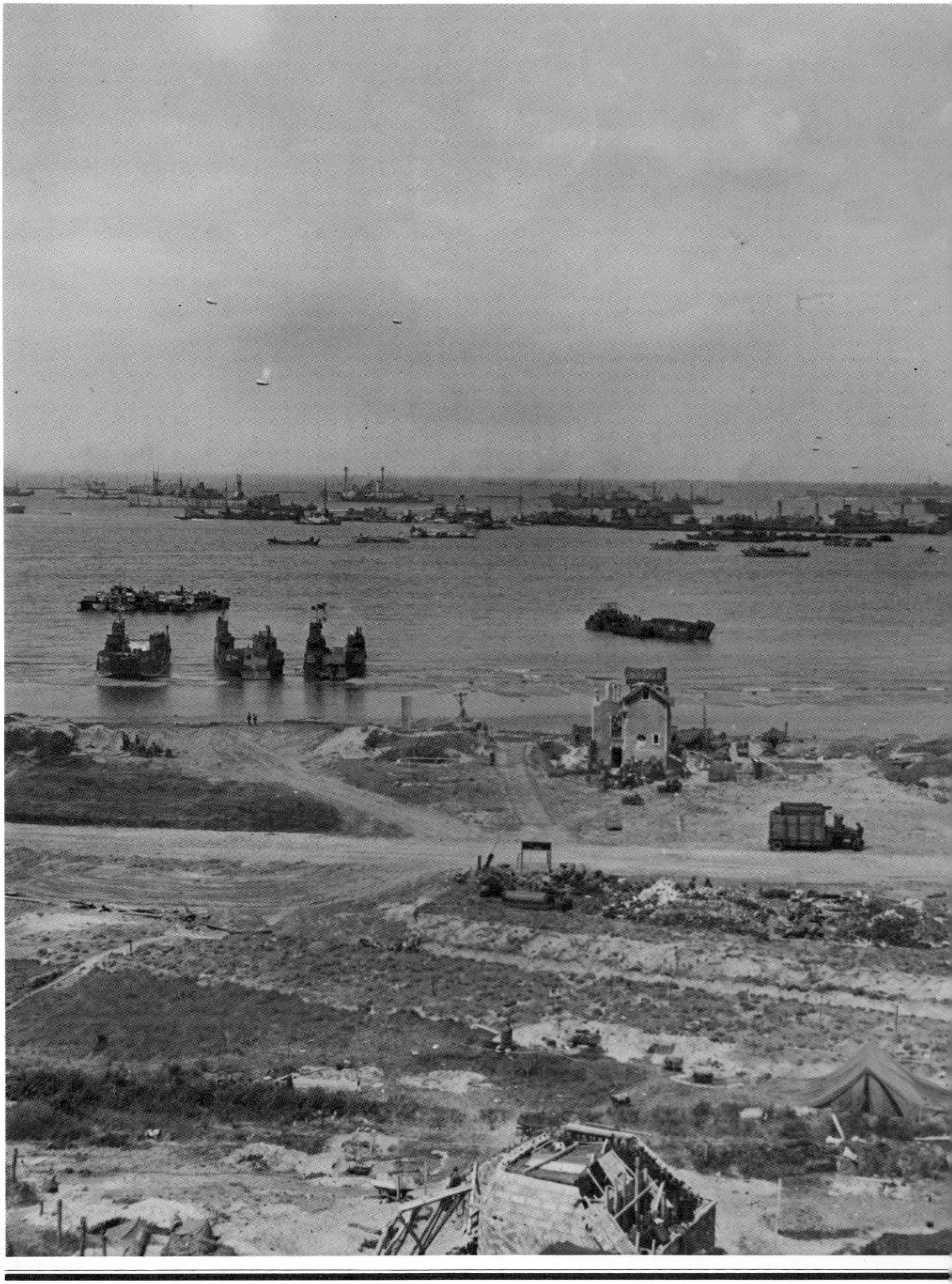

Left: LCTs landing supplies on one of the Normandy invasion beaches. Surplus ships form an artificial breakwater.

Above: Utah Beach from the air, shortly after the initial assault, showing troops swarming up the beach.

future supply route. With all this done, Third Army would then turn east *en masse* and charge through the German rear echelons, doing as much damage as it could. The plan would be aided by constant intelligence; Ultra would give Patton the 'big picture' and 'Patton's Household Cavalry,' more properly the 6th Cavalry Group, would act as his eyes and ears on the ground, constantly probing ahead and on the flanks to produce up-to-the-minute information on the immediate tactical picture. With this information to guide him, his orders to his commanders were simply that they had to push forward up to and beyond the limits of endurance. If they ran into an obstacle, one group would contain it while another would outflank and continue the advance. The whole plan was the old cavalry spirit revived, revolving around dash and audacity.

Cobra was scheduled for 24 July, but the weather had turned so bad that flying was almost impossible. At the last minute the aerial attack was cancelled, but unfortunately much of the force was in the air by this time and failed to receive the cancellation. Fighter bombers strafed the prescribed area, heavy bombers dropped several hundreds of tons of bombs, but due to the poor visibility and high winds which shifted marker smoke, many of the attacks fell on US troops. Lieutenant General Leslie McNair, who had replaced Patton in charge of the 'Fortitude' operation and was in France merely as an observer, was caught in the raid and almost killed.

After the usual recriminations the air attack was re-mounted, this time for the 25 July, when better weather was forecast. Again the troops stood by for the advance, again the fighters and bombers roared in, and again sloppy planning and inaccurate bombing caused hundreds of American troops to be killed. This time the Air Force made up for their near-miss of the day before and killed the

Below: The assault wave making for Omaha Beach on D-Day, using DUKW amphibian trucks in the rough sea.

unfortunate General McNair.

As the noise died away, so the advance began. The German Panzer *Lehr* Division, directly in front, had been badly battered, but the flanking divisions had been less affected by the bombing and were soon putting up a stiff resistance. By nightfall the Americans had pushed about 2000 yards forward, and the follow-

ing morning Collins sent in two mobile divisions. The first, advancing east of Marigny, met little resistance, but the other, moving towards Coutances, had a much harder time of it. It was now time to make the move to take Avranches, and Bradley sent for Patton and ordered him forward to act as Bradley's deputy commander on this front. This was something

of a shock to the First Army formations who had not encountered Patton before, but he rapidly inspired them with some of his fire, and on 27 July two armored divisions moved off southwards. The German forces sidestepped, in order to avoid the direct blow and then to take the advancing Americans in the flank, but their sidestep brought them straight into the path of VII Corps and they were cut to ribbons. All obstacles were now removed and Avranches fell on the 30th. Now Patton was poised for the starter's gun; he had VIII Corps at Avranches, and behind them XV and XX Corps. Behind them again was XII Corps HQ marshalling the final units of Third Army as they arrived across the beaches and moved forward to where Patton waited. A general post was performed in the US Command structure. Hodges was to take over First US Army, Bradley became the commander of 12th Army Group, and, on 1 August, Third US Army became officially operational as part of that group. The grand strategy had worked, the road was clear, and Patton was ready.

7: THE IRRESISTIBLE FORCE

At noon on 1 August 1944 the US Third Army became operational, though the news was kept under wraps: 'In the interests of cover and deception there will be no announcement of this for some time' ordered Eisenhower. At the same time, on the other side of the lines, there was an equally momentous reshuffle of responsibility. At a conference at Hitler's 'Wolf's Lair' in East Prussia, the Führer announced that he no longer had faith in von Kluge, the Commander in Chief West, and that henceforth he would direct the operations against the invasion himself. All the French ports in German hands were to be made into fortresses and held to the bitter end; in the event of any withdrawal, all railway facilities and similar key installations were to be destroyed and the Allies presented with a 'scorched earth' area for occupation. Von Kluge was to take his orders from Hitler and 'keep his eyes riveted on the front and on the enemy, without even looking backward.' This move had two important consequences for the Allies; first, with Hitler in charge the guidance would be militarily inept, and second, because Hitler's HQ was some 1800 miles away from the fighting, all orders would have to be sent by radio, using the Enigma codes which the Allies could read.

General Wood, commanding 4th Armored Division, had been ordered by General Middleton, commanding VIII Corps, to advance and take Rennes, but when Patton assumed control of the operation on 1 August he told Wood to continue on and take Quiberon, 60 miles further, and so seal off the entire Brittany peninsula. Wood was a go-ahead cavalry-man and took Patton's orders as final. By the evening of the 1st his armor was knocking at the door of Rennes, where he met with a vigorous defence from the German garrison, reinforced by an additional 2000 infantry sent up from Le Mans. That night General Koenig, commanding the US 91st Division, arrived outside Rennes with more troops. Being senior, he assumed command in place of Wood, who suggested that the operation against Rennes was now more of an infantry attack than an armored thrust. Middleton agreed and furnished more infantry, so Wood withdrew his tanks, refuelled, reformed, swept around Rennes and took off for Quiberon.

The 6th Armored Division was commanded by General Grow and his orders from Middleton were to aim for Dinan, but before his column was well started Patton appeared and told him to go instead for Brest and to bypass any resistance he met. Patton had made a bet with Montgomery that he would have Brest 'by Saturday night,' that was in five days, and it was 200 miles away. Grow advanced 'with no boundaries to worry about, no definite information, in fact nothing but a map of Brittany and the knowledge that resistance was where you found it.' By the evening of the 2nd they were outside Dinan, having advanced 35 miles.

Dinan turned out to be strongly fortified and resolutely defended, so Grow decided that it should be left to the 79th Infantry Division to deal with when they caught up, while he pushed ahead for Brest. Accordingly, on the 3rd he left Dinan and advanced another 30 miles but was then halted by a furious order from Middleton, directing 6th Armored to return to Dinan and take it as part of the preparation for a corps attack on St Malo. Grow protested, but to no avail; the orders stood. The next morning, while Grow and his staff were still mulling over their orders to attack Dinan, Patton burst in upon them like an avenging deity. 'What the hell are you doing here? I told you to go to Brest!' he shouted. Grow produced the written order which had halted him and explained why the division was halted. Patton read the order, stuffed it angrily in his pocket, then said to Grow 'I'll see Middleton; you go ahead where I told you to go.' But

Right: US wounded awaiting evacuation at a Field Hospital in Normandy, early June 1944.

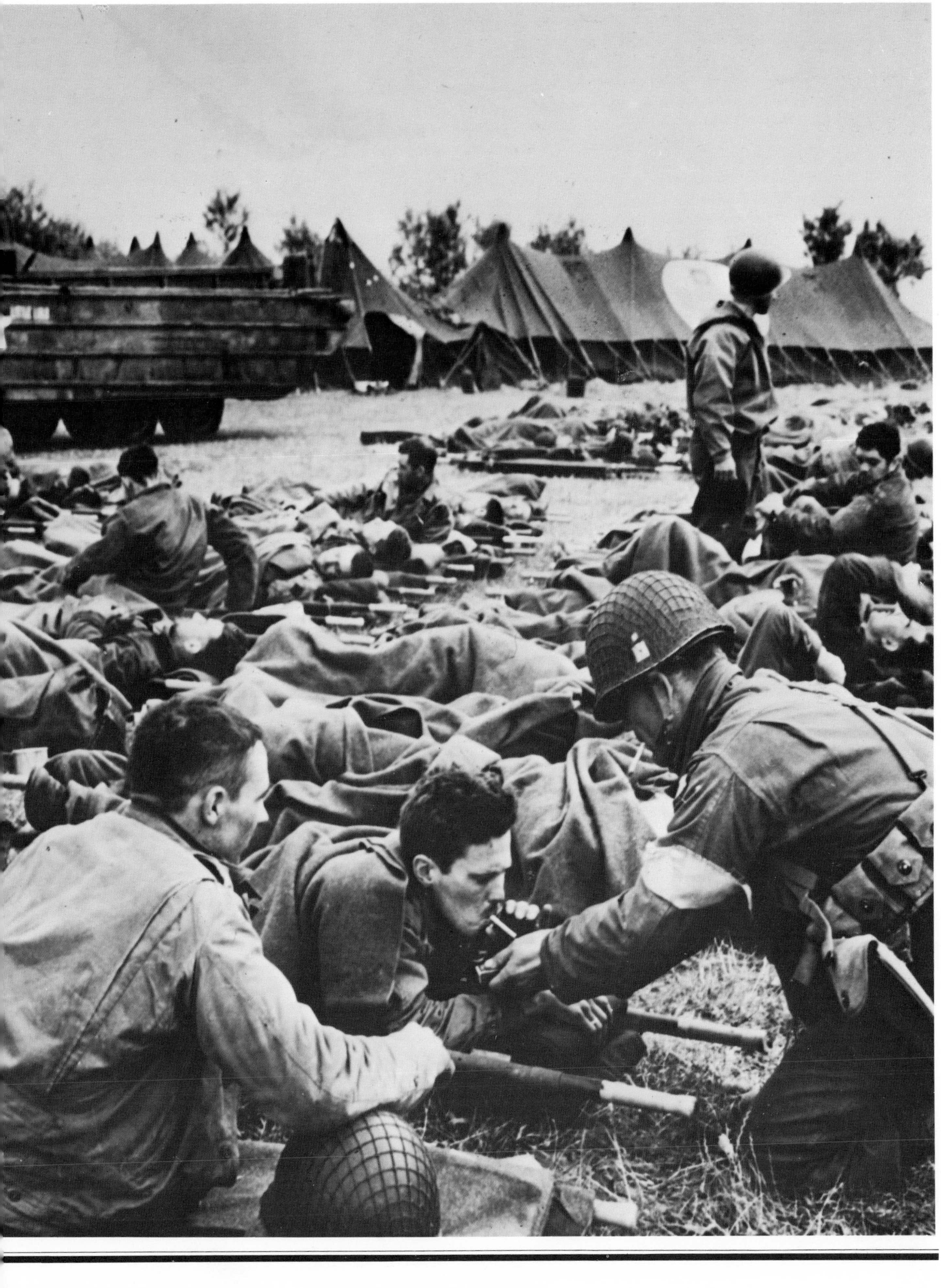

Left: An American advanced dressing station on the Cherbourg peninsula; one GI gets a plasma transfusion.

be prepared for further armored action to the east and south-east.

Patton had already sized up the tangled situation as well as anyone. His eye was on the large numbers of Germans west of the Seine, and he reasoned that a very rapid eastward advance followed by an equally rapid northward swing would encircle them so that they could be destroyed. He sent XV Corps off to the line of the Mayenne River, between Mayenne and Chateau-Gontier, and XX Corps due south towards the Loire. This marked his first 'bound', which would be followed by a second 'bound' to the Le Mans area. What happened after that would depend upon what reactions the Germans made, but he warned the commander of XV Corps not to be surprised

it was too late; the day's delay imposed by Middleton's order was sufficient to allow the Germans to get troops into Brest to reinforce the garrison and put the defenses in readiness for the American attack. With a tough German paratrooper, Lieutenant General Hermann Ramcke in command of 40,000 troops and auxiliaries, it was to be several Saturdays before US troops finally took Brest.

While this had been going on, the strategic situation had changed. There was a rapidly widening gap between the beach areas and the German Army. Due to withdrawals to strengthen the forces in the eastern part of the front, the German troops in Brittany were now only enough to hold the ports. The French Forces of the Interior, the armed resistance movement, were coming to life, and it was estimated that they plus one US corps would be all that was needed to clear the Brittany area. Bradley therefore made a change of plan, ordering Hodges with First Army to advance towards Mayenne and Domfront, and cancelling Patton's previous orders. Patton and the Third Army were now to secure the Brittany ports 'using minimum forces' while the bulk of Third Army set off eastward to clear the country south to the Loire and

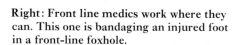

Right: Front line medics work where they can. This one is bandaging an injured foot in a front-line foxhole.

if he suddenly received orders to swing north.

However, the Germans were quite capable of surprising everybody, and on 2 August the Ultra listeners picked up the first of many significant messages from Hitler to von Kluge. This one instructed him to 'ignore the American break-out, which can be dealt with later' and then went into detail about collecting four of the armored divisions from the Caen front, adding some infantry divisions, and then aiming this at Avranches in a lightning counterattack. This caused a flurry in the Allied camp as Bradley would have to make preparations for a defensive battle round Avranches but do it in such a manner as not to reveal that he had been forewarned and so compromise the Ultra secret. On the next day came a long message from von Kluge, arguing with Hitler and pointing out some of the dangers: 'Such an attack, if not successful, would lay open the whole attacking force to be cut off in the west.' This thought had already occurred to Eisenhower, and it was one of the reasons for Bradley's instruction to Patton to move quickly eastward so as to be in a position to do the cutting-off.

Hitler, of course, had his way and he signalled von Kluge 'The attack to split the American force must be carried out.' Eisenhower now ordered Montgomery to be prepared to surround the Germans from the north while Bradley's 12th Army Group moved from the west and south. The trap was prepared and waiting for its victim.

At dawn on 7 August the 4th Panzer Division suddenly erupted and stormed through the American lines and into Mortain. Although Bradley had prepared a defense-in-depth position to absorb the blow, the thrust had such momentum that it went through Mortain and seven miles beyond before it was halted. There it ran into massed artillery fire, and while halted was attacked by rocket-firing aircraft and fighter-bombers. Half the tanks were destroyed while the rest were driven into static positions to fight a slow battle. By that evening von Kluge was signalling Hitler that the attack had stalled and that he intended to pull back in view of a possible British threat from the north. Hitler's reply was rapid and incisive: 'I command that the attack be prosecuted daringly and recklessly towards the sea, regard-

Above: Loading wounded soldiers on to a C-47 Dakota transport to be flown back to hospitals in England.

less of risk . . .' He then instructed von Kluge to withdraw more forces from the east to reinforce his attack. Three Panzer divisions were ordered up from the Caen area, but before they could move, the Allied attack began.

The first element was an attempt by the Canadians to reach Falaise, aided by a heavy 1000-bomber air assault. Even with this preliminary, the attack was halted by the German armor some eight miles away from the town. It was unfortunate that aerial bombardment was such a vital part of the plan, because once such an attack is set in motion it is nearly impossible to stop or amend. Ground forces can be halted minutes before a planned attack, but not aircraft who have been assembling from distant airfields for several hours. In the case of the Falaise assault, the news of the withdrawal of three Panzer divisions from the area, to reinforce von Kluge's attack, came too late. If Montgomery had known of the Ultra signal in time, he could have stopped the air operation, cancelled the ground attack, and waited until the Panzers had cleared the area before restarting. As it was, the attack went ahead, and it was the same three Panzer divisions which were instrumental in stopping it.

On 8 August Eisenhower, Bradley and Montgomery conferred on the situation and decided that it was time the trap was sprung. Bradley's Army Group should now be diverted northwards towards Flers and Argentan so as to slice across the rear of the Germans and meet up with the Canadian and British forces near Falaise. Orders were sent to Patton directing him to turn XV Corps due north from Le Mans and 'advance on the axis Alençon-Sees to the line of the Army Group boundary.' This boundary was a line drawn between Sees and Carrouges, south of Argentan. To strengthen his attack Patton was given 2nd French Armored Division, recently arrived in the theater. Hodges was ordered to thrust up towards Flers on Patton's left. It appears from these orders that Bradley envisaged Patton and Hodges arriving on the Army Group boundary to serve as the anvil for the hammer blow which was to come from the British-Canadian advance from the north. Strategically sound as this may have been, it was not the sort of active role which appealed to Patton, and he therefore modified the orders, instructing XV Corps to advance to the boundary but to be prepared to continue northward until such time as they met the Canadians or British coming south. Thus the encirclement and destruction of the German Armies would be completed.

That, at least was the promise, but somewhere along the line came misunderstandings and mistakes of colossal proportions which came near to negating the whole manoeuvre. Argument has since raged over the question of responsibility for the mishandling of the Falaise Pocket, but military organizations are designed to pinpoint responsibility, and the inescapable fact is that Eisenhower, the Supreme Commander Allied Expeditionary Force, was in France, on the ground, physically in charge, and therefore the final responsibility has to be his. At a critical juncture he vacillated and finally left decisions to his subordinates, instead of giving firm orders, and as a result the rout of the German Army was not completed.

In brief, the sequence of events went as follows: Patton's XV Corps stormed northward, but on 12 August came the first delay when the French 2nd Armored under Leclerc trespassed on to the Alençon-Argentan road and so delayed the American advance on Argentan. When this finally got under way the delay had, as usual, allowed the Germans to strengthen their defences, and the American attack made little progress. In the north, the Canadian and Polish Armored Divisions prepared a fresh assault, 'Operation Tractable', against Falaise, but late that evening a Canadian officer carrying the plans of the operation

lost his way, strayed into the German lines and was killed. On his body the Germans found the orders and were able to make hurried but effective alterations to their defenses which ensured that when 'Tractable' was launched on 14 August it was firmly resisted. Moreover the usual errors occurred with the initial air bombardment; the attack fell short and 65 Polish and Canadian troops were killed and 241 wounded before the attack even began. Progress was slow and the day ended with the attackers still three miles from Falaise.

To the south, Patton had now reached the Army Boundary line – indeed, had over-stepped it and was quite prepared to continue to Falaise. But at this point he was stopped by orders from Bradley: all further movement northwards was to stop; any troops in the vicinity of Argentan were to be pulled back; XV Corps were to be concentrated preparatory to 'operations in another direction.'

It was this order which has caused all the subsequent controversy. Bradley's

stated reason for giving it was that had XV Corps been allowed to continue northward they might have collided with the incoming Canadian, British and Polish forces and caused what he called 'a calamitous battle between friends.' This is a very thin excuse; armies have staffs trained in arranging this sort of thing, soldiers in the field have agreed systems of recognition signals, there were ample radios capable of listening to each other's frequencies, there were ample observation aircraft capable of checking to see exactly where each force was on the ground – it was for this very reason that every Allied vehicle in the invasion force had a large white star painted on its upper surface. It has also been alleged that Montgomery deliberately withheld the formal permission for XV Corps to cross his boundary out of spite. This is not worth consideration, since it is a matter of

Below: American troops advancing to take a German fortified position outside Cherbourg, June 1944.

Above: Infantry of the British 3rd Division fighting their way into Caen, Normandy, early in July.

halt was a great mistake, as I was certain that we could have entered Falaise and I was not certain that the British would.'

Eventually, the gap was closed when Canadian and Polish troops fought their way south at an immense cost in blood and finally met the Americans near Chambois on the evening of 19 August. Over 10,000 German troops were killed and 50,000 captured, while hundreds of tanks, guns and vehicles were either destroyed or captured, but by that time Patton and the Third Army had moved on. On the 17th Bradley had ordered Patton to move two divisions eastward to take the Seine river and effect a crossing, and shortly afterwards First Army relieved Third Army in the south of the Falaise Pocket and Patton was free to

begin his war of movement once more.

The XII Corps, under Major General Gilbert Cook, tore ahead to such good effect that by 19 August he was at Orleans and Chartres. As might be imagined, the liberation of Orleans, with its association with Jeanne d'Arc, caught the fancy of the world's press, and it was considered apt, at this juncture, to release the news that the liberators were none other than Third US Army under the command of General George S Patton. Unfortunately, at this point, Major General Cook fell ill and had to be relieved of his command, which dis-

Below: A P-51 Mustang of the Royal Air Force over Conde-sur-Boireau in the Falaise Gap, July 1944.

record that he had already urged the American force to advance further north to take Chambois and Trun, and he was too set on destroying the Germans to sit pedantically on his boundary rights. Admittedly, Montgomery was over-optimistic about the ability of 21st Army Group to drive south and close the gap, but at no stage had he made any veto on further movement of XV Corps. The best that can be said is that probably Montgomery, busy with other affairs, overlooked the formality of sending formal permission to Bradley, while Bradley equally overlooked the possibility that Montgomery needed reminding. Eisenhower, in his overseeing position, should have spotted this and done something about it. More than any other situation in the European campaign, the Falaise Pocket reveals his prime defect as a commander, his lack of actual combat experience and his inability to 'read' a battle as could men like Patton and Montgomery.

At the time, Patton was philosophic about it. Questioned by reporters as to why XV Corps did not advance, he implied that it was not his idea but that 'Some of the greatest pursuits in history have been planned to leave an escape hole, through which the enemy's forces funnel, only to be annihilated as they flow through.' Later he was to write 'XV Corps could have easily entered Falaise and completely closed the gap . . . this

tressed Patton since he was a first class soldier who could be relied upon to forge ahead, and Patton could well have done with him in the future.

Aided by Ultra information as to the disposition of the principal German forces, Third Army now forged ahead. Leaving Orleans and Chartres behind, a task force of 79th Division found that the Germans had abandoned Mantes-la-Jolie, some 30 miles northwest of Paris. A patrol found a small weir over which they were able to cross the Seine and by the afternoon of 20 August a bridge had been thrown across and a bridgehead established. Leaving this for future use by First Army, the bulk of Patton's force aimed to the east of Paris, first crossing the Seine at Fontainebleu, Montereau and Sens (where their arrival was so unexpected that they rounded up German officers taking their Sunday constitutional in full dress uniform). Consolidation and the construction of bridges sufficient to carry armor took a little time, but by 25 August there were four major bridgeheads across the river to the east of

Paris and one to the west. On that day General Dietrich von Choltitz, commander of the Paris garrison, surrendered the city, with all its bridges intact, to the First US Army. While things were moving easily in this quarter, there were still problems further west. Despite the disaster at Falaise, the German Army was still a formidable fighting force and they were now making a fighting withdrawal to cross the Seine near Rouen, closely pursued by the British and Canadian armies. If the crossings could be denied, then the Germans would again be encircled and another Falaise enacted. Accordingly, Patton was ordered to turn his XV Corps to the left and drive along the left bank of the Seine, west of Paris, to Louviers, while XIX Corps moved against Elbeuf. The Germans had anticipated this and it was to take XV Corps five days to cover the 20 miles to Louviers, while XIX Corps had equal trouble in reaching Elbeuf. In that time much of the German strength managed to get across the river and away. Had Patton crossed the river and moved along

Above: American troops, accompanied by a Sherman tank, clearing the last German defenders out of St Lô.

the east bank, to catch the Germans as they came over their bridgeheads, the carnage would have been far more effective and, at least in the view of General Speidel, Chief of Staff of Army Group B, the German force would have been annihilated. Instead, anything up to 50,000 men escaped to fight another day. Patton never expressed an opinion on this, but it is possible that the significance of it escaped him, although it is equally possible that he was not really excited about it, viewing it as being Bradley's concern and not his. At that stage of the pursuit he was more interested in striking forward and spearheading his way into Germany than he was in what were essentially, in his view, 'mopping-up operations.'

The speed of Third Army's dash across the center of France and over the Seine had engendered an ebullient enthusiasm among the soldiers. Battle fatigue cases dropped to zero, while the rapturous welcome accorded them by the civil population was guaranteed to make any soldier feel good. One point which many soldiers commented on was that the French, far from being the starved and ragged victims of Nazism that they expected, appeared to be reasonably well dressed and well nourished. Indeed, they were to have a harder time in the next six months than they had had throughout the war so far, due to supply problems. Now that Paris had fallen, De Gaulle turned to Eisenhower and demanded – and got – 1500 tons of food, medical supplies and petrol daily to supply Paris, including 500 tons which were to be delivered by air, all at the expense of the military supply system.

With the crossings of the Seine completed, Third Army had set the seal on its performance since Normandy. They had advanced 400 miles in 26 days, had accounted for over 100,000 German troops, 500 tanks and 700 guns, and had done this for a cost of a little over 16,000 casualties, less than 13 percent of total US losses since D-Day.

On 26 August Third Army took up the pursuit once more, having been ordered by Bradley to follow the line of the principal roads towards the east and make for the area of Metz and Strasbourg, the area which Patton called 'The Nancy Gap.' There was satisfaction for Patton in these orders, since it was this line which his mentor Pershing had indicated for his planned advance in 1919, and Patton had long cherished the thought that it was his military destiny to complete Pershing's plan and win the victory which had been denied them in the previous war. So XII Corps headed for Chalons while XX Corps made for Reims. Behind them stretched a supply line carrying stores and gasoline, some of which was being air-lifted to Orleans for onward movement by road. On the 28th the advance columns crossed the Marne at Chalons and Château Thierry without serious opposition and began heading over the familiar country of the Meuse-Argonne, ground which Patton had fought across in 1918. The speed of the advance was such that German road-blocks and bridge guards were simply brushed aside or encircled. There seemed to be no coherent German plan of defense and prisoners were being scooped up before they even realised that Allied troops were within miles of them. To the delight of Third Army troops they began catching up with trainloads of loot evacuated from Paris before the fall, food, clothing, liquor, cameras, every sort of portable valuables, all of which were joyfully parcelled out among the GIs.

The plan of action was relatively simple: first to clear the Marne, then go for the line of the Meuse, then the Moselle, then the Saar and finally the Rhine. These rivers were all about 30 miles apart and thus created a regular series of bounds to help the planners. The pursuit of the Germans was going very well but was soon to come to an abrupt halt. Patton later claimed that 29 August was the crucial day and he was probably right. On that day it became obvious to him that the German Army had, as an organized resistive force, collapsed and so long as the pressure was kept up there was no way that Third Army could be stopped. He ordered Walton Walker's XX Corps and Eddy's XII Corps to cross the Meuse at Commercy and Verdun before the Germans could blow the bridges and then go as fast as possible for the next river line, the Moselle. Walker and Eddy set off in high spirits, but shortly afterwards came Patton's first inklings of trouble: the supply column back in Orleans reported that the day's shipment of 140,000 gallons of gasoline had not arrived. On questioning this, Patton was told that there was a plan afoot to drop paratroops ahead of First Army and therefore the transport aircraft had been withdrawn from his supply line; in spite of protests, the order stood. Before he could decide on his next move, a message came from Eddy to say that XII Corps would have to halt at Saint Dizier, 30 miles short of the Meuse, because they were short of gasoline. Patton's reply was an order to push on until the tanks ran out of gas, then get out and walk, but take the Meuse crossings. By juggling with his remaining fuel, draining some vehicles to keep others moving, Eddy succeeded in getting to the river and making a crossing near St Mihiel.

On the following day Patton intended to push forward for the Moselle, and he now flew off to Bradley's headquarters to plead for the necessary fuel. 'Damn it, Brad,' he cried, 'just give me 400,000 gallons of gas and I'll put you inside Germany in two days!' But, as Bradley later put it, 'George might as well have asked for the moon.'

The simple fact was that the Allies had outrun their supply lines. This situation had been foreseen and prophesied by a number of officers concerned with supply, but in the heady days following the

Below: A French railroad yard in Normandy after its destruction by the RAF to prevent German supplies reaching the front.

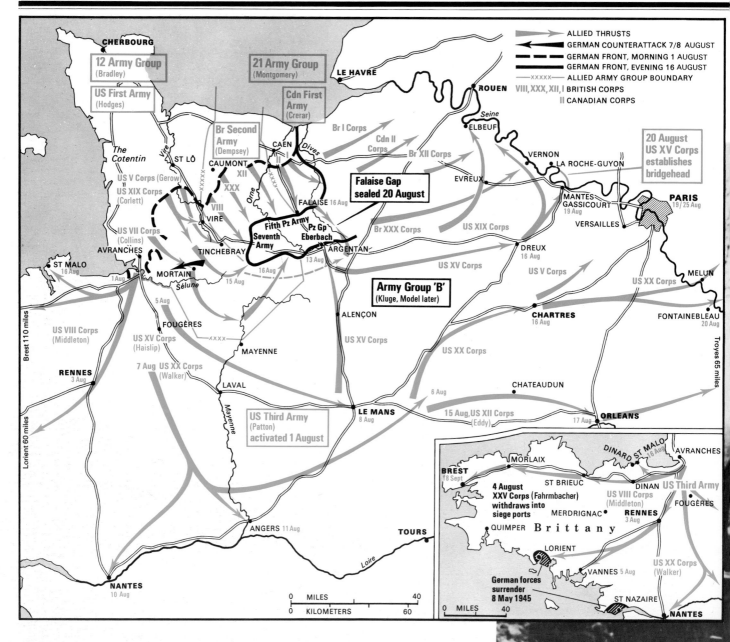

CHERBOURG

12 Army Group (Bradley)

US First Army (Hodges)

21 Army Group (Montgomery)

LE HAVRE

Cdn First Army (Crerar)

ROUEN

ALLIED THRUSTS
GERMAN COUNTERATTACK 7/8 AUGUST
GERMAN FRONT, MORNING 1 AUGUST
GERMAN FRONT, EVENING 16 AUGUST
—×××× ALLIED ARMY GROUP BOUNDARY
VIII, XXX, XII, I BRITISH CORPS
II CANADIAN CORPS

Seine
ELBEUF

Br I Corps

Cdn II Corps

Br XII Corps

Br Second Army (Dempsey)

CAEN
Dives

The Cotentin

ST LÔ
Vire

CAUMONT
XII
XXX

VERNON
LA ROCHE-GUYON

20 August US XV Corps establishes bridgehead

MANTES GASSICOURT 19 Aug

PARIS 19/25 Aug

EVREUX

FALAISE 16 Aug

Falaise Gap sealed 20 August

US V Corps (Gerow)
US XIX Corps (Corlett)

VIII
VIRE

US VII Corps (Collins)

AVRANCHES

Orne

Fifth Pz Army
Seventh Army

Pz Gp Eberbach

ARGENTAN
13 Aug

Br XXX Corps

US XIX Corps

VERSAILLES

DREUX 16 Aug

MELUN

ST MALO 16 Aug

1 Aug
MORTAIN

Sélune

TINCHEBRAY

16 Aug
15 Aug

5 Aug

Army Group 'B' (Kluge, Model later)

US XV Corps

US V Corps

US XX Corps

FONTAINEBLEAU 20 Aug

Brest 110 miles

US VIII Corps (Middleton)

FOUGÈRES

US XV Corps (Haislip)

ALENÇON

US XV Corps

US XX Corps

CHARTRES 16 Aug

Troyes 65 miles

RENNES 3 Aug

7 Aug US XX Corps (Walker)

MAYENNE

CHATEAUDUN

Lorient 60 miles

Mayenne

LAVAL

6 Aug

15 Aug, US XII Corps (Eddy)

ORLEANS 17 Aug

US Third Army (Patton) **activated 1 August**

LE MANS 8 Aug

ANGERS 11 Aug

TOURS

Loire

NANTES 10 Aug

0 MILES 40
0 KILOMETERS 60

MORLAIX
DINARD ST MALO 16 Aug
AVRANCHES

BREST 18 Sept

ST BRIEUC

DINAN

US Third Army

4 August XXV Corps (Fahrmbacher) withdraws into siege ports

MERDRIGNAC

US VIII Corps (Middleton)

RENNES 3 Aug

FOUGÈRES

QUIMPER

Brittany

LORIENT

VANNES 5 Aug

US XX Corps (Walker)

German forces surrender 8 May 1945

ST NAZAIRE

NANTES

0 MILES 40

Falaise battle their warnings had gone unheeded. The main cause of the trouble was the lack of port facilities. Only Cherbourg had so far been liberated, and the greater proportion of the supplies for all the Allied armies was still flowing across the invasion beaches. Second to this came the difficulty of moving those supplies forward. The original Allied predictions had assumed that the Seine would be reached on D+90, after which there would be a pause to allow stocking of supplies, whereas in fact the Seine went on D+74 and there had been no pause. The French railroad system was so damaged by Allied air attack and subsequent combat that it was in no condition to move large quantities of stores. The situation was finally hindered by the demand to divert 1500 tons daily,

Right: A US column moves through the shattered French countryside on its way inland from Avranches in August 1944

Above: How the Third Army crossed France.

with the requisite transport, to the civil population of Paris. If contemporary reports are any guide, these supplies mostly found their way on to the black market. (The author can recall hearing tales in late 1944 of 'Patton's tanks stuck outside Verdun while his gasoline is being sold in the back streets of Paris.')

In an effort to break this deadlock, the 'Red Ball' system was invented. Two routes from the Normandy Beaches to a dump area north of Paris were segregated and labelled 'Red Ball UP' and 'Red Ball

DOWN'. Along the 'Up' route sped a stream of trucks, day and night, carrying stores forward; on the 'Down' route the empty trucks thundered back for more supplies. Both routes were off limits to other traffic and were patrolled constantly by military police and maintenance crews who dragged off any vehicle which broke down. In this way 7000 tons of stores were moved daily, but the cost was enormous. Units were stripped of their transport and immobilised, while far too much of the precious gasoline was burned up in moving the remainder forward. On top of all this there was discontent among the field armies, who felt that the supply services were not doing their work efficiently. While most of supply troops were undoubtedly hard-working and conscientious, what did annoy the soldiers' was the sight of Major

Left: A German self-propelled four-barrel anti-aircraft gun watches for Allied fighters in August 1944.

promptly went into the tanks of Third Army. Mysterious raids took place on the fuel dumps of neighbouring formations. French towns were combed for stocks of gasoline, which were promptly commandeered, while whenever a Third Army truck had to go into another Army's area it started out with the minimum of fuel and always filled its tanks at someone else's expense. All this was no more than a drop in the bucket against a daily requirement of 400,000 gallons. Third Army's supply dropped first to 300,000, then, drastically, to no more than 32,000. Patton was going to have to halt.

Had Patton been the only Allied army there would have been no trouble, but the same supply system was also having to produce fuel for Hodges and Montgomery. It is here that the argument between the 'single thrust' and the 'broad

General Lee's inflated headquarters moving up from Normandy to commandeer some of the most luxurious hotels in Paris, in spite of Eisenhower's directive that no rear echelon headquarters was to enter the city. This ill-timed jaunt swallowed 25000 tons of gasoline and took a vast number of trucks out of the Red Ball system while the move took place.

Nevertheless, Patton managed to keep moving somehow. His supply officer conveniently 'forgot' to report back stocks of captured gasoline, which

Below: The remains of a shot-up German staff car after an Allied air attack on the Falaise Gap.

Above: A dump of damaged vehicles of both sides from which Allied troops could 'cannibalise' spare parts.

front' begins to have some point. Briefly, the argument ran like this: if we concentrate all the available energies into a single thrust, we can drive into the middle of Germany immediately. If, on the other hand, we spread the supply, we shall move on a broad front, all Allied armies working in concert, and so do a more thorough job but do it more slowly. After all, a single thrust leaves itself open to being chopped off, and think what a disaster that would be.

The practical soldiers – Patton and Montgomery – were adamant that the single thrust was the answer. The only thing on which they disagreed was, naturally, who was going to do the thrusting. Patton wanted to go through the Nancy Gap and swing up into the Ruhr, while Montgomery wanted to strike in from the Belgian flank, also for the Ruhr. Both plans were equally valid, but Montgomery's was perhaps slightly more

advantageous in that it was hoped that his sweep through Belgium would give the Allies some more port facilities. Eisenhower, though, was set against this idea and was firmly convinced that the broad front solution was the only correct one. Moreover, giving Montgomery his head would have meant that the American armies would have been reduced to a secondary role, which was politically unthinkable, particularly in view of the upcoming Presidential elections in the USA. Patton's spectacular progress had caught the American public's eye, and stopping him in mid-flight in order to give Montgomery the go-ahead would have resulted in an uproar and a probable loss of votes.

Eisenhower's decision, given to an army commander's conference on 2 September, was that the current operations of the First US and Second British Armies around Mons would continue until completed, whereupon First and Third US Armies would remain static until supplies had been built up. Then they would attack the German 'West

Wall' defenses. In concert with this the British 21st Army Group would advance into Belgium, clearing the Channel coast and the V-1 and V-2 sites. Thus the 'Broad Front' policy was laid down. Patton protested, but in vain. In spite of the fact that Ultra information indicated a complete collapse of German defenses, there was to be no lightning thrust to take advantage of it. There can be little doubt that Eisenhower's decision was wrong in every particular, and if Patton had been given his supplies, and his head, there is every likelihood that the war could have been shortened by six months. It is a matter of record that two-thirds of all the Allied casualties in Europe were suffered after the September check. It is perhaps more a matter for speculation that if Patton's troops had been able to crack the German defenses at that time and thus open the gate to permit rapid occupation of the country, the political map of Europe might well have taken a completely different shape and many postwar problems might never have arisen.

8: THE IMMOVABLE OBJECT

It was on 4 September that Eisenhower, considering that the necessary supplies had now been brought forward, gave Patton permission to renew his advance on the Saar. At the same time 21st Army Group and First US Army were to take Antwerp, break through the West Wall above the Ardennes, and head for the Ruhr. But the five day halt had changed the situation which confronted the Allied armies. In the first place Hitler had ordered von Rundstedt to take over as Commander in Chief West and had appointed General Westphal, a brilliant soldier, as his Chief of Staff. Their orders were to hold the British as far west as they could, maintain control of the Low Countries, and in due course to mount a counterattack towards Reims and Paris. Opposite Patton was General Otto von Knobelsdorff, a Panzer veteran of the Russian campaign, and a highly competent and confident soldier. He had succeeded in rounding up sufficient troops and equipment to be able to set up a defensive front with seven infantry divisions and a Panzer brigade. The Germans were short of tanks, short of artillery, and short of men, but they were well provided with small arms and Panzerfausts, the throw-away portable recoilless guns which could master any tank in existence when used by a determined soldier. They also had the advantages of the terrain which was not suitable for attacking armor.

Patton was now leaving the open farmland which had been so easy for his tanks to cover and entering the Lorraine area, in which three principal rivers ran northward and intersected the country with deep ravines. Their tributaries also sliced up the country into hilly, wooded tracts difficult to clear on foot and impossible to clear thoroughly by armored sweeps. Moreover, late September and October were, statistically, the wettest months in that area. Last, but far from least, Patton was about to advance in an area which was a traditional battleground. As he could see, the Meuse-Moselle-Saar-Rhine leapfrog was the logical method of

driving from France into Germany. Unfortunately, since topography is fairly constant, this line of approach had been well understood since Roman times. Because traffic could obviously flow both ways the French had fortified it for centuries in order to keep the Germans out, and after the war of 1870 the Germans had strengthened the fortifications to keep the French from regaining their lost territory of Alsace-Lorraine. Patton was headed straight for an area which had been prepared for his reception for generations.

Although there seem to be no recorded comments on the matter, it seems certain that neither Patton nor his Corps Commander Walton H Walker had the slightest idea of what was in store for them. In all its previous history the US Army had never been called upon to attack fortifications as the Europeans understood them. The US Army certainly knew of the existence of such things and their engineer manuals gave brief descriptions of defensive works, but most of these manuals were devoted to 'field fortification,' the construction of makeshift works by a field army to stave off raids and patrols. We can be fairly certain that any engineer speaking of bastions, counterscarps, casemates or ravelins would have baffled the American soldier of the 1940s. It was thought that tanks, aircraft and modern artillery had rendered such fortifications obsolete.

The anvil against which the hammer of XX Corps was about to beat was by no means a battlemented medieval castle; leaving aside what had been done in the 17th and 18th centuries, the French had refortified the Metz area in the 1860s. The work had been interrupted by the War of 1870 and was then continued by the Germans. Improvements in artillery led them to build more works in the 1890s, and finally, in the early 1900s, the area was vastly strengthened in order to

Right: Troops of the Third Army rounding up the remnants of German resistance in a small French town.

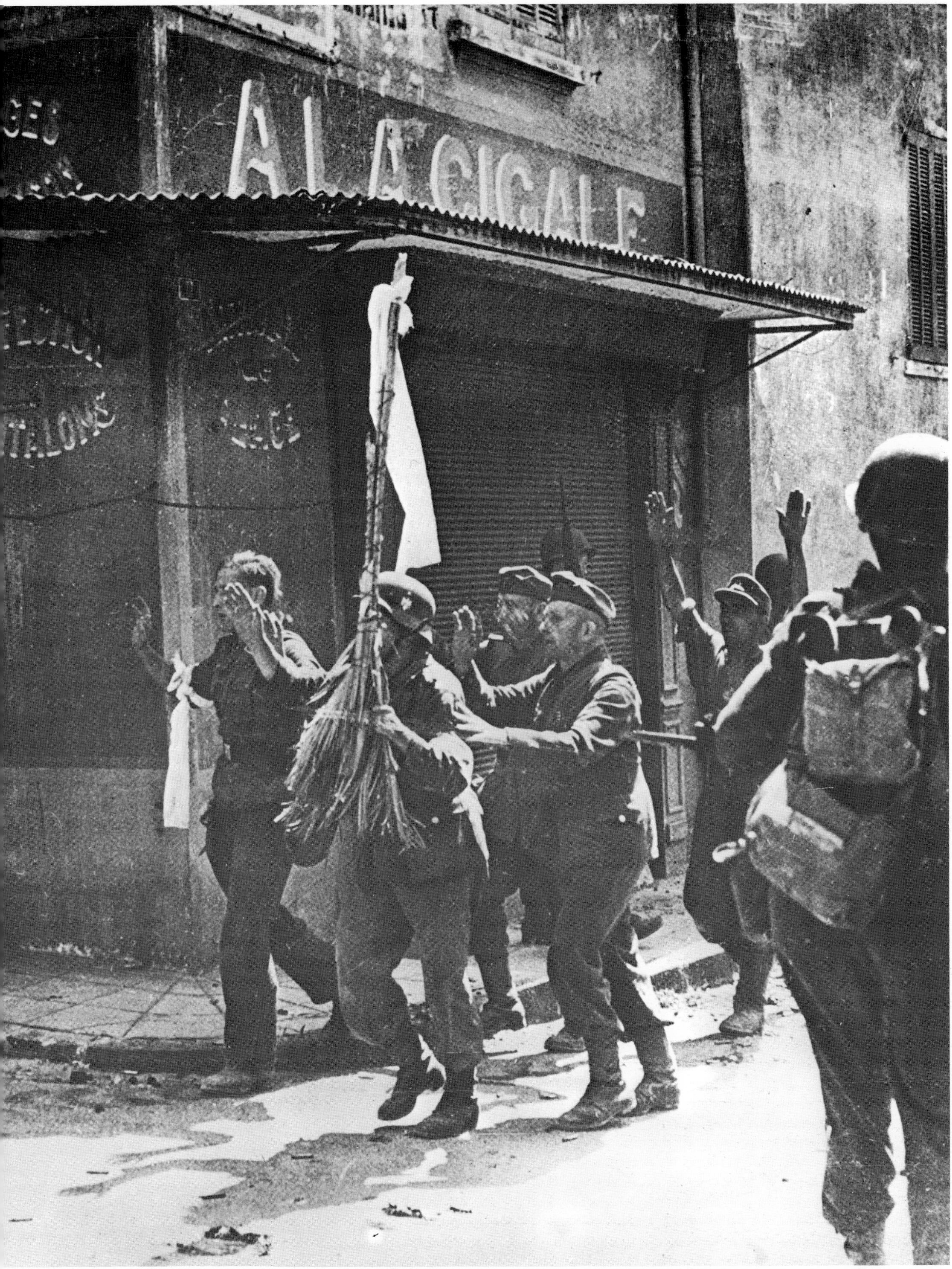
A LA CIGALE

become the pivot of the great Schlieffen Plan. This envisaged a wheeling action of the German Armies, through Belgium and into northern France, with Metz acting as the turning point and as the block to prevent a French advance which could upset the plan. To provide this block the *feste* was perfected, the culmination of years of experience in the art of fortification.

The *feste* broke away from the traditional idea of a fortress being a block of granite towering over its neighborhood. Instead, it was almost invisible; it was simply a suitable piece of terrain into which were emplaced armored gun batteries, command posts, infantry shelters, machine gun pillboxes, observation posts and whatever was deemed desirable, all buried or concealed, and all connected by tunnels and trenches. At the rear of the *feste* area would be multi-level subterranean barracks with hospital, messhall, power station, telephone exchange, workshops and every necessity for command and control of the work. Surrounding the area would be a thick barbed wire fence, deep ditches, 'unclimbable' steel

fences and other obstacles. Within the area the various strongpoints were separated from each other by wire, minefields, traps and obstacles, and the underground tunnels were prepared for demolition so that if an enemy managed to get a foothold in any part of the *feste*, he did not, thereby, gain access to the rest of it.

Eight of these *festen* had been built around Metz, others around Thionville to the north, all disposed so as to block any advance across the Moselle. During most of the war years they were, of course, far from any fighting and became military stores, depots, schools, magazines or administrative establishments. Now, as the war suddenly drew closer, orders were given to put them into working order and prepare them for action. As the Americans drew closer and as German units began falling back through the area, order, counter-order and disorder held sway, but on 2 Sep-

Below: Generals Montgomery and Patton run a professional eye over a parade.

tember, as the first US patrols entered Thionville, Lieutenant General Walter Krause was appointed Fortress Commander, and he soon began imposing order on the scene. By raiding local military establishments he assembled a fighting force to defend the area, one which was much more formidable on the ground than it looked to be on paper. Basically the troops to man the fortress were from an Officer Candidate School, an NCO School, and the 1010 Security Regiment. The latter was understrength and had been formed in France for line-of-communications guard duties from men who were mostly over-age or medically downgraded, and of questionable efficiency but the other two units were a different matter entirely. Both numbered about 1600 men and were largely composed of battle-hardened veterans of the Russian front, attending professional schools as a result of having received battlefield promotion for skill and bravery. They were highly skilled and highly motivated and because the worth of fortification is measured by the efficiency of the troops inside, garrisoning the *festen* with troops of this caliber increased their worth by a considerable factor.

Once Patton had his orders, there were some delays while the Third Army was organized. The first priority was to distribute the new supplies of gasoline to all the transport, bridging equipment, engineer vehicles and tanks scattered between Verdun and Reims where they had run dry, after which they had to be brought up to concentration areas. The infantry divisions had to be gathered up and positioned ready for the advance. What was most annoying was that the SHAEF map section had been surprised by the speed of the advance, and the only maps available to Patton's force were Michelin tourist maps at a scale of 1/100,000, maps which gave a good idea of where the roads ran but which were quite useless when it came to analysing terrain or planning a small-unit action.

On 6 September the advance got under way, with a strong reconnaissance force intending to move across the Moselle towards Metz. They had been preceded by light cavalry screens but most of these ran into trouble and had been driven back from their objectives. At this time elements of 17 SS Panzer Division were still retreating towards Metz and it was

their rearguard who had chased off the patrols. The river Moselle was reached but all the bridges had been blown. However four or five fordable areas were reported and the reconnaissance column headed towards them. Because the Moselle lay in a deep valley the roads down to it ran through ravines, and all of these turned out to be covered by German troops, guns and mines. It took a great deal of perseverance to get the first US forces to the water's edge, and then they had to wait for engineers and bridging equipment to come forward. Eventually 5th Infantry Division was ordered to make a crossing at Dornot and made its way there; but 7th Armored Division had already got to Dornot, and the result of the arrival of 5th Division was a monster traffic jam as the arriving infantry units tried to struggle through the backed-up armor to reach the village. The place was jammed with men and vehicles, and to add to the misery rain and sleet began to fall.

What the advancing force did not know was that across the river from Dornot were two forts, Sommy and St Blaise. They were, like most of the older forts, marked on the Michelin map, but not very accurately, and those people who had noticed them on the map had ignored them as probably being ancient monuments. But when dawn broke on 8 September the two forts came to life and began pouring fire across the river into Dornot and the American units clustered there.

By afternoon a force of 11th Infantry Battalion had managed to cross the river in assault boats, and two companies set out to capture Fort St Blaise. Their advance was relatively uneventful, up a hill and through a wood, until, suddenly, they found themselves outside the fort and one company commander was shot by a sniper. The 11th Infantry went to ground and contemplated what was in front of them: five rows of barbed wire, a 4 meter-high steel fence and a dry ditch

Above: Standing in his jeep, Patton crosses the River Seine at Melun, France, followed by a troop of light tanks.

15 meters wide and 5 meters deep. Added to this, a prisoner they had captured on the way said that there were 1500 SS men inside. The Battalion Operations Officer decided that the obstacles and 1500 SS fanatics were beyond the capability of his two companies, so he pulled back and radioed for artillery fire. When it came, it fell short and landed on the 11th Infantry, causing several casualties. The fire provoked a response from the guns of the fort, and at the same time German infantry appeared around both sides of the fort and began attacking. The only course open was a quick retreat, and the remains of the 11th made their way back to the bridgehead.

The 5th Infantry Division now requested permission to pull the bridgehead out, but this was refused. Another bridgehead was in the process of being

Left: Cheering crowds and a giant-sized flag greet the first US troops to enter Paris on August 25th 1944.

with heavy bombs, and on the following day three sorties of P-47 Thunderbolts, with 500-pound armor-piercing bombs, attacked the forts in front of them. The bombs did little or no damage and when the infantry tried to attack they met with the same resistance as before. On 14

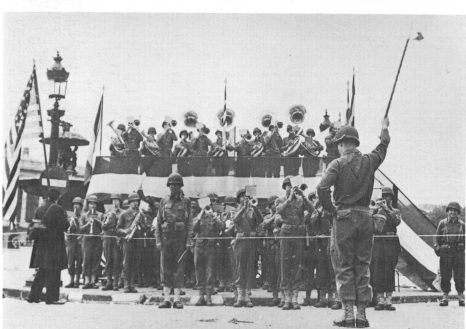

Above: A US Army band plays in the Place de la Concorde, Paris, to celebrate the liberation of the city.

established further south, and the longer the Dornot party could hold out and draw German fire, the longer the new bridgehead at Arnaville would have to become established. The Dornot bridgehead held until the night of 10 September, when the troops were finally withdrawn with only two officers left fit for duty and a total of 200 casualties.

The Arnaville bridgehead was successfully established, even though it was constantly under fire from various forts, and this was expanded so that units could begin working around the south of Metz. Meanwhile 2nd Infantry, advancing northwards beyond Dornot, had run into a string of forts which pinned them down. Artillery was called up, but many of the works bombarding the American troops were on reverse slopes and could not be located. By the evening of 9 September the CO of 2nd Infantry Regiment reported that he had lost 14 officers and 332 men, and protested volubly against sending infantry against 'twenty-odd forts.' He suggested an aircraft attack

September General Walker called off the attack and decided to concentrate his energies into the Arnaville bridgehead; he tried to break out there in order to encircle Metz from the south but his advance was soon stopped.

The 5th Infantry Division was withdrawn and replaced by the 90th Infantry Division who now tried to advance toward Metz down the road through St Privat. This brought them head-on against two groups of forts, the Canrobert group and the Lorraine group, backed up by Forts Kellerman, De Guise and Jeanne d'Arc plus an infinite number of field works. It was a hornet's nest of interlocking fire and 90th Division was stopped dead.

By the third week in September the entire Allied line was running into problems. The weather had deteriorated into highly unseasonable rain, rivers were flooded, tracks and fields turned into quagmires, and the effects were being felt in the supply lines. Once again forward movement was halted and Patton's Third Army was restricted to purely local offensives. Priority was being channeled northward in an endeavour to

Below: American troops fill the Champs Elysées, Paris, during a march to celebrate the liberation.

clear the Scheldt estuary and open the port of Antwerp. Colonel Charles W Yuill, commanding 11th Infantry Regiment, felt that taking a fort fell within the definition of a 'local offensive' and was confident that Fort Driant, the key to the south-western sector of Metz, could be stormed and taken. One battalion was detailed for the attack, which went in on 27 September and was preceded by an air strike using bombs and napalm. An artillery bombardment followed, after which two infantry companies accompanied by a troop of tank destroyers, moved toward the fort. The defenders, who had remained quiet during the bombardment, now opened fire with everything they had, the assaulting troops went to ground, and the attack was withdrawn. The divisional commander wanted to simply contain the fort and starve it into submission, but he was overruled. Orders came from Patton to General Walker to the effect that the fort *had* to be taken; 'If it takes every man in the Corps,

Below: Well to the front, General Patton studies the terrain from a forward observer's post in Northern France.

I cannot allow an attack by this Army to fail.'

By this time a set of plans of the fort had been found, together with a French officer who was familiar with it and, with somewhat better knowledge of what they

were about to encounter, another attack went in on 3 October. With air, artillery and tank support two infantry companies managed to get inside the fort perimeter and establish themselves on top of it. As they clung there they were subjected to violent attacks by parties of Germans who appeared from concealed entrances all over the area, fired, and slipped back into hiding again. Engineers with satchel charges tried to blast their way into the fort without success; most of them were shot by hidden marksmen before they could reach their objectives. The Americans held on for two days but at dawn on 5 October they were severely bombarded by guns of other forts and the survivors had to be withdrawn.

A fresh attack went in on the 7th and gained the top of the fort. Armed with the plans they were able to get inside a tunnel but found their way blocked by a steel door, which they blew down, but the passage beyond was blocked by a tangle of steel scrap. A welding torch was brought up during the night and the scrap cut away, but fifty yards further on was another steel door. This was attacked by a beehive demolition charge, but as soon as a hole was made in the door, the German defenders beyond opened up with a machine gun, ending the advance through the tunnel.

It was at about this juncture that the French officer advising on the attack was approached by an American commander who proposed to blow down the steel door and charge his troops through. The French officer called for the services of an interpreter. 'What for,' asked the American, 'You speak pretty good English?' 'Yes, perhaps I do,' said the Frenchman, 'But if I am to send a hundred or two of your soldiers to their deaths, then I feel that they should be told about it before they start.' The American officer took the hint and abandoned his plan.

By the morning of 9 October the attacking force had suffered terrible losses for such a small action and 21 officers and 485 men had been made casualties. A commanders conference discussed ways and means of taking the fort, but the only feasible idea – to drive the enemy underground and keep him there – was ruled out since it would have

demanded four infantry battalions. Eventually the Americans gave up, and on the night of 12/13 October they withdrew from the fort. It was the first time Third Army had been defeated, and it rankled.

For the rest of October there was little action, while the staffs planned a fresh assault on the forts of Metz. At the same time the Germans took advantage of the lull to reorganize their defense. Most of the officer candidates and NCOs were withdrawn from the fortress and sent back into Germany to rejoin their units, and by the beginning of November the garrison consisted of about 14,000 second-grade troops commanded by Lieutenant General Heinrich Kittel, a man who had built a reputation as a defender of cities on the Eastern front.

At last the Third Army decided to encircle Metz in strength. The plan called for a fresh division, the 95th Infantry, to hold the Germans in the west while the 90th would force the Moselle above Thionville. This would then be exploited by 10th Armored Division who would swing around to the southeast of the fortress area. Meanwhile the 5th Infantry Division in the south would break out of the Arnaville bridgehead and drive across the south of Metz, finally to swing north and meet the 10th Armored as it came south. The orders actually specified 'the destruction or capture of the Metz garrison without the investiture or siege of the Metz forts.'

The attack started on 9 November when 90th Infantry seized two bridgeheads at Cattenom and Gavisse, north of Thionville. However, they then discovered that Thionville was heavily fortified too, and the fire from the forts severely hampered operations. One had to be taken by costly assault before bridging operations could be completed. By the 14th the 90th Infantry had a secure foothold in Thionville, and now Major General Henry L Twaddle, commanding the 95th Division, asked permission to change his assignment from simply holding the Germans to active attack. Despite the plain orders not to attack the forts, he was given permission and he moved forward with three infantry regiments and a composite task force. The attack began well when 378th Infantry Regiment moved around the Canrobert group of forts and managed to take them in the rear. The loss of this group included the

loss of the Germans' principal artillery observation post, which effectively blinded them in that quarter. On the next day the 379th Infantry attempted to try the same tactics against a group of works known as the 'Seven Dwarves' but they were less lucky. They were cut off by a German counterstroke and had to be supplied by air for three days, during which they achieved very little.

Once past the Canrobert screen, though, it became possible for the 95th Division to fight its way into the town of Metz, bypassing forts wherever possible. Meanwhile the two arms of the pincer movement moved closer until eventually the encirclement was completed. Elements of 90th Division now moved into Metz to assist the 95th in clearing the town. General Kittel was actually found on an operating table in the German field hospital, about to have a wound attended to. He refused to surrender the town or its forts and thus there was never any formal capitulation of Metz. The Americans simply carried on until it was considered secure on the afternoon of 22 November. Even then there were still German garrisons holding out in seven forts, but they were left to submit in their own time. The last, Fort Jeanne d'Arc, held out until 9 December when it finally ran out of food and water.

The notable thing about the Metz

battle is the absence of Patton. Apart from presiding over the conference which decided on the final encirclement, he played very little part in the affair except to emit exhortations from time to time. He handed the difficult operation to Walton Walker and left him to get on with it. It is hard to resist the conclusion that in this affair Patton was out of his depth and knew it. The abortive, piecemeal attacks on Fort Driant would have been unlikely if Patton's usual decisive leadership had been present.

However, he had not been idle while XX Corps hammered at Metz. He was active in chasing up supplies, making sure that winter clothing and equipment, rations and mail all reached the troops in sufficient quantities and in good time before the worst of the winter arrived. He was also busy preparing plans for the next advance which had been decided upon by Eisenhower at a conference in Brussels on 18 October. First Army would attack early in November from Aachen and secure a bridgehead over the Rhine south of Cologne. Ninth US Army would protect its northern flank and then move northward to meet Montgomery's 21st Army Group south of Nijmegen.

Below: Sherman tanks of the Third Army roll through a shattered village in Northern France en route to Verdun.

Above: General Patton and Gen Walton H Walker, commanding XX Corps, congratulating the officers and men of the corps in France.

Ninth Army would then swing east across the top of the Ruhr, while First Army swung across the bottom and then north until the area was encircled. Third Army was to play a secondary role in all this, and was to cross the Rhine somewhere between Worms and Mainz 'when logistic conditions permit.' The weather, however, was terrible and the start of the operation was indefinitely postponed until such time as conditions would permit the necessary preliminary air bombardment. Provisionally, this was set for 8 November, on which day XII Corps would launch a major attack. The weather showed no sign of improvement and on the evening of the 7th one of the corps commanders and a divisional commander appeared in Patton's HQ, pointed out that the weather was still dreadful, and requested a postponement of the attack. Patton's reply was typical: 'Would you care to make recommendations as to your successors?' They returned to their own units to prepare for the next day.

On the following morning a 700-gun bombardment hammered the German

Right: Ever-vigilant for his supplies, Patton makes a visit to an Ordnance Maintenance workshop behind the lines.

positions across the Moselle while the rain still poured down. But it soon slackened off to a drizzle and then the sun came through the clouds. Almost immediately hundreds of aircraft appeared and began bombing and machine-gunning all the known German positions. By late afternoon XII Corps was able to report that almost all the day's objectives had been taken. That night the rain resumed, heavier than ever and by next morning units were stranded by floods, bridges had been swept away, and the rivers had burst their banks. In spite of the terrible conditions Third Army struggled forward until by the beginning of December they had closed up to the West Wall defences of Germany. Preparations were put in hand for a final attack through the West Wall on 19 December, providentially aided by a talkative prisoner, a German officer with comprehensive knowledge of the defences facing Third Army. The attack never came off because of events elsewhere.

Colonel Oscar Koch, Patton's intelligence officer and among the shrewdest of his type, had been worrying for some time over indications that the Germans

Below: 'Behind the last battle of this war stands our Victory'. German graffiti on a French farmhouse.

were building up reserves in front of the First Army. These appeared to be all first-class troops: Panzers, Panzer Grenadiers and parachute divisions. Ultra intercepts gave no clue as to what this build-up was intended for, and, indeed, the indications were so slight that many people ignored them. Koch, however, had reports of heavy rail

Above: A front line soldier attempts a bath in a foxhole, somewhere in Northern France.

movements within the German lines and continued to worry. At a conference on 9 December he drew Patton's attention to these features, pointing out that in front of VIII Corps, to their northern flank (in a 'quiet sector') there were two and a half more divisions than faced the entire Third Army, three and a half more than faced Seventh Army; why this enormous preponderance against a single Corps? It meant that the Germans had a three to one superiority on a front with few natural obstacles, while the American strength, in VIII Corps, consisted of two green divisions and two which had suffered badly in earlier battles and were 'resting.' He suggested that the Germans might be thinking of trying a spoiling attack. There was silence when Koch had finished his exposition, then a long discussion on the possible moves. Patton finally decided that planning for the 19 December attack must go on, but, just in case, plans should be drawn up to cover the possibility of an attack against the Ardennes, including securing Third Army's northern boundary and also preparing for a counterattack towards the north. If these things were taken care of, said Patton, 'We'll be in a position to meet whatever happens.' It was a prophetic remark.

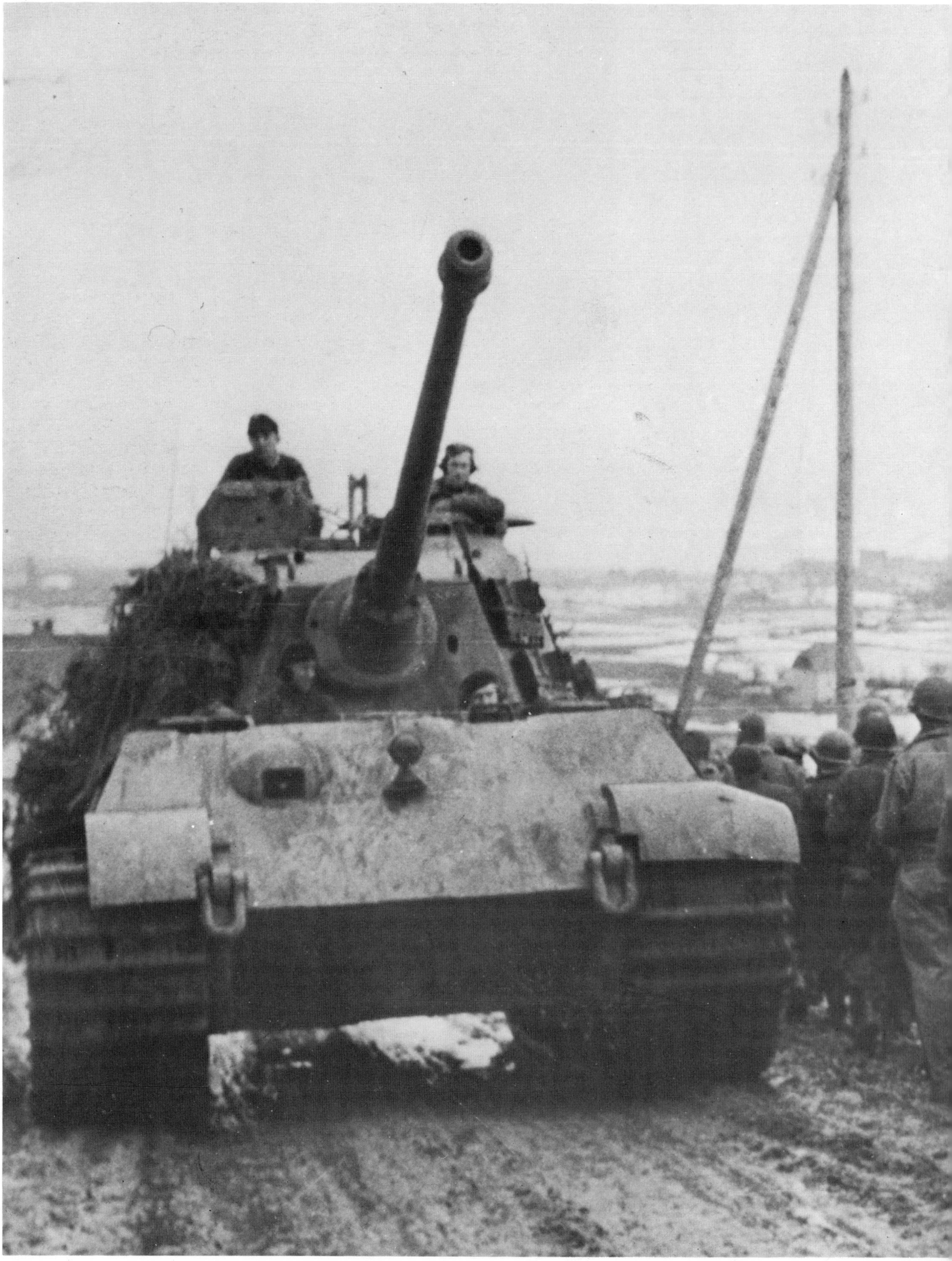

9: THE FINAL ACTS

The 16 December 1944 dawned with low clouds, mists and fog, promising yet another day of the bad weather which had plagued the front for weeks; it was, indeed, to be a particularly bad winter. A thunderous artillery bombardment burst out of this gray shroud on to VIII Corps. Before the astonished Americans could appreciate what was going on, German infantry with Panzers following closely behind came pouring out of the woods and into the attack. The German Fifth and Sixth Panzer and Seventh Armies, consisting of 13 infantry and seven armored divisions at the cutting edge with a further 10 divisions following, all supported by 2000 pieces of artillery, were about to make Hitler's last throw.

It was afternoon before the news of the sudden onslaught trickled through to Eisenhower's HQ at Versailles, where Bradley was conferring with Eisenhower. At first they were inclined to treat the news as an exaggerated reaction to a minor spoiling attack, but as the reports flowed in it became obvious that this was something more serious. Bradley was painfully aware that his dispositions in the area were sensitive. He had no reserves in that sector and his own head-quarters in Luxembourg were perilously close to the scene. Eventually he decided to reinforce VIII Corps by removing the 7th Armored Division from Ninth Army in the north and 10th Armored Division from Third Army in the south.

Patton, poised for his breakout to the Saar, was less than pleased at the prospect of losing one of his armored divisions. In spite of Koch's warnings he considered, in the light of what little information he had, that this attack was designed princi-pally to throw him off balance and delay his Saar offensive, and taking one of his divisions away from him was playing into the German hands. Bradley agreed that this was a possibility, but suggested in guarded phrases that there might be more to it than was immediately obvious and that he wanted the 10th Armored Divi-sion. Patton now thought back to the

Left: American troops captured during the Battle of the Bulge are marched into captivity past an advancing King Tiger tank.

conference in which Koch had unfolded his theories, saw the light, and sent the division north within the hour.

By next day, when Bradley finally got back to 12th Army Group HQ, the situation was frightening. Identification had been made of no less than 14 German divisions confronting VIII Corps. Twenty miles away the 4th US Infantry Division had just managed to stem the latest attack by bringing cooks, bakers, truck drivers and clerks into the line, and a message from the divisional commander to Bradley suggested that unless 10th Armored got there soon, then Bradley himself might have to get into a foxhole with a rifle. Communications were poor and rumors were flying. Droves of German commandos, dressed as Ameri-cans, were sweeping through the area sabotaging and murdering and units had been cut off, annihilated, lost, redis-covered, nobody knew what was going on. In fact the panic seems to have been confined to higher formation HQs who, in default of solid facts, tended to seize on rumors and embellish them. On the ground, as it later turned out, things were rather different. Junior officers and NCOs had rallied their men into self-defensible areas and although the Ger-man forces had covered a great deal of ground, they had by-passed many Ameri-can sub-units which were holding their own and defending themselves quite effectively. If any affair in American history can be said to be a 'soldier's battle,' the Ardennes qualifies. Thrown on their own resources the lower echelons of the US Army responded magnificently and fought valiantly to disrupt and delay the German build-up.

The weather was on the German side, with the low cloud, overcast and fog preventing Allied air forces from flying over the battle area, whether recon-naissance or strike forces. Eisenhower reacted with unusual promptness and despatched his only reserves, the 82nd and 101st Airborne Divisions from Reims to Bastogne, a vital road junction in the path of the advancing Germans. On 18 December Patton reported to Bradley's HQ to find that things were worse than had been thought and that, in fact, all

Koch's most pessimistic fears were coming true. The only bright spot was that the German drive seemed to be intent on going forward and not spreading outward, so that the Allied forces on the flanks of the 'Bulge' (as it was now being called) were holding fast. In the north the Sixth SS Panzer Army had reached Malmédy, where they were being held. St Vith was being securely held by 7th US Armored Division, while Fifth Panzer Army was headed for Bastogne in what appeared to be a race between them and 101st Airborne. Bradley told Patton that he intended to move up a corps of three divisions from the south to aid VIII

Corps, and that Patton would have to cancel his proposed Saar offensive and give assistance.

Because of Koch's prevision, Patton was ready for this situation, and plans were made and orders were ready for three or four possible moves. So without hesitating, Patton offered to pull out 4th Armored Division and have it concentrated near Longwy by midnight, pull 80th Infantry Division out of the line and start it marching by dawn, and have 26th Infantry Division following them within 24 hours. Bradley, and a few of his staff, were somewhat skeptical of Patton's ability to meet such a schedule, but they

should have known better. Patton returned to his HQ and the necessary orders were ready for issue within the hour. That evening he had a call from Bradley to say that Eisenhower was coming up to Verdun to hold a conference at 1100 hours next day. Patton called his own staff conference for 0800 next morning.

He opened the conference then went on to say that if they thought they were capable of rapid movement, they had a surprise coming, because they were going to move a damn sight faster than they'd ever done before. Third Army were going to strike upwards and slice off the German intrusion. Where this took place would depend upon events, and he sketched in three possible lines – due north from Diekirch, or from Arlon towards Bastogne, or on the Neufchateau –Bastogne road. Outline plans were made for each of these moves and a simple word code was arranged so that Patton could telephone from the Verdun conference and indicate which attack line was to be used.

The Verdun conference opened on a note of gloom as Major General Kenneth Strong, Eisenhower's intelligence chief, outlined the various disasters which had occurred. Eisenhower then attempted to rally the meeting, and Patton put the seal on it by suddenly bursting out 'Hell, let's have the guts to let the bastards go all the way to Paris, then we'll really cut 'em off and chew 'em up!' This cheered everybody up. When asked what steps he could take, he promised a strong attack with his three divisions within 48 hours. He could assemble a stronger force but that would take more time, and time was something they did not have because waiting would give the Germans more time to consolidate and would ruin the surprise effect of a quick strike. Not knowing how well Patton was prepared, this statement caused no small amount of surprise. Could Patton hold von Rundstedt in the south? 'Hold von Rundstedt? I'll take von Rundstedt and shove him up Montgomery's ass!' Patton replied. After more discussion Eisen-

Above left: A German 'Sturmgeschutz' assault gun in a camouflaged ambush position in the Ardennes, 1944.

Left: A wrecked German transport column on a road near Givroulle, Belgium, after an Allied air attack, one of many which marked the defeat of the German advance.

withdrawn from Sauerlautern and started towards Luxembourg within 24 hours.

The next morning, though, brought news of a decision by Eisenhower which was to start an argument which still raises blood pressures. The trouble was that the German thrust had split Bradley's 12th Army Group into two parts: Bradley's HQ, Patton's Third Army and a portion of First Army were in the south, while the Ninth Army and the remainder of First Army were away on the north side of the Bulge. Bradley was therefore unable to take effective control of the northern part. Eisenhower suggested that he move his HQ to Namur but Bradley refused to do this since he felt it would have a bad effect on his troops' morale. Eisenhower therefore had no choice, on logical military grounds, but to transfer control of the northern sector to Montgomery, who was better-placed to exercise command. Bradley was extremely upset by this and protested to Bedell Smith, Eisenhower's Chief of Staff. But Bedell Smith was a practical man who later observed that 'There was ample justification to the Army Group in the north taking temporary command on the side of the penetration.' So Bradley bowed to the inevitable and stood more or less on the sidelines for the rest of the battle. His only responsibility was Patton who was quite capable of looking after himself.

Patton now drove to Arlon to be with his forward troops and also to visit VIII Corps and get some first-hand information about what was happening. The

Below: Troops of the 82nd Airborne Division with a collection of prisoners amid the snows of the Ardennes forest.

Top: Roles reversed, American troops watch as a column of German troops march past on their way to the POW cages.

Above: Well wrapped up against the winter cold, a group of German prisoners under the eye of a US Military Policeman await orders to march into captivity.

hower summarised; the north would be held firm while Patton attacked from the south. Patton went to a telephone, called Gay, his Chief of Staff, and gave the word for the Arlon-Bastogne maneuver. The 26th Infantry and 4th Armored were to move to Arlon, and the 80th Division to Luxembourg. The 5th Division was to be

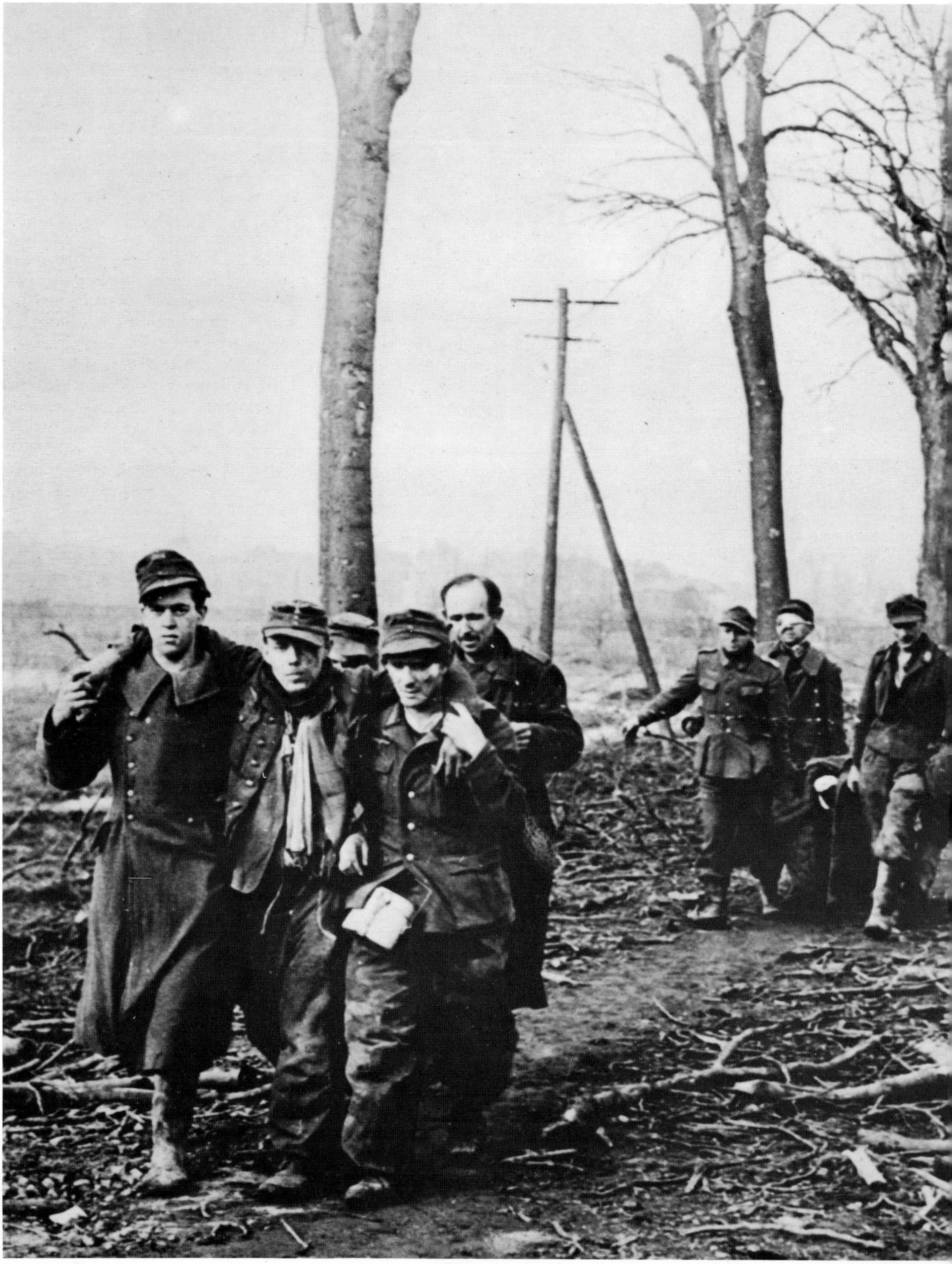

remains of the corps were fighting back as well as they could. The 101st Airborne had beaten the Panzers to Bastogne, and together with a combat command of 9th Division, one from 10th Armored Division, the 705th Tank Destroyer Battalion and various remnants and stragglers that had rallied to the town, were holding off three German Panzer divisions.

Patton had ordered the advance to relieve Bastogne to begin at 0040 hours on 22 December. To execute the necessary movements to get his troops out of the Saar area, turned through a right-angle and started north, all with the minimum of confusion, was a piece of staff organization which, among military experts, ranks among the all-time master-pieces. Within 48 hours of receiving orders he would have two divisions attacking with a third following up, and within a week he was to move 250,000 men and 133,000 vehicles over 50 miles, in freezing weather over ice-bound roads and in a major snowstorm. The only thing which really worried Patton was the thought of the weak front he was leaving behind in the Saar. If von Rundstedt had any more reserves up his sleeve and threw

Left: German troops, carrying their wounded, march to the rear after capture by the US 9th Army somewhere east of the Roer River, in Germany.

Below: Corpses and wreckage strew the streets of Bastogne after the battle for its ownership had raged through and around the city.

an attack into that area, the effects could be disastrous. He was, however, able to feed replacement units into the Saar front to maintain the semblance of a presence and keep up the pressure, so that the Germans did not know that the bulk of Third Army had been withdrawn and was moving away from them.

The principal worry for everyone was the vile weather. Patton decided to call on the highest possible echelon and sent for his Senior Chaplain, to whom he gave orders to pray for better weather. He even went as far as having Christmas Cards printed for distribution to the troops, complete with a pertinent prayer:

"Almighty and most merciful Father, we humbly beseech Thee, of Thy great goodness, to restrain these immoderate rains with which we have had to contend. Grant us fair weather for battle. Graciously hearken to us as soldiers who call upon Thee that, armed with Thy power, we may advance from victory to victory, and crush the oppression and wickedness of our enemies, and establish Thy justice among men and nations. Amen."

Whether it was Patton's luck, his Senior Chaplain's prayer, or the combined prayers of Third Army, the rain and snow stopped. Patton deployed his troops and, at long last, the skies cleared and the Allied air forces were able to add their weight to the battle.

If the men of Third Army expected another glorious charge across Germany,

they were to be disappointed. They came up against the 5th German Parachute Division, a very tough outfit indeed who gave them a hard fight. After two days of slogging the Germans actually managed to mount a counterattack which pushed some of 4th Armored Division back for several miles. Patton later blamed himself for this setback, admitting that he had pushed his troops beyond their endurance, insisting that they continued fighting by night and day, without rest, hoping to catch the enemy off balance. All this succeeded in doing was to exhaust the Americans, and he realized that this sort of extreme endeavor can only be kept up for a short time. He even went to the astonishing length of apologising to Eisenhower for his slow advance, as if anyone else could have done any better. The Bastogne perimeter was slowly shrinking, though it is said that once they

heard the news that Third Army was on the way, their spirits rose. 'If Georgie's coming, we got it made' said one sergeant.

On Christmas Day, with the Panzers making a final desperate attack on Bastogne, III Corps' advance was still stuck and General Milliken decided to try and move sideways to work around the German flank. General Gaffey of 4th Armored asked Patton if he could take a chance and try to break his Combat Command B through the German lines to Bastogne. Patton agreed, CCB moved off, and by the evening they had managed to open a 300 yard wide corridor into the beleaguered town and make contact with 101st Airborne. Once the way was clear a light tank battalion was thrust in to convoy 40 truckloads of supplies and 70 ambulances to remove the wounded.

Boxing Day was the turning point. The Panzers had reached their furthest in-

cursion at Celles, whereupon Collins with VII Corps and the British 29th Armoured Brigade fell upon them and threw them back. Fighter bombers ranged the whole area to such effect that von Rundstedt ordered his tanks not to move during daylight for fear of attack. Moreover the fuel shortage was beginning to bite, and tank spares and ammunition could not be brought into the Bulge to resupply the Panzers because there was no gasoline for the supply columns. Even so, the remnants of the German forces fought back with vigor and it was not until 2 January that von Rundstedt called off the attempt to regain Bastogne.

On 27 December Patton, reading the battle as well as ever, saw that the time had come for a rapid thrust northward to chop off the entire salient and encircle the remaining German troops. He put the idea forward to Eisenhower. Bedell

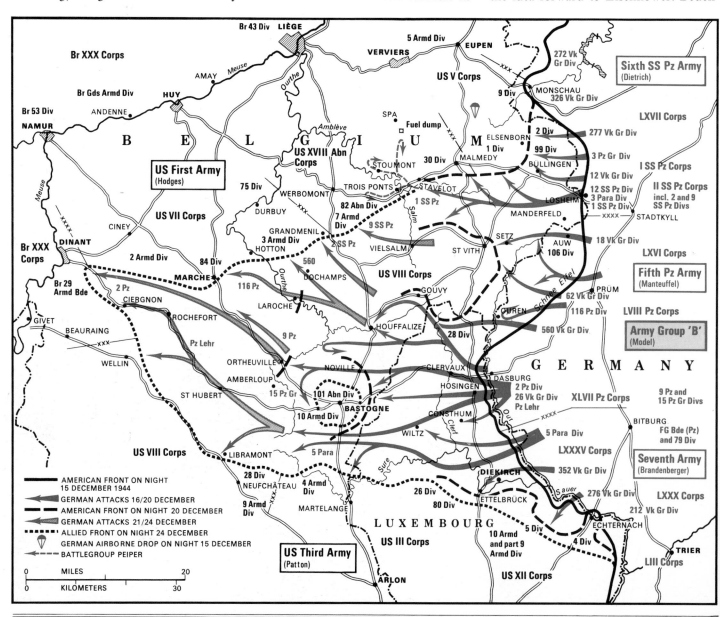

Above: Brigadier-General McAuliffe, of
'Nuts' fame, receives the Distinguished
Service Cross from General Patton.

Smith thought it sensible, even though
the road lay-out was awkward. But
Eisenhower turned down the idea because it would upset his 'Broad Front'
plans. Instead, First and Third Armies
would attack from north and south, not at
the base of the Bulge as Patton wanted,
but about half-way along it, to meet near

Left: The magnitude of the German
advance can be judged from his map
which shows the farthest points reached.

Right: The counterstroke by the Allies,
with Patton's Third Army moving in from
the South.

Below: Troops of 101st Airborne making a
sortie from besieged Bastogne to link up
with the relieving troops of Third Army.

Houffalize. The attacks were duly mounted, against stiff opposition, and by 16
January the operation was completed
when the two armies met. First Army
went on to take St Vith on 23 January,
and for all practical purposes the 'Battle
of the Bulge' was over. Although the
encircling movement had worked, it had
not netted the quantity of German troops
and equipment that would have resulted
if Patton's idea had been followed. Nonetheless Hitler had lost about 85,000 troops
and a vast number of valuable tanks and
guns. The offensive had cost nearly
70,000 Allied, mostly American, casualties and there had been heavy losses in
American artillery. It also gave German
morale a boost just when it needed one.

In early January, while the advance to
Houffalize was still going forward, the
German reaction which Patton had feared
took place; a diversionary attack was
launched against Seventh US Army
north of Strasbourg. Worried by this,
Eisenhower instructed Bradley to stop
Patton's attack to Houffalize and pull
Third Army back to its previous front.
This is the second time I've been stopped
in a successful attack by the Germans
having more nerve than us' complained

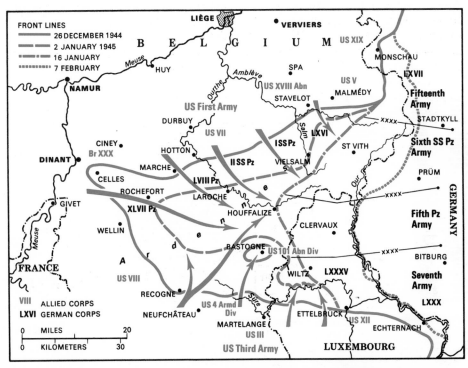

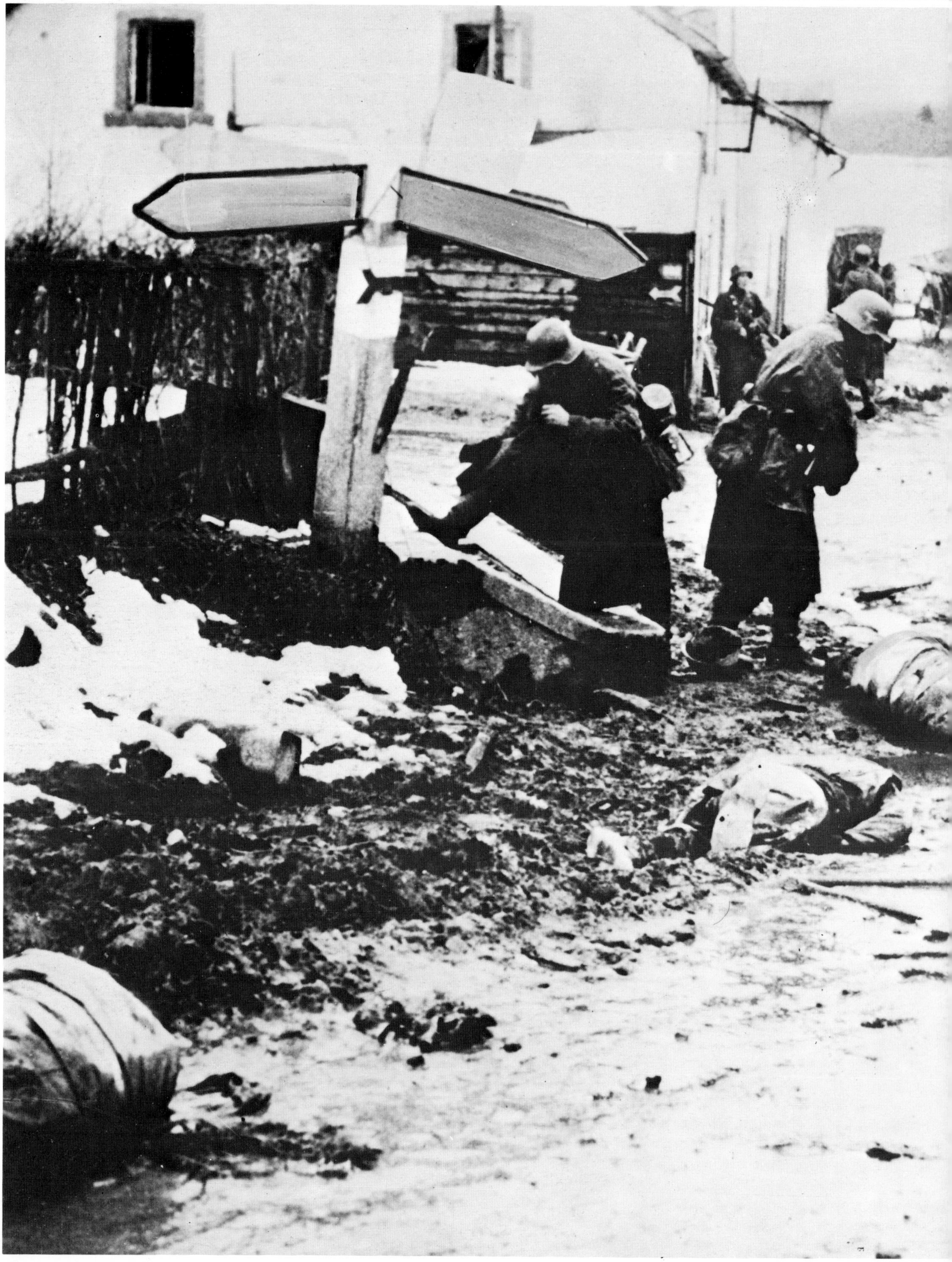

Left: A typical scene during the Battle of the Bulge; note that the censor has blacked out the names on the signpost.

Top: Infantrymen of a German Volks-Grenadier regiment feeling sorry for themselves after their capture by Third Army troops.

Above: Germany was feeling the man-power pinch by December 1944 as this parade of the Volkssturm in Berlin shows. Most are armed with Panzerfaust anti-tank weapons.

Right: Brigadier-General Anthony G McAuliffe, commander of 101st Airborne Division in the heroic defense of Bastogne.

Left: Bastogne, after its liberation, became a focal point on the supply routes to the front line.

Patton, and although he acquiesced in the order, he took his time about it and allowed the pincer movement to be completed before he began withdrawing.

However, he was not to be granted his freedom to burst out from the Saar line as had been his previous intention. On 1 January, Eisenhower had issued a directive stating that on reaching the Rhine, the main effort of the Allied armies would be north of the Ruhr. To implement this Montgomery and 21st Army Group (Second British and First Canadian Armies) were to move, accompanied by the Ninth US Army, to seize the west bank of the Rhine from Düsseldorf to Nijmegen. The First US Army would take the Roer Dams, so as to prevent any German attempt to inundate areas, and protect the Ninth Army's southern flank. Once Ninth Army had

Below: A souvenir not to be resisted! A GI removes the name plate from a street in a small German town.

Below left: Generals Hodges, Bradley and Dempsey, with Field-Marshal Montgomery, after conferring on the next moves.

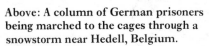

Above: A column of German prisoners being marched to the cages through a snowstorm near Hedell, Belgium.

reached the Rhine, First Army would strike towards Cologne, take it, and then move south to cut off any German troops west of the Rhine. Since the available supplies could not sustain five armies in attack, Third Army was to remain static. Patton, it hardly needs saying, was not pleased with that. His army was already making probing attacks in the Saar region, and he was in no mood to sit around while others did the fighting. Moreover he knew that he had a sound and well-trained army at the top of its morale, and to let such an army sit on its hands was asking for trouble. Patton therefore looked closely at his front to see what excuse he could come up with to justify some action, and shortly appeared before Bradley asking for permission to mount a limited advance in the Eifel Mountain region 'so as to prevent the enemy withdrawing troops for use against other sectors.' This was a very reasonable

Top left: Adolf Hitler congratulates a Hitler Youth member after awarding him the Iron Cross in Berlin, March 1945.

Center left: Doktor Goebbels takes the salute at a parade of the Volkssturm through Berlin in December 1944.

Left: Possibly the youngest recipient of an Iron Cross, one of twenty Hitler Youth given awards by Hitler in March 1945.

Above: Men of the 39th Infantry, 3rd Armored Division, hitch a ride on a tank through the 'dragon's teeth' of the Siegfried Line.

purpose, and Bradley gave it his blessing, with permission to 'pierce the Siegfried defenses north of the Moselle and advance quietly to the Kyll,' this being a small river some 12 miles inside Germany. There he was to set up a bridgehead for future use when the time came to advance to the Rhine.

On the evening of 7 February the various operations got under way. First Army took the Roer Dams but not before the Germans had opened the sluices and blocked Ninth Army's route. First Canadian Army struck from Nijmegen, and Third Army swept into the Eifel. They all met the same problems: rain, mud and floods. Nevertheless, nothing stopped Third Army and by 22 February they had captured a sizeable slice of the Siegfried Line defenses between Bitberg and Prum. They had also made a bridgehead over the Sauer river near Trier. Seeing this, Bradley telephoned and suggested that he should now go on the defensive. Patton replied that he was the oldest and most experienced soldier in the US forces in Europe, and if they wanted him on the defensive he would damn well ask to be relieved. Bradley dropped his line of argument.

What Patton was up to now was his favorite tactic; 'reconnaissance in force.'

He would send out a patrol, ostensibly with orders to reconnoiter but usually with some objective in view. To everyone's surprise the patrol would radio through 'we have entered village X and it is unoccupied' or 'We have reached X and have come under fire.' Either way, Patton would immediately say 'Goodness me, we must do something' and send a back-up force to either occupy the vacuum or reinforce the patrol. Of course, once the back-up force had taken the place, the American line had advanced

a little; flanks had to be pushed forward, lines adjusted, and so there was always a slight forward impetus on Patton's front, even when he was, nominally, standing still. This process was happening in the Eifel and by the end of the month the Kyll river had been passed. On 2 March XX Corps took Trier and captured a bridge over the Moselle. Now Bradley came along with orders for Patton to drive through the Eifel for Koblenz, at the same time as First Army's move on Cologne.

On 5 March First and Third Armies struck together, with 4th Armored Division leading the way for Patton and 11th Armored on their left. In spite of rain and mud 4th Armored dashed through the close country of the Eifel and inside two days had carved through 35 miles of German defenses. On 7 March 4th and 11th Armored converged, thus encircling a pocket of German troops. Organized resistance collapsed west of the Rhine and the civil population hurried to surrender the towns and villages. As Third Army came up to the Rhine, so First Army found the unblown bridge at Remagen which Bradley immediately exploited, giving his army group a useful entrance into Germany in case other operations should fail. Bradley now had the bit between his teeth and, anxious not

Below: General Patton, well wrapped against the January cold, visits the HQ of the 87th Division.

Above: Three in harmony – Generals Eisenhower, Bradley and Patton meet in Bastogne after the end of the battle.

Below: Patton poses alongside his bridge, built across the Sauer River, between Luxembourg and Germany.

Above: Eisenhower and Bradley listen attentively as Patton describes the battle for Bastogne, the ruins of which lie around them.

Above: A Boston newspaper celebrates Patton's drive to the Rhine.

nightfall, had 14 battalions of infantry beyond the river. The 4th Armored Division now moved into the lead and within two days they were on the River Nahe, halfway across the Palatinate. Patton now reasoned that at this point the Germans should counterattack, if they had anything left at all, and so he halted his force on the Nahe and brought up more troops, packing artillery behind his defensive zone. As he had predicted, the counterattack came, and it was blown to pieces by artillery fire and then rolled back by XII Corps. By this time XX Corps had dealt with its opposition and had rolled forward to join up with XII Corps, and the two Corps swept east to strike the Rhine between Mainz and Mannheim. The pressure generated by Patton had caused the West Wall front to weaken and Seventh Army were coming through. By 21 March virtually all German resistance in the Palatinate was at an end. Third Army had taken over 70,000 prisoners in four days.

That day found XII Corps attacking Mainz, the 4th and 11th Armored Divisions were outside Worms, and 12th Armored Division of XX Corps was nearing Mannheim. Patton now had his forces in positions which he had foreseen

to lose any of his group to other operations and anxious to keep Patton and Hodges occupied, he now decided to commit them to an operation from which it would be impossible to withdraw them. To the southwest of Koblenz stretches the Palatinate, a roughly triangular area bounded by the Rhine and the Moselle. At the base of this triangle lay the US Seventh Army, fighting against the West Wall defences. If Patton was now to swing right and move into this area he would capture a large piece of Germany and would also come up behind the West Wall and thus open the door for Seventh Army to advance with fewer casualties. He discussed the idea with Patton, then went to sell the idea to Eisenhower's

headquarters who were not particularly enthusiastic but did not actually forbid the operation. This was just as well, because Patton was not waiting for approval and was already aligning his formations, issuing orders and preparing for the advance with the usual Third Army alacrity.

By 13 March there were five divisions on the line of the Moselle and another four close to Trier, and they moved off with their infantry leading. The move from Trier by XX Corps attracted the German main reserve, a mountain division which put up a stiff resistance. However, this pulled defenses away from XII Corps who were able to put four bridges across the Moselle and, by

months before and he knew exactly what to do. General Eddy, commanding XII Corps, had spotted a likely crossing point on the map weeks before, and Patton had a naval squad who had been rehearsing their moves back in Tours for a month or more. They were now sent for, together with their dozen amphibious carriers, while Major General Conklin, Patton's Chief of Engineers, had all the bridging equipment moved up under cover. Assuming that the Germans would expect a crossing to be attempted in Mainz, Patton arranged for the artillery to blind the defenders with a prolonged smoke screen, while XII and XX Corps drove south on the west side of the Rhine. The 5th and 90th Divisions then dropped out of the line of march, turned due east and dashed for the river at Oppenheim, some 15 miles from Mainz. The amphibians were driven up, rubber boats arrived on trucks, and at 2000 hours that night, without air attacks, bombardments or any other diversions, the 23rd Infantry Regiment slipped across the river. By dawn they had six battalions across for

Below: Patton the tourist, examining a monument commemorating Zeppelin, the airship pioneer.

Top: Patton and General James A Van Fleet, commanding III Corps, examining a photomosaic of the River Rhine.

Above: A glowering Patton after reprimanding a tank driver for an excess of sandbag protection on his tank.

the loss of 8 men killed and 20 wounded. A few amphibious tanks were also put across in the dawn, and the bridgehead was secured. Conklin's engineers now moved in and began building a treadway bridge as fast as they could go.

What particularly pleased Patton was that this crossing was going to upset several people. The crossing of the Rhine had become the Holy Grail of the Allied advance, and, in the north, 21st Army Group had been making massive preparations, including a powerful artillery barrage, airborne drops and amphibious use of vehicles of all kinds. Now Patton seized his phone and called Bradley, who was breakfasting in his HQ. 'Brad, don't tell anyone, but I'm across!' 'Well I'm

Above: Patton shares a map with Maj Gen Eddy, commanding XII Corps, as they watch 5th Infantry cross the Rhine at Oppenheim.

damned!' said Bradley, 'You mean across the Rhine?' 'I sure am,' replied Patton, 'I sneaked a division over last night. There are so few Krauts around, they don't know it yet, so don't make any announcement. We'll keep it secret and see how it goes.'

The Germans soon found out, however, and they reacted violently, sending in some 150 air strikes against Conklin's bridge. Patton had ensured plenty of antiaircraft protection, however, and the bridge survived. In the evening he rang Bradley once more: 'Brad, for God's sake tell the world we're across. We knocked down 33 Krauts when they came after our bridge today. I want the world to know that Third Army made it before Monty starts across!'

On the next morning Patton himself went to Oppenheim to inspect progress. After satisfying himself as to the arrangements, he led his party across the bridge. Halfway over he stopped. 'Time for a short halt,' he said, then turned to the edge of the bridge, unbuttoned his breeches, and urinated into the Rhine. 'I've been looking forward to this for a long time' he said. Then he walked on, across the Rhine and into the heartland of Germany.

Once across the river, Third Army swung north and made for the line of the River Main, with Frankfurt as their next major objective. It was at this juncture that the peculiar episode of the Hammelburg Raid occured. It is doubtful if the truth about this affair will ever be known, because most of those principals in a position to know the truth are dead, and those who have any inkling remain silent. We can, therefore, only speculate on the motive. As to the raid itself, the facts are scarce but amply confirmed.

On 24 March Patton passed orders to General Eddy, who then relayed them to General Hoge, commanding 4th Armored Division, that he wanted a raid mounted against a German camp at Hammelburg which contained several hundred Allied prisoners of war. Hoge was surprised because he saw little point in despatching a Combat Command about 300 strong some fifty-odd miles into German-held territory simply to liberate some prisoners who, in any event, would probably be freed in a short time as the general advance rolled forward. Moreover taking a Combat Command would seriously weaken his front. He argued the point but without success.

Some 300 officers and men set out from Aschaffenburg, on the Main on the evening of 26 March. They moved on 10 Sherman tanks, 27 halftracks, six light tanks, six Command and Reconnaissance cars and an amphibious Weasel cargo carrier. The raid was launched by a limited attack into the village of Schweinheim, on the northern bank of the Main, which punched a hole in the German defenses for long enough to slip the raiding party through, after which the attack was run down and withdrawn, allowing the Germans to reform their line. The raiding party were now on their own. Unfortunately for all concerned, the leadership was inept, and instead of quietly driving through the countryside to their destination, doing the job, and driving home, the force appears to have gone out of its way to stir up trouble by shooting-up railroad trains and launching unnecessary attacks on villages it encountered. Even at this late stage of the war, it was inadvisable to be too impertinent with the German Army, and the inevitable reaction soon appeared. The area around Hammelburg had been a military training area for generations (it still is) and there were several arms schools and depots within easy call. Among them was a Waffen SS Officer candidate school, which promptly turned out a 300-strong force of veteran NCOs, and a Panzerjäger school which sent a squadron of tank destroyers. The latter were equipped with the formidable

Below: Gaston Thibeault, Mayor of Verdun, presents General Patton with the Verdun Medal.

Jagdpanther mounting an 88mm gun which could destroy Shermans at 800 yards range, before the Sherman, with its 75 or 76mm gun, could get close enough to do any damage. Tracked by observation aircraft, who were able to describe the precise strength and composition of the raiding force, the Americans drove on and into an ambush mounted by the Jagdpanthers which cost them most of their armor. They disengaged, moved around the ambush, and eventually reached the prisoner-of-war camp. Here their conduct was even more peculiar. When, greeted by machine-gun fire from the camp guards, the remaining tanks stopped some 800 yards from the camp and began to shell the prisoners' compounds. Eventually, after some three

Below: Into Czechoslovakia – and out. Patton says farewell to the 8th Armored Division at Rokycanym September 1945.

hours, the raiding force managed to liberate the prisoners, loaded the American prisoners on to their halftracks, and set off back. By now, of course, every armed German within 50 miles was waiting for them and the result was a foregone conclusion. They were surrounded, shot to pieces, and the remnants surrendered. Rescuers and rescued were returned to the prison camp, and that was the end of the Hammelburg Raid.

That it was a fiasco there can be no denying, but the most fundamental question is *why*? What made Patton mount such an expensive and abortive mission in the first place? Hammelburg Camp was, in fact, liberated on 6 April – nine days after the raiding party had succumbed – so why did nearly 300 men have to die in order to save a mere nine days? Then rumors began to circulate throughout Third Army and even higher. It seemed that one of the prisoners was a

Lieutenant Colonel Waters, who was Patton's son-in-law. That Waters was in the camp cannot be denied. Indeed he was severely wounded in the fracas, but Patton stoutly denied that he had any knowledge of this when he ordered the raid, and maintained that his only concern was for the Allied prisoners in general who were in the camp. Bearing in mind that many other prison camps were liberated and that even concentration camps were unearthed by Third Army, yet that none of them was ever raided in the same manner, this explanation seems to lack credence. Patton called a press conference to explain his ignorance of Waters' presence and to give his reasons for the raid, and he then added a further explanation, that by mounting this raid in an eastward direction he had hoped to mislead the enemy into thinking his next advance would be in that direction, when, in fact, he intended to move south.

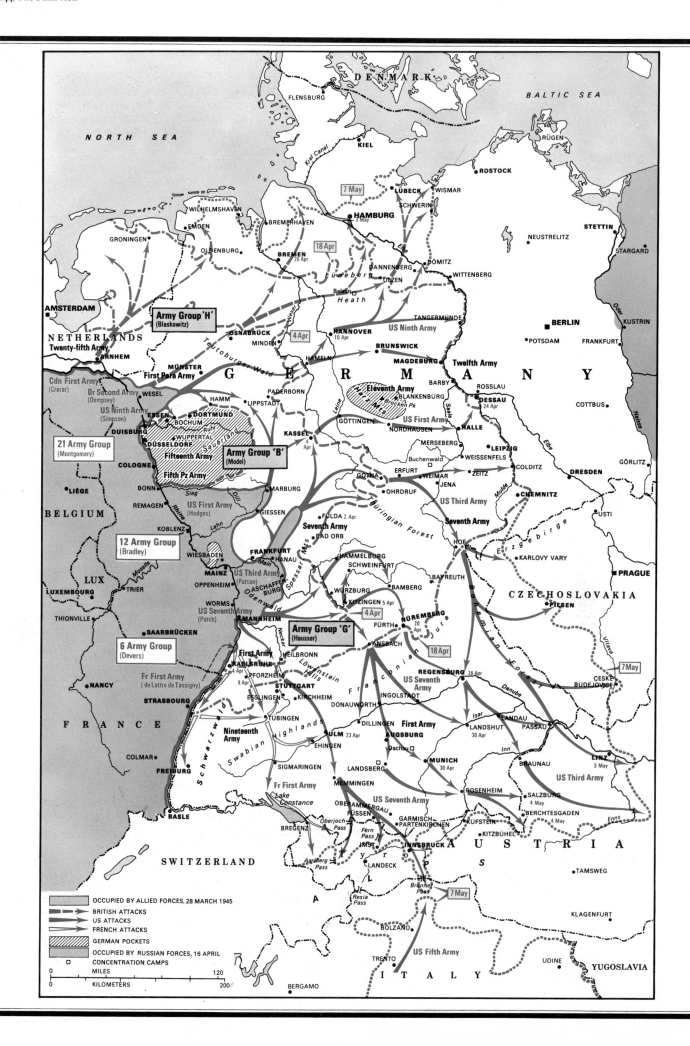

DENMARK

BALTIC SEA

NORTH SEA

FLENSBURG

KIEL

RÜGEN

ROSTOCK

Kiel Canal

7 May

LÜBECK WISMAR
SCHWERIN

HAMBURG
3 May

STETTIN

WILHELMSHAVEN

BREMERHAVEN

NEUSTRELITZ

STARGARD

EMDEN

18 Apr

BREMEN
26 Apr

Elbe

DANNENBERG

DÖMITZ

GRONINGEN

OLDENBURG

Lüneberg

WITTENBERG

ULZEN

Belsen

TANGERMÜNDE

BERLIN

AMSTERDAM

Weser

Heath

US Ninth Army

KUSTRIN

Army Group 'H'
(Blaskowitz)

OSNABRÜCK

HANNOVER
10 Apr

POTSDAM

FRANKFURT

NETHERLANDS

MINDEN

4 Apr

BRUNSWICK

Oder

Twenty-fifth Army

ARNHEM

G E R

M A N Y

Teutoburger Wald

HAMELN

MAGDEBURG

Twelfth Army

Cdn First Army
(Crerar)

MÜNSTER

PADERBORN

Eleventh Army

BARBY

ROSSLAU

COTTBUS

First Para Army

Br Second Army
(Dempsey)

WESEL

HAMM

LIPPSTADT

BLANKENBURG
Brocken Pk

DESSAU
24 Apr

US Ninth Army
(Simpson)

ESSEN
DORTMUND
BOCHUM

KASSEL
Apr

GÖTTINGEN

NORDHAUSEN

US First Army

HALLE

Saale

LEIPZIG

Neisse

GÖRLITZ

21 Army Group
(Montgomery)

DUISBURG

DÜSSELDORF

WUPPERTAL

Ruhr

Sauerland

MERSEBURG

WEISSENFELS

DRESDEN

Elbe

COLOGNE

Fifteenth Army

Army Group 'B'
(Model)

MARBURG

Buchenwald

ERFURT

WEIMAR

ZEITZ

COLDITZ

LIÈGE

Fifth Pz Army

BONN

Sieg

Dill

GIESSEN

GOTHA

JENA

CHEMNITZ

USTI

BELGIUM

REMAGEN

Rhine

Lahn

FULDA 2 Apr

OHRDRUF

US Third Army

KOBLENZ

12 Army Group
(Bradley)

Seventh Army

Thuringian Forest

HOF

Erzgebirge

KARLOVY VARY

PRAGUE

WIESBADEN

FRANKFURT

BAD ORB

Seventh Army

CZECHOSLOVAKIA

LUX

Moselle

Main

HANAU

HAMMELBURG

SCHWEINFURT

BAYREUTH

LUXEMBOURG

TRIER

MAINZ

US Third Army
(Patton)

ASCHAFFEN-
BURG

Spessart Mts

WÜRZBURG

BAMBERG

PILSEN

THIONVILLE

OPPENHEIM

Odenwald

KITZINGEN 5 Apr

CESKE
BUDEJOVICE

WORMS

US Seventh Army
(Patch)

MANNHEIM

4 Apr

NUREMBERG
20
Apr

FÜRTH

18 Apr

7 May

SAARBRÜCKEN

Army Group 'G'
(Hausser)

ANSBACH

Bohemian Jura

REGENSBURG
26 Apr

6 Army Group
(Devers)

First Army

HEILBRONN

US Seventh
Army

Danube

NANCY

Fr First Army
(de Lattre de Tassigny)

KARLSRUHE
4 Apr

PFORZHEIM
8 Apr

Löwenstein
Hills

Franconian Jura

LANDAU

PASSAU

STRASBOURG

STUTTGART

ESSLINGEN

KIRCHHEIM

DONAUWÖRTH

INGOLSTADT

Isar

LANDSHUT
30 Apr

Bohemian Forest

CESKE
BUDEJOVICE

F R A N C E

TÜBINGEN

Swabian Highlands

DILLINGEN

First Army

AUGSBURG

LINZ
5 May

COLMAR

Nineteenth
Army

Schwarzwald

ULM 23 Apr

Dachau

Inn

BRAUNAU

US Third Army

FREIBURG

SIGMARINGEN

LANDSBERG

MUNICH
30 Apr

ROSENHEIM

SALZBURG
4 May

BERCHTESGADEN
4 May

Enns

BASLE

Fr First Army

MEMMINGEN

US Seventh Army

Lake
Constance

OBERAMMERGAU

GARMISCH-
PARTENKIRCHEN

KUFSTEIN

KITZBÜHEL

SWITZERLAND

Oberjoch
Pass

FÜSSEN

Fern
Pass

IMST

INNSBRUCK

A U S T R I A

TAMSWEG

BREGENZ

Aarlberg
Pass

LANDECK

T y r o l

A L P S

A

Resia
Pass

Brenner
Pass

7 May

KLAGENFURT

OCCUPIED BY ALLIED FORCES, 28 MARCH 1945

BRITISH ATTACKS

US ATTACKS

FRENCH ATTACKS

GERMAN POCKETS

OCCUPIED BY RUSSIAN FORCES, 16 APRIL

CONCENTRATION CAMPS

BOLZANO

0   MILES   120

US Fifth Army

0   KILOMETERS   200

TRENTO

BERGAMO

I T A L Y

UDINE

YUGOSLAVIA

Far left: The great sweep of the Allies into Germany, from the Baltic to the Swiss border.

Above left: Patton enjoys some duck hunting near Ceeb, Czechoslovakia, in the company of Major General Harmon.

Above: General Patton receives a cut-glass vase from a grateful Czech town – and a bonus went with it.

Left: The white horse 'Favory Afrika', which Hitler intended to present to Emperor Hirohito of Japan, has a new owner.

On 28 March Third Army's advance began once more. Frankfurt fell the next day, Kassel on 2 April, and by 4 April they had crossed the River Werra and halted to allow the infantry to catch up. On 11 April they moved off again, part of Eisenhower's drive to the River Elbe in order to meet up with the advancing Soviet Army. At this time a new scare appeared on the horizon when statements by prisoners and German radio propaganda indicated that a 'National Redoubt' was being formed in south Bavaria, in which a fanatic core of Nazis would resist until the bitter end. Most of the Allied intelligence officers scorned the idea, but it was given enough credence to make an investigation worthwhile. So Third Army turned southward, and by 15 April they were in Chemnitz, by the 17th they were on the Czech border. Here Patton was halted to regroup before driving down the Danube valley to seek out the mysterious redoubt.

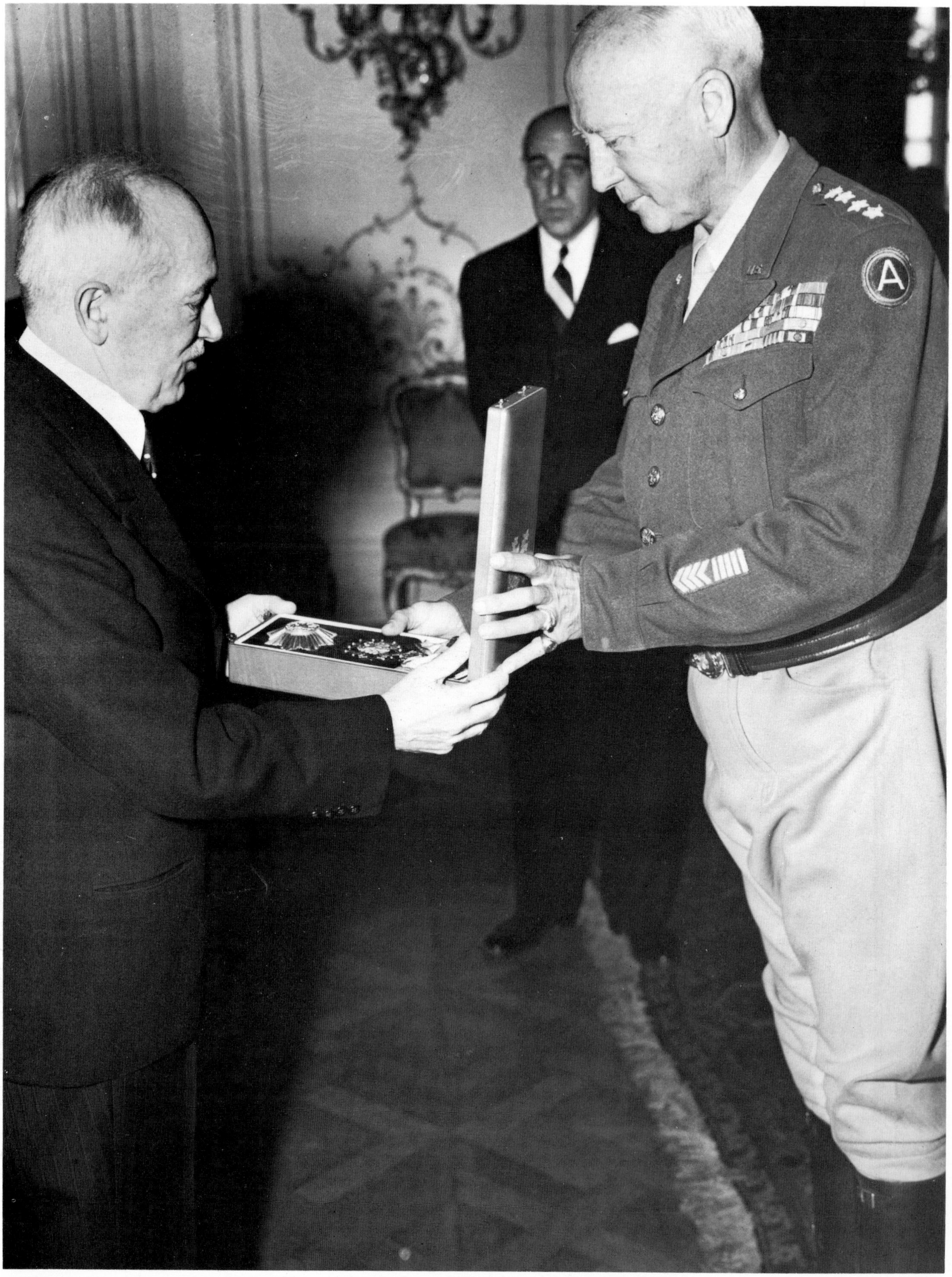

Far left: More honours as General Patton receives the Order of the White Lion and Military Cross First Class from President Benes of Czechoslovakia.

Left: An unusual picture, showing General Patton bedecked with all the various honors received from grateful Europeans.

Pilsen-Budejovice and be ready, if called upon, to advance and clear Prague of Germans. Patton moved forward, but this immediately called forth a protest from the Soviets, even then with their eye on postwar political advantage, and Patton was firmly ordered to stop on the Pilsen line. It is noticeable today that in Czechoslovakia every town, village and hamlet east of Pilsen has a large monument outside, commemorating its liberation by the victorious Red Army in 1945, while behind the Pilsen line, no such monuments to the American liberators exist. Only the older residents, quietly, will tell you of the far-off happy days when the Third Army briefly lifted the yoke from their necks.

It was while Patton sat on this line that the inhabitants of Prague, with liberation in sight, rose against the German occupying troops. Having done so, they appealed to Eisenhower and to Patton for help. To Eisenhower's eternal discredit, he replied that by agreement with the Soviets he had halted Patton's army, and that any calls for aid should be sent to the Soviet Army in the east. It was Eisenhower's final chance to perform a telling manoeuver, and one which could have had far-reaching effects.

On the 8 May 1945 the war in Europe ended, and Third Army could look back on some notable achievements. They had killed 144,500 enemy soldiers, wounded 366,000 and captured 956,000 prisoners. They had captured 2447 tanks and 3454 guns, plus uncounted thousands of other vehicles and pieces of equipment. Their own casualties were much less; 21,441 killed, 99,224 wounded and 16,200 missing, with 308 light tanks, 949 medium tanks and 175 guns lost. Between 29 January and 22 March 1945 they had captured 6484 square miles of German territory and cleared 3072 towns and cities. They had practically wiped out two entire German armies, the First and Seventh. 'History records no greater achievement in such a limited time' said Patton in an Order of the Day quoting these figures.

The Third Army was 437,000 strong at this time, with four corps of 12 infantry and six armored divisions plus three armored cavalry groups, and it was probably the most formidable of the Allied armies. This mighty force now swung into Austria and Czechoslovakia, finding no trace of any National Redoubt but capturing tens of thousands of prisoners, over-running POW camps and concentration camps, capturing enormous stocks of equipment. On 4 May they reached Linz, in Austria. By this time the Soviet Army was on the far side of Czechoslovakia, some 70 miles from Prague, and Eisenhower now ordered Patton to move into Czechoslovakia and take up positions on a line Karlsbad-

FIRE EXTINGUIS
LOCATED INS!

EPILOGUE

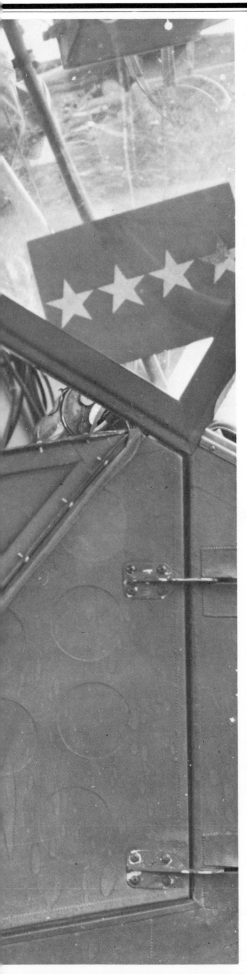

With the end of the war in Europe, Patton contemplated taking his victorious Third Army off to the Pacific and repeating his triumphs against the Japanese but he must have realised this was mere day dreaming. The Pacific Theater was well supplied with troops and generals, he was 60 years old and entitled to rest on his laurels, and besides, his troops were fast evaporating as they returned to the USA for furloughs and discharges. Patton had left the USA in 1942 for North Africa, confiding to his wife that he did not expect to return, for his ideal was that of the Spartan warrior, to return either with his shield or on it, and because his idea of glory was death on the battlefield he had fair expectations of achieving that end. However, as one rises through the ladder of command, it becomes less likely that one's end will be violent and glorious, and so Patton eventually returned to his wife and to a hero's welcome in the city of Boston, in June 1945. To the cheers of the assembled crowds, Patton was driven through the streets in an open car, caparisoned in all his glory – burnished helmet with four stars, medal ribbons of 30 awards on his chest, gold-buckled belt with his famous pistols, riding breeches, polished boots and a riding crop. The crowd loved it, and so did he. This was followed by a state reception, the first such dinner given by the Commonwealth of Massachusetts since Marshal Foch was their guest in 1919. After Boston he went to Los Angeles to another rapturous welcome. Then, after enjoying a well-earned rest, he returned to duty in Germany.

What remained of Third Army was now in Bavaria, with headquarters at Bad Tolz. The army was now the occupying force and George Patton became the *de facto* military governor of Bavaria. In practise the military were being shouldered aside by an army of bureaucrats attempting to bring order into the civil administration, and Patton found little in common with these people. Nonetheless

Left: General Patton, with his four stars well displayed, leaves Kirchdorf, Germany, after the final review of the 103rd Div.

Below: 7th June 1945 and the warrior returns to greet his wife in Boston after three years overseas duty.

he had nominal control and was not loath to exercise it. As he saw it, the best man to perform the job of postmaster, or town clerk, or ratcatcher was the man who had been doing the job before, and if he happened to have been a member of the Nazi party, it mattered little. After all, membership of the party was a stock requirement for almost any responsible post in Hitler's Germany, and (as in some Communist countries today) people took out membership of the party in much the same way as people in democracies joined trade unions, simply as job insurance and without any sort of political conviction. That, anyway, was the way Patton saw it, and as a result he reinstated numbers of minor party members in civil service posts. This, naturally enough, brought him into conflict with some of the more politically-minded administrative staffs of the Allied Military Government and some of the more virulently anti-Nazi press. At long last his patience cracked, and at a press conference on 22 Sep-

Above: General von Rundstedt, together with his son and a German medical orderly, after their capture by US troops in Bavaria.

Below: Slightly embarrassed, Patton receives the 'accolade' from General Juin, together with the Legion d'Honneur.

tember he made a typically ill-considered remark. Questioned about his policy in restoring party members to various jobs, and about his slowness in 'de-Nazification' of the province, he observed, mildly, that he saw little difference between Nazis and non-Nazis. One lot had had control and the others had not. This simplification caused one reporter to ask if, in that case, Patton might consider the two as comparable to, say, the Democratic and Republican parties in American politics. Unwisely he agreed that this was exactly so. That was enough; the next day's American newspapers headlined it 'NAZIS JUST LIKE REPUBLICANS AND DEMOCRATS' and poor Patton was in trouble once more.

He had already upset several people by his outspokenness on his new allies, the Russians. 'I have no particular desire to understand them except to ascertain how much lead or iron it takes to kill them' was one such remark. Another was recorded after he had visited a liberated prisoner-of-war camp and had seen a detatchment of Red Army prisoners marching out in good order. 'That's it, that's the Russian infantry,' he said, 'Hard to beat.' He then added, in a quieter tone, 'But it can be done, and that is undoubtedly just what we will have to do.'

Expressions of this sort, followed by his press conference, led to him being called up by Eisenhower. He was ordered to retract the statement and make clear

the Allied policy towards the defeated Germans. He did, but in his own way:

'I believe that I am responsible for the death of as many Germans as almost anyone, but I killed them in battle. I should be un-American if I did not try my uttermost to prevent unnecessary deaths after the war is over. With the exception of these few people it is my opinion, to the best of my knowledge and belief, that there are no out-and-out Nazis in positions of importance...'

When Eisenhower heard that, he came to the conclusion that Patton was unrepentant. On 28 September he was relieved of command of Third Army.

In his own words, 'That (press) conference cost me the command of the Third Army, or rather of a group of soldiers, mostly recruits, who then rejoiced in that historic name. But I was intentionally direct, because I believed that it was time for people to know what was going on. My language was not particularly polite, but I have yet to find where polite language produces successful government.'

His new appointment was to command the Fifteenth Army; this was little more than a headquarters staff charged with writing the official history of the American campaigns in Europe. Although it was, in most respects, a demotion, in fact

Eisenhower could hardly have chosen a better man for the task, since military history had always been Patton's principal study. However, he was not to enjoy his new post for long.

On Sunday 9 December he set out with Brigadier General Gay, his Chief of Staff, to enjoy a day's shooting in the country. Passing through the northern outskirts of Mannheim, through an area littered with wrecked vehicles and other detritus of war, Patton commented to Gay on the litter, 'Look at all those derelict vehicles! And just look at *that* heap of rubbish!' He was so emphatic that the driver of his car automatically reacted and looked too. Just then a truck coming in the opposite direction turned across the road in front. By the time the car driver had turned his eyes back to the road, it was too late to avoid a collision. He braked, but struck the truck's fuel tank. It appeared to be a relatively minor accident, but Patton had been thrown forward and had struck his head; he was bleeding profusely from cuts in his forehead and scalp. Yet he was the first to speak. 'Are you hurt, Gay?' 'No, not a bit, sir. Are you?' 'I think I'm paralysed...' Patton replied. 'I'm having trouble breathing. Work my fingers for me.' Gay worked his fingers until Patton suddenly said 'Go ahead, Hap, work my fingers!' At which point Gay realised that Patton had no sensation in his fingers; 'I

Below: General Patton, wearing his four stars for the first time, with Lowell Thomas, NBC commentator, Hershfeldt, Germany.

don't think it's advisable to move you, General' he said.

A military police squad now arrived and Patton was rapidly taken to the station hospital in Heidelberg, which had been set up in the old cavalry barracks. News of the accident was telephoned to SHAEF and Major General Kenner, Theater Chief Surgeon arrived to take charge. From London, Brigadier Hugh Cairns, a famous professor of neurosurgery from Oxford, flew in. The diagnosis was short and brutal: 'Fracture, simple, third cervical vertebrae, with posterior dislocation of fourth cervical. Complete paralysis below level of third cervical. Condition critical, prognosis guarded.' Patton had a broken neck and

Above: Generals Bradley and Patton outside the house in Rheims where the Germans signed the terms of surrender to Patton.

was paralyzed from the neck down.

Mrs Patton was flown in and arrived on 11 December to find George resting quietly and taking nourishment. By the 13th he showed such improvement that the doctors began discussing the possibility of flying him back to the USA. But on the 20th he had an acute attack of breathlessness and pallor, lasting for about an hour. It was apparent to the watching doctors that he had suffered an embolism; a blood clot had got loose into his bloodstream and had been pumped into his lungs. His condition deteriorated

Left: General Geoffrey Keys and Mrs. Patton follow Patton's casket as it leaves the station in Luxembourg.

Below left: A grief-stricken M/Sgt Meeks, Patton's personal orderly since 1942, stands with the color guard at the funeral.

make his mark both among the military and on the public, are we able to make some sort of an analysis of his performance as a General? Is Patton to be numbered among history's Great Captains? Since he never had an independent command, but was always subordinate to another, this is something nobody can say with certainty, but it seems unlikely. In the first place, he was no strategist. The 'big picture' totally eluded him. Allied to this, he was no politician, and the political consequences of any action he contemplated or took never entered his head. As examples of these failings we can point to his constant 'reconnaissances in force' with Third Army, always pushing farther than his orders warranted without a backward glance and without troubling himself about how his maneuvers were unbalancing Eisen-

as his lung filled with fluid. In the early afternoon of the 21st he fell asleep; at 1500 hours Colonel Spurling, his doctor, looked in and found him awake and saying how much better he felt. Then he dozed off again. But at 1750 hours another embolism struck his other lung, and he died of acute heart failure.

General George S Patton Jr lies among his Third Army soldiers in the American Military Cemetery at Hamm, just outside Luxembourg City. His grave is marked by the same simple cross as all the others:

GEORGE S PATTON JR
General, Third Army
California. Dec 21 1945

In May 1954 his son, Captain George S Patton III, was present when the Prince of Luxembourg unveiled a monument at Ettelbruck to commemorate Patton and the Third Army who liberated the country. Nearby is a Sherman tank and a statue of Patton, helmeted and in his combat clothing, with his pistols, and holding a pair of binoculars, ever vigilant, like the soldier he was.

Now, 40 years after Patton began to

hower's plans or how his appetite for fuel was paralyzing other units. His lack of political acumen can be seen throughout his career from Morocco onward, culminating in his maladroit statements in Bavaria.

As a tactician he undoubtedly had a gift amounting to genius for high-speed mobile warfare, and he was one of the few generals capable of handling armored forces rapidly and effectively. Against this must be set his somewhat lesser ability when confronted with really solid resistance, such as confronted him at Metz. So long as he could keep his enemy off balance and moving, Patton rarely made a mistake, and he was quick to spot weakness and exploit it but if his enemy was able to regain his balance and prepare a defensive position, Patton's touch was less sure and he was prone to reinforce his own weaknesses and persist in courses of action even when they had been demonstrated to be wrong or ineffective. He was prone to sneer at other generals, notably Montgomery, for being slow in pursuit and slow to mount attacks against well-prepared positions. He may have been right in the first case,

but he was wrong in the other. Montgomery, Bradley and others may not have had the same dash when it came to chasing, but they were more successful with set-piece attacks, because they took their time in preparing. With a fluid battle it is possible to obtain tactical surprise in space or time, launching sudden moves against weak points, but when the enemy is firmly emplaced and knows that attack is inevitable and from which direction it must come, then the only surprise possible is that of time and scale, and to achieve them, precise preparations must be made. This was entirely alien to Patton's character, and for all his lifelong study of military history it seems to have been a lesson he failed to digest properly.

To most of the soldiers he commanded, Patton's reputation is secure. He is reputed to have once said, in a speech, that 'When your grandchildren ask you what you did in the war, you can tell them "I fought with Patton." You won't have to shift them to the other knee, cough, and say "I shovelled dirt in Louisiana."' This is more or less what has happened, and those who fought with Patton are never loath to talk about it. It is probable

that Third Army held him in more regard than did the troops he led in Sicily, but on balance he *was* liked and respected by his troops, and this is largely because soldiers always prefer to be commanded by a character than by a nonentity, even if the nonentity is a better soldier.

As an individual, Patton was a complex character who would have given any psychiatrist a lifetime's work, had one ever been allowed within earshot of him. He was a martinet in matters of dress, deportment and discipline because he was convinced that soldierly behavior stemmed from soldierly appearance. His early days with Pershing, a man of similar convictions, may well have influenced him in this, but there is little doubt of the correctness of his theories. His scale of fines for dress faults in Third Army were legendary throughout the European Theater and were the subject of countless jokes, but Third Army took a perverse pride in it and Third Army was a very superior force because of it.

Below: Led by M/Sgt Meeks, the pall-bearers prepare to place the casket on a half-track en route to the funeral service.

Left: General Patton and General Zahvatieff, commanding the Russian 4th Guards Army, salute the flags during an official meeting at Linz, Austria.

Below left: The General relaxes with troops of 10th Armored Division during their third anniversary celebrations at Garmisch-Partenkirchen, July 1945.

On the other hand, although he drove his troops up to and beyond their limits of endurance, he was ever watchful to see that they received their just dues, that they had hot food, fresh clothing, were rested, had ample medical support, and were denied nothing that would ease their task. He had been brought up in the old school which decreed that an officer thought first of his horses, then of his men, and finally of himself, and he followed this rule implacably and hammered it into his junior officers at every opportunity.

Against this, he was capable of some incredible misjudgements. Witness the slapping incidents in Sicily and the crassness of the Hammelburg Raid. In the one he ran the risk of alienating public opinion, while in the other he ran the even greater risk of alienating his own soldiers. No soldier objects much to attacking the enemy as part of the general scheme of the war, which after all, is what he is there for. But to go into battle simply to satisfy a personal whim of the commander, or to be sent off on a virtual suicide mission which bears no relationship to the conduct of the battle as a whole, is something which few soldiers are prepared to accept, and it must be taken as a measure of Patton's belated recognition of this that the Hammelburg incident was hushed up at the time and is still something of a mystery.

He had a great deal of the actor in his make-up, and the showy uniforms, the shining helmet, the pistols, his love of parades and ceremonial, all point to his love of the theatrical gesture. Again, this is something which paid off in making him known to his troops, and the commander who is known is the one who is followed. For the same reason he believed in commanding from the front as often as he could, so that his men could see that their general was taking the same risks as they were and knew what battle was by first-hand experience.

It is this histrionic streak which is at the heart of much of Patton's behavior. Like any star performer, he hated to be upstaged, and it is noticeable that those among his contemporaries whom he befriended were those who had no particular desire to shine in the press or the public eye – men like Bradley, Hodges and Hughes. On the other hand any general who was intent upon publicity was automatically Patton's enemy and the focus of his acute jealousy. Much, for example, has been made of Patton's 'anti-British' attitude, but on closer examination this was largely directed at Montgomery, who was as much a *prima donna* as Patton and as adept at handling the press to good advantage. Had Montgomery carried out his military duties as efficiently but without press publicity, Patton would have exhibited far less spleen toward him. Among his own army, General J C H Lee

was singled out for opprobium on the basis of his poor showing in providing Patton with supplies, but, again, Lee was something of a showman himself and this must have attracted Patton's temper to a greater degree than did his military shortcomings. There were no shades of gray in Patton's view – either you were with him or you were against him – and the transition from one status to the other could be easily made by a very casual step.

Patton was a soldier, whose sole aim was to make war in as efficient and rapid a manner as possible, and any person or thing offering obstruction was immediately condemned without further argument. Moreover he was often right in his tactical analyses, and the fact that his superiors failed to see his reasoning or failed for other reasons to adopt his

Below: Jodl faces a battery of Allied generals and Admirals to sign the instrument of surrender at Rheims.

Right: A fine portrait of General Patton taken shortly before his untimely death.

proposals, was enough to make anyone short-tempered. We have seen that, in Europe, Patton offered Eisenhower many opportunities which, if properly exploited, could have shortened the war and, into the bargain, left the Allies in a better postwar strategic posture. First, in August 1944, he was halted at Argentan instead of being permitted to close the Falaise Gap, thus allowing several thousand German troops to escape.

Below: General Bradley congratulates General Patton after having presented him with an Oak Leaf Cluster to his DSM.

Right: Wearing, for once, his issue pistol, Gen Patton presents battle streamers to the 231st FA Bn of 8th Armored Division, in a parade held at Zellhausen, Germany.

Secondly, when he forced a crossing of the Seine a week later, had he cleared the northern bank instead of the southern, it is probable that the German Army Group B would have been eliminated. Thirdly, at the end of August, had he not been held back by Eisenhower's fuel restrictions, he could probably have crossed the Rhine with the momentum he had, and thus caused chaos in the German defenses. Fourthly, when he moved up in the Battle of the Bulge, his suggestion to chop off the German salient at its base, rather than half-way along its length, was one which could have had far-reaching effects. Finally, who can say what the consequences might have been had he been permitted to thrust into Czechoslovakia and relieve Prague?

This line of thought brings us back, inevitably, to his personality. If you wish to persuade someone to a course of action, it is not always the best course to do it by punching him on the nose. You catch more flies with honey than you do with vinegar, and people who had once been upset by Patton were unlikely to be receptive to his ideas a second time. In a perfect army, of course, personalities would be submerged by a common cause, but unfortunately personalities still count for a great deal.

In the final reckoning, Patton was the right man, in the right place, at the right time. He fitted the World War II scene more perfectly than he would have fitted, say, Korea or Vietnam, and he would certainly never have survived for long in the postwar US Army. In World War II

Above: The Victory Parade in Berlin, and General Patton stands alongside Marshal Zhukov of the Soviet Army.

Left: After the Victory Parade, Patton poses for his portrait alongside Zhukov.

there was still room for the flamboyant leader, the man who could impress his own personality on the troops he led and, to some extent, on the enemy. It was still a war in which the thrusting commander could get forward in the battle and see for himself. Twenty years later the United States Army (and, let it be admitted, several others too) had changed from being soldiers led by officers to, according to one critic, 'Trade union operatives led by Management Consultants,' and there is no possible way that George Patton could have fitted into that formula.

Patton wasn't perfect, few people are, but those of us who were alive when Patton and the Third Army were storming across Europe will never forget him.

INDEX

Page numbers in italics refer to illustrations

ACKNOWLEDGMENTS

Bison: 42/3, 82/3, 99, 102/3, 110, 131, 149
Bundesarchiv: 38 top, 38 bottom, 41, 42, 43, 58 below, 60, 62, 63, 93 top left, 125 bottom, 128 top, 128 below, 129 top, 129 center, 129 bottom, 130–1, 135 top, 135 center, 136 below right, 137 top left, 137 center, 137 below
Library of Congress: 140
H. R. U.: 111, 113 (MARS), 114 top (MARS), 114 below (MARS), 115 (MARS)
Robert Hunt Library: 101, 134–5, 136 top, 150 below
Imperial War Museum: 26/7 (MARS), 39, 40/41, 52, 66/7 (MARS), 69

below (MARS), 90, 92, 93 top right, 98/9 above, 106 bottom, 108 (MARS), 109 top (MARS), 109 below (MARS), 136 below left
Richard Natkiel: 112 map, 132 map, 133 map, 144 map
Peter Newark's Western Americana: 10 above and below, 77 top
New York Times: 77 below
George S. Patton Museum: 6, 8 top, 8 below, 9 top, 37 top
US Air Force: 62/3, 70 top (MARS), 71 (MARS), 75 (MARS), 78/9 (MARS), 84
US Army: 1, 2/3, 4/5, 9 below left, 13 below, 30/1, 31, 33, 34, 34/35, 35, 36 top, 40, 48/9, 53, 54, 54/5, 55, 56,

56/7 top, 56/7 below, 58 top, 58/9, 60/61, 64, 65, 68, 69 top, 72, 73 top, 73 bottom, 74/75, 76, 78, 81, 86/7, 87, 88, 88/9, 89, 91, 94 top, 94 below, 95 top, 95 below, 96/97 top, 97 below, 104/5 (MARS), 106 top (MARS), 107 (MARS), 110 (MARS), 118, 119, 122 top, 122 bottom, 123, 124 top, 124 bottom, 125 top, 126–7, 133 top, 133 below, 135 bottom, 137 top right, 138 top, 138 below, 139 top left, 139 top right, 139 below, 140–1, 141 top, 141 below, 142 top, 142 below, 143, 145 top left, 145 top right, 145 below, 146, 148–9, 150 below, 151 top, 151 below, 152 top, 152 below, 153, 154 top, 154 below,

155, 155 top, 155 below, 156 top, 156 below
US Coast Guard: 98/9 below
US Information Service: 12 above, 12 below, 120 top, 120 below, 120/1
US National Archives: 9 right (MARS), 11 above, 11 below, 13 above, 14 top, 14 center, 15, 16 top, 16/17, 17, 18 top, 18 below, 18/19, 19, 20, 20/21, 22 top, 22 bottom, 23, 28, 29, 32, 36 below, 37 bottom, 44/5, 46, 50, 50/51, 84/5, 92/3, 97, 100/1
US Navy: 45, 49, 80 top (MARS), 80 below (MARS)
US Signal Corps: 6/7, 14, 24